LITERATURE AND THE DISCOVERY OF METHOD
IN THE ENGLISH RENAISSANCE

LITERATURE AND THE DISCOVERY OF METHOD IN THE ENGLISH RENAISSANCE

Patrick Grant

THE UNIVERSITY OF GEORGIA PRESS
ATHENS

Published in 1985 in the United States of America
by the University of Georgia Press,
Athens, Georgia 30602

Library of Congress Cataloging in Publication Data
Grant, Patrick.
Literature and the discovery of method in the
English Renaissance.
Bibliography: p.
Includes index.
1. Literature and science—Great Britain—Addresses,
essays, lectures.   2. English literature—Early modern,
1500–1700—History and criticism.   3. English litera-
ture—18th century—History and criticism—Addresses,
essays, lectures.   I. Title.
PR438.S35G7   1985   820′.9′356   84–23920
ISBN 0–8203–0764–5

For
Nicholas, Erinn and Damian

Contents

Preface   ix

1 Introduction: Literature, Method and Metaphysics   1

   I   Critical options   1
   II The meaning of method   5
   III The problem of metaphysics   11
   IV The contribution of literature   16

2 Thomas More's *Richard III*: Moral Narration and Humanist Method   19

   I   More's Humanism   19
   II *The History of King Richard III*   24
   III More and the Erasmian manifesto   35
   IV Metaphysics and tradition   44

3 Ben Jonson's *Bartholomew Fair*: Physiological Determinism and Balanced Judgement   48

   I   Jonson's values and *Every Man in his Humour*   48
   II Physiological theory   55
   III Puppets and vapours in *Bartholomew Fair*   62

4 John Donne's *Anniversaries*: New Philosophy and the Act of the Heart   77

   I   The poems and their problem   77
   II Donne and the heart   80

vii

III *The Anniversaries* 89
IV The new science and the disoriented heart 96

5 Thomas Browne's *Religio Medici*: Baconian Method and the Metaphysical Cross 102

I Metaphysics and imagination 102
II *Religio Medici* and the metaphysical cross 109
III Kenelm Digby's argument from method 117

6 William Law's *Spirit of Love*: Rationalist Argument and Behemist Myth 124

I Rigour and imagination in *A Serious Call* 124
II Malebranchiste theory and *The Case of Reason* 128
III Hume's *Dialogues* and Law's predicament 132
IV Boehme's metaphysics and *The Spirit of Love* 138

7 Conclusion 146

Notes 155

Index 185

Preface

In this study, I suggest that the discovery of scientific method precipitates a characteristically modern divorce between physics and metaphysics, and in so doing challenges poets to investigate with new self-consciousness the relationship between fictive images and truth. Clearly, not everyone who wrote English literature during the Renaissance felt compelled to engage such issues. But I have chosen five authors who did, in order to suggest that they recognised a new responsibility and a new opportunity in the intellectual and cultural challenges posed by the rise of science. On each of the five I believe I have also something new to say: on the narrator and Humanist epistemology in More's *Richard III*, on the physiological meaning of puppets and vapours in Jonson's *Bartholomew Fair*, on the imagery of the heart in Donne's *Anniversaries*, on the 'metaphysical cross' in Browne's *Religio Medici*, and on the 'Humean critique' of Malebranche in William Law. My strategy thus requires that my general conclusions depend upon critical judgements made specifically about literature in each of these cases.

I acknowledge with gratitude the help of Laurence Lerner and A. D. Nuttall, who read the typescript and, as ever, made valuable suggestions. I also thank E. I. Berry, Robert Schuler, Terry G. Sherwood, and Marvin Shinbrot for their comments on individual chapters. I am grateful to the University of Zurich, Columbia University and the University of Winnipeg for inviting me to lecture on parts of the work in progress, and to the University of Edmonton for hosting a conference where I was permitted to venture some opinions on Thomas More. Acknowledgements are owing also to *Renaissance and Reformation* for permission to reproduce materials from my article 'Thomas More's *Richard III*: Moral Narration and Humanist Method' (August 1983), and to the Social Sciences and Humanities Research Council of Canada for a Leave Fellowship enabling me to complete the research.

CHAPTER ONE

Introduction: Literature, Method and Metaphysics

I CRITICAL OPTIONS

We often accord to great ideas of the past a certain identity and stability. History, we feel, has tested them, and they take on the appearance of a tried, if sometimes antique, currency. Plato's theory of Forms, Aquinas on individuation, Leibniz's monadology, Hume on induction: these are part of the repertoire of Western thought, and we the patient initiates.

And, yet, this kind of approach to ideas cultivates also a potentially misleading attitude to the great thinkers of pre-modern times. It assumes that they faced their problems in the same terms as we do – that the problems, that is, have a stable identity – whereas our critical vocabularies and assumptions have in fact been transformed by the very manner in which the problems themselves were formulated. If a man of the sixteenth century, let us imagine for the sake of clarity, found a woman charming, he may have wanted, as a result, to burn her alive; in the twentieth century he may want to marry her. The difference here is more than semantic (meaning, I agree, is not determined by derivation);[1] 'charming' still implies that she casts a spell, but we have since learned that witches do not have direct power over physical phenomena.[2] The word has been transformed, and it would misrepresent the sixteenth-century man's position if we interpreted his reaction to the charming woman in our sense of what 'charming' means, rather than in the sense, say, in which it was used of one Alice Prabury: 'She taketh upon her to help by the way of charming. . . .'[3] But this is exactly what happens when we accord to ideas, no less than words, too firm a present

1

identity by looking at them without historical imagination. When Copernicus defined the earth as a planet, or when, by way of Harvey and Descartes, the heart came increasingly to seem a kind of engine,[4] or when Van Helmont invented the word 'gas' (deriving it from 'chaos'), the meanings of 'earth', 'planet', 'heart' and 'chaos' were transformed. They had not been seen quite that way before, and it would, afterwards, require an act of imagination to apprehend them in the old way again.[5]

The methodological consequences of such observations for scholarship are fairly plain: to understand the real profundity of, say, Newton's contribution to human thought we should first try to discover something of the state of mechanics and astronomy as he received them. This inquiry will then soon lead to our further discovery of Newton's quasi-theological attitudes to these subjects, and we shall learn how his mathematics, for instance (inherited from the Copernican and Keplerian tradition through the Cambridge Platonists), was tinged with Hermetic and magical elements. These in part encouraged Newton to seek for nature's hidden harmonies and secret signatures, while simultaneously preventing him from seeing just how much his own theories would eventually divest classical scientific thinking altogether of Neo-Platonist metaphysics.[6]

Today, in short, a child can readily enough apprehend and apply Newton's laws,[7] but only a patient reconstruction of the context within which the great man worked will educate a just admiration of his achievement. How often true knowledge of profound things follows such a pattern of initial, apparent simplicity followed by patient rediscovery is teasing to consider. But it is worth noting also that such a pattern can operate in reverse. For instance, it is not difficult to imagine our ingenuous child as an adolescent first picking up Plato, the seminal genius of Western thought to whose mathematical interests (he might now know) Newton's discoveries can be traced. How does such a young reader react, at first, to those fabulously boring Socratic arguments which dispose, by such dubious means, of one dupe after another, all alike unable to see through the tirelessly blithe perpetrations of false analogies and inconclusive demonstrations? The reaction is likely to be (mine was) a kind of fascinated puzzlement, crossed with moments which are, simply, flabbergasting.

The issue here clearly enough resembles the one raised for

Newton, but as its mirror image. Newton's major conclusions are straightforward and useful: they are the consequence of certain methodological procedures, and we need to acquire an appreciation of how difficult these procedures were to come by. By contrast, Plato's conclusions are perplexing and speculative, and we need to acquire an appreciation of how they can be applied, usefully, to the ordinary facts of human experience. Education, in this case, may come to our assistance by enabling us to see, for instance, how there is in the Dialogues a special amalgam of drama, sophisticated humour, challenging intellectual arbitrariness, and mytho-poetic speculation which requires a special tuning of our receivers, so to speak, and which then takes on a quality of life distinctively its own – majestic, and infinitely fruitful. Plato comes alive, that is, when we begin to feel what he is getting at, how he attempts to marry a Socratic ethical individualism with the claims of metaphysics and Sophist rhetoric; to discover how Homer's representation of the gods bears upon the philosopher's abstract monotheism; how the perennial intuitions about the unity and diversity of the world, as pre-Socratic cosmologists had described it, are to be stabilised and reconciled; in what sense the problem of justice calls for exercise of individual reason, for an understanding of cosmic order, for a reliance on traditional mores and on eschatological hope. The pressing issues of philosophy are all here, somehow massively coherent and yet creatively tentative, in process of formulation, dramatically rendered, provocative, inconclusive, yet gathering and synthesising an extraordinary range of past knowledge and endeavour. There had been no synthesis like it before, and nothing after it – including the scientific revolution – was untouched by it. Clearly, there is much more to learn by trying to read Plato on such terms, appreciating the vitality with which he presents the subjective life of ideas, than by concentrating alone on the logical nonsense of Socrates' arguments, or the deficiencies of the doctrine of Forms.

With Newton, therefore, we might say that objective clarity is of first importance, and the amalgam of theology and alchemy which constitutes the subjective life of his thought is secondary. With Plato, the objective doctrines are less significant than his brilliant expression of the mind's kaleidoscopic energies in search of truth. Still, the nonsense and deficiencies which pertain to certain aspects of the thought of both Newton and Plato should not be ignored. No matter how deeply we come to understand the state of mind, say, of the sixteenth-century man who would burn a woman thinking her a witch, we must not deny that it is morally wrong to burn someone alive, and we should try to give our reasons. But in giving them let us be careful also to stop short of self-righteousness. Witch-hunting, after all, assumes a variety of forms, and the impulses underlying it – for instance, of fear and superstition and the desire to find scapegoats – remain with us, as a little reflection (and a little Freud) will quickly confirm.[8]

So far, then, I have suggested that we might best approach ideas from the past by means of a twofold critical procedure. First, we should attempt to place an idea in a historical setting in order to understand its true originality. Second, we should ask how, in the original text, an idea is clothed in flesh and blood, so that it remains interesting even at a later period when the argument itself is outmoded. Although these two approaches can be distinguished, however, they cannot be completely separated, and together they make up a binary yet single activity of historical imagination, which will remain central in the ensuing chapters of this study, as we look at our principal authors in ʾlation to the rise of science and the discovery of method. For, as is ɪow well known, modern science emerged from a complex relationship to a variety of metaphysical and theological beliefs: from a richly subjective life, that is, of a sort necessarily ignored by the epitomised versions of ideas which come down to us in scientific textbooks, divested of all that would occlude objective clarity. In claiming, therefore, that some appreciation of the subjective life of ideas is required for an understanding of scientific method I am also opening the door to a specifically literary approach to the subject, if only because literature might well be expected to record with special insight the quality of subjective life in question.

I do not mean, of course, that poets necessarily speak with authority on scientific matters; merely that poets who engage issues having to do with science can furnish convincing evidence of the mind's dramatic, tentative, self-contradictory and intuitive participation in the process of discovering new ideas. Literature in this sense not only records the historical development of culture in an especially intimate way, but also shows us how objectivity, and the methods by which it is pursued, are always in question – how we shall continue to be challenged, in the way poetry itself challenges us, by the task of ordering and clarifying what we know, and of monitoring the interactions between what we feel and desire, and what we think. Not only culture at large, but each individual mind, it seems, requires its Plato as well as its Newton. Indeed, one highly significant tendency of modern history and philosophy of science has been to recognise anew the pertinacity of this fact, and in so doing to call in question exactly how we should apply the word 'objective' to scientific progress. Let us consider, briefly, in this respect, the relationship of Newton to Einstein, and try to put the issue baldly. If we agree that Einstein is right, does this mean that Newton is wrong?

II THE MEANING OF METHOD

One answer to this question is, simply, that Newton is right as far as he goes, that his discoveries are truly objective, but that Einstein added to what Newton knew. Newton's theory, in short, seems to be derivable from Einstein's, of which it is a special case, and, since no theory can be in conflict with one of its special cases, Newton remains today as correct as he ever has been; Einstein contradicts only certain incautious and extravagant claims of Newtonian theory.[9] This is a fairly straightforward and commonplace view, suggesting that progress occurs by accretion and is therefore increasingly objective.

Another opinion, however, suggests that Newton's universe is *transformed* by Einstein's and reconceived from within, rather than just added to. The physical events that Newton saw remain before us, but they are observed in a new way. 'To make sense of Einstein's universe', writes Thomas Kuhn, 'the whole [Newtonian] conceptual web whose strands are space, time, matter, force, and so on, had to be shifted and laid down again on nature whole. Only men who had together undergone or failed to undergo the transformation would be able to discover precisely what they agreed or disagreed about.'[10] Karl Popper likewise points out that the new theory explains the same things as the old theory, but it '*corrects* the old theory: it contains the old theory, *but only as an approximation*'; 'similarly', Popper goes on, 'Einstein's theory contradicts Newton's, which it likewise explains, and contains as an approximation'. Einstein in turn, however, as Popper elsewhere says, is not himself proof against the process that led him to correct Newton; Einstein assumed that his own theory was provisional and hoped to find it wrong: 'Einstein *consciously seeks for error elimination*. He tries to kill his theories.'[11] He tries, that is, to make the ideas of the past obsolete, and, in so far as such an impulse is necessary for scientific progress, science indeed remains anti-historical. It declares the old theories wrong, because the new theory is more comprehensive, stands up to tests better, is less easily falsified.

The value of this second view of scientific progress is that it respects objectivity without being overconfident, for it acknowledges that science does not develop by starting from scratch, basing knowledge on certainty and proceeding, step by step, to clear conclusions.[12] Einstein appreciated this by the very fact that he assumed his theories would be found wrong, just as, presumably, countless working scientists admit that their own ideas are not likely to be definitive. But such an admission can, in turn, entail varying degrees of imaginative range. Spoken from a conviction, for instance, that today's science is the best and most sophisticated that ever has been, it can mean simply that progress *has* been cumulative, so that (no doubt) more will be added to what we have so far achieved. Such thinking, I am keen to stress, is a far cry from the kind which sees progress as an imaginative reconstitution perilously and ambiguously dependent on cultural and historical circumstances, mingling the improbable with the provocative, the well known with the new, old vocabularies with fresh insight: a sense, in short, of the development of science which makes it sound more anxious than assured, more organic than structured, more reminiscent of the development of literature and, thus, more completely part of a society which also expresses itself in art and history as well as in the languages of quantification. All of which brings me again to Plato, for it is more difficult to say of him (than of either the imaginary witch-hunter or of Einstein in relation to Newton), that he is, objectively, right or wrong. One reason is that the Dialogues so often achieve literary distinction; they show us character in action, arguments in process of formulation, speculation rendered as myth, ideas expressing the character of the speaker as well as his logic. They show us, that is, how formative is the influence of subjectivity on ideas.

It is also fair to point out, however, that this special amalgam of effects was unavoidable for Plato because philosophy had not yet achieved an independent universe of discourse, distinct from that of the poets and theologians and scientists.[13] Historically, the path towards division and secularisation of the sciences was arduous, and the fact that it took a major step forward during the Renaissance is, largely, what I mean by the 'discovery of method'. Such a discovery entails, indeed, that Newton *is* more objective than Plato, Copernicus more objective than Ptolemy, while maintaining none the less that method is not to be reduced to a clearcut procedure into which scientists are somehow initiated and which guarantees their continuing success; the creative impulse which enables the development of science would inevitably diminish within the confinement of that kind of dogmatism.

On the one hand, therefore, we must avoid assuming that Ramus and Bacon and Descartes and Hobbes used the term 'method' (which they used often) in a clear or univocal sense, as some shared objective notion, as it were, which could be developed and added to as knowledge progressed. On the other hand, we must avoid losing sight of the revolutionary fact that a new scientific attitude and set of procedures did emerge with striking distinctiveness during the Renaissance, and have subsequently transformed Western thought and culture. Many useful studies can illuminate both sides of this issue. Neal Gilbert's *Renaissance Concepts of Method*,[14] for instance, reviews uses of the term 'method' from Plato through the Middle Ages and into various areas of Renaissance speculation. In its original sense, says Gilbert, 'method' means 'following after', and indicates both the acquisition of a sound knowledge of an art, and the qualification to teach it (p. 40). We are reminded that 'However divergent the various trends of this discussion may appear, the ancient Greek basis of it can always be traced' (p. 221). In his introduction, not surprisingly, Gilbert points out that much 'talk of method in the Renaissance may not have concerned *scientific* method in our modern sense at all' (p. xv), and he provides a great deal of information on the application of the word to theology (Erasmus), to history (Jean Bodin), to medicine (Galen's commentators), to logic (Peter of Spain), to the arts (Sturm), and to the general educational curriculum (the *Ratio Studiorum* of the Jesuits). He discusses a single method for the teaching of all subjects (Ramus), and proposals for a plurality of methods, each appropriate for a different area (Giulio Pacius). At the same time, he acknowledges the emergence from all this of a modern scientific attitude, and, in consequence, of a distinctively modern temper in seventeenth-century methodologies, such as Descartes's.

We are thus provided with a wealth of evidence, so that any 'modern' sense of what 'method' means will soon, inevitably, be found to blur, becoming absorbed by its antecedents. Nevertheless, certain points do remain tolerably clear, and Herbert Butterfield puts the main issue plainly: the scientific revolution, he says, is so momentous that it

> outshines everything since the rise of Christianity and reduces the Renaissance and Reformation to the rank of mere episodes, mere internal displacements, within the system of mediaeval Christendom. Since it changed the character of men's habitual mental operations even in the conduct of the non-material sciences, while transforming the whole diagram of the physical universe and the very texture of human life itself, it looms so large as the real origin both of the modern world and of the modern mentality that our customary periodisation of European history has become an anachronism and an encumbrance.[15]

There *was* a palpable challenge to old authorities in the name of new modes of inquiry which involved different presuppositions, which the phrase 'discovery of method' can describe. For instance, despite Galileo's indebtedness to medieval impetus theory,[16] his peculiar genius is expressed especially in the declarations of *Siderius Nuncius* and in the mathematical results of his experiments on motion. Likewise, despite a covert attachment to Aristotle, Bacon remains significant for the history of science through his strenuous journalistic sense that progress lay with the kinds of experiment which would vex nature, and would be conducted in an atmosphere of co-operative mutual criticism. Those who appreciate Kepler's laws of planetary motion do not need to dwell on his magical reverence for the sun;[17] nor did the followers of Newton need to consider seriously his alchemy and theological opinions. The New Philosophy which for Donne called all in doubt may indeed have arisen along no clear or single line of development, but rather as a kind of organic upheaval occasioned by a number of causes working together, but it was a palpable and disturbing process, felt as such, both implicitly and explicitly. In Galileo's case, we might say, the departure from tradition was predominantly explicit; by contrast, in Descartes's careful submission to orthodoxy in the *Principia* (as in his equally careful avoidance of outright Atomism),[18] we can detect a tacit awareness of the unsettling implications of the kind of enquiry he, no less than Galileo, knew himself to be promoting.

How, then, should we describe the new thing? Walter Ong's common-sense suggestion that method entails a certain 'routine of efficiency'[19] in collecting, organising and promulgating knowledge about nature is a convenient place to start. But Giorgio de Santillana[20] is also correct to avoid defining such a 'routine' conceptually; rather in terms of a disposition or attitude, a distinctive habit of mind or desire based on a certainty for which one assumes responsibility: 'It is the resolute assumption of responsibility', he writes, 'which forms the criterion' (p. 45). Thus, in face of the anti-Copernican decree of 1616, stood Galileo: 'He stated in no uncertain terms that in such grave matters his authority was fully equal to that of the Church Fathers themselves' (p. 47), and this new attitude entails something like a 'feeling of *immanence* as against the former sacramental transcendence' (p. 39). The visual arts especially exemplify the point: whereas the invisible field of force in the background of medieval paintings is God's mysterious presence, in the Renaissance this background is space, not manifesting transcendent mystery, says Santillana, but asserting intelligible reality.

Santillana of course wants to highlight the importance for the rise of science of painting and architecture, and so his argument draws mainly from these fields. But the attitude he describes has to do, in a larger sense, with the objective world itself – the book of the world, as it were – conceived not primarily as the bearer of ontological mystery, but as a configuration of things in space: the book of the world, as Galileo says in a famous phrase, which is written in mathematical symbols.[21] The 'routine of efficiency' which marks the discovery of method, we might therefore venture, deals especially with matter moving in space; its procedures are mathematical and empirical, and its disposition is to treat nature as intelligible, not mysterious. It follows that Copernicus is revolutionary because he deployed mathematics to describe the spatial movements of the heavenly bodies, and

Galileo's 'perspective glass' vindicated not only the Copernican theory, but also the spirit of Copernican inquiry, just as his experiments with the pendulum and with rates of acceleration of spheres on an inclined plane took as their first concern the movement of mass in space, empirically observed and accounted for in terms of quantity. Likewise, Brahe's careful observations of the heavenly bodies (albeit for astrological reasons), when interpreted mathematically by Kepler, resulted in the laws of planetary motion: the movements, that is, of mass through space. Although Bacon did not accept the Copernican theory,[22] by his resolute empiricism he advocated the new attitude; his House of Solomon was a model for the Royal Society, and the famous experimenters who belonged to the Society – such as Boyle and Hooke – saw him as their prototype.[23] Although Descartes, in turn, was not an empiricist on Bacon's model, his mathematical method – arising from his invention of analytical geometry, which assumed that relations in space could be represented numerically by arithmetic or algebra – assumed that true scientific knowledge was mathematical. His famous (or infamous) theory of vortices – whereby the ether, or prime matter made up of corpuscles, was held to move in a series of whirling centres – was an attempt to render the universe amenable to mathematical analysis by representing its basic components as material bodies in motion. And in England, when Sir Kenelm Digby introduced his friend Thomas Hobbes to Cartesian thought, Hobbes combined parts of it with elements from Galileo and Bacon, intending to explain reality solely in terms of bodies moving in space. One result was that for Hobbes thinking itself became a kind of motion, an agitation of the primary corpuscles, a mechanical function to be conceived in material, quantifiable terms. And at last, most supremely, for Newton (as the title of his *opus magnum, Philosophiae Naturalis Principia Mathematica* – 'Mathematical Principles of Natural Philosophy' – suggests), mathematics was fundamental, though Newton also insisted on the empirical verification of mathematical deductions. Like the others, he held a corpuscular theory of matter, and suggested, even, that new, powerful microscopes might enable us to see some of the atomic particles. Despite his quasi-theological notions on ethereal spirits and on space conceived as God's *sensorium*, Newton's major contribution to science rendered cogent, as never before, an interpretation of nature as a vast system of mechanical motions definable mathematically in terms of mass, space and time.[24]

The discovery of method I therefore take to mean a certain efficient organisation of knowledge, based on the assumption of responsibility for a mathematico-empirical investigation of nature, espousing a corpuscular theory of matter and, for practical purposes, depicting the universe in terms of geometrical configurations of mass in space. The new method departed not only from the standard medieval model of the universe based on Ptolemy, but also from the metaphysical spirit which had informed and regulated it. The assumption of responsibility of which Santillana talks therefore entails, I wish now to suggest, a willingness to do without traditional metaphysics as far as possible, for practical scientific purposes.

III THE PROBLEM OF METAPHYSICS

A. R. Hall summarises the relationship between the old and new attitudes to metaphysics as follows:

> Christianity furnished the scientist with God as the First Cause of things. But if this First Cause had, so to speak, set the universe to run its course and endowed man with free-will to make his own destiny, the phenomena of nature could only be the result of determined processes, manifestations of a mechanistic design, like an infinitely complex automaton or clock. A clock is not explained by saying that the hands have a natural desire to turn, or that the bell has a natural appetite for striking the hours, but by tracing its movements to the interconnections of its parts, and so to the driving force, the weight. If God was the driving force in the universe, were not its motions and other properties also to be ascribed to the interconnections of its parts? The question, slowly compelling attention over three hundred years, received a positive answer in the seventeenth century. The only sort of explanation science could give must be in terms of descriptions of processes, mechanisms, interconnections of parts. Greek animism was dead. Appetites, natural tendencies, sympathies, attractions, were moribund concepts in science, too. The

universe of classical physics, in which the only realities were matter and motion, could begin to take shape.[25]

The new scientists, that is, did not reject God as the first cause, nor were they without metaphysical interests. But, as we see by hindsight, a mechanised model of the universe did in the end displace, as an adequate explanation of phenomena, such schemes as the magical Neo-Platonist correspondences and sympathies, and the Aristotelian organic metaphysics.[26] In the midst of that complex manifold which makes up the thinking of the new scientists, a drift to mechanism was inherent, and constituted a part of that threat to traditional metaphysics which accompanied the discovery of method from the beginning. One consequence, as Hall says, was to render the first cause responsible merely for keeping together the elegant machine which it had created and set in motion. A providential God, immanent in nature and caring for nature's every movement is, simply, difficult to reconcile with a nature whose every movement is reducible to the strict determinism of quantity. Thus the kind of metaphysical language (the kind developed especially in scholasticism) which describes the world as a series of perfections ordered upwards on a scale or ladder towards the highest, originating perfection was not a fit tool for empirical and mathematical science. The reasons *why* we find nature intelligible (by the apprehension of forms) become a less pressing issue than *how* nature operates (in terms of the laws governing its movement). Covert inheritances from scholasticism notwithstanding (such as scholars keep detecting in Galileo and Bacon and Descartes and Locke),[27] the explicit anti-scholastic polemic of the new science remains one of its distinguishing factors, and is endlessly reiterated.

Clearly, the major proponents of the new method wanted not only to do without the kinds of abstract questions raised by scholastic metaphysics, but also to do without the entanglement of ecclesiastical authority with natural philosophy which scholastic metaphysics seemed to entail. The scorn, for instance, which Hobbes directs at scholastic thought is based partly on his hatred of a corrupt priestcraft which used arcane metaphysical arguments to bolster illegitimate authority, and also on a firm conviction that 'there is nothing in the world universal but names'. Words do not discover essences or substances, and are merely images which, in turn, are residual impressions of *'decaying sense'*.[28] Ordinary language, for Hobbes and those who thought like him, is laced with misleading qualitative judgements which we wrongly assume belong to the objects we observe. Colour and sound, heat and cold, moisture and dryness, beauty and ugliness, no less than the conventional metaphysical 'essences' and 'quiddities' with which these terms belong, are subjective conditions and states of the knower, not useful for determining the nature of the thing itself. As early as Galileo, this theory took the form of a distinction between primary and secondary qualities, with subjective quality relegated to a secondary role and condemned as 'occult'. By contrast, primary qualities (those really belonging to the object) were held to belong to the mathematically quantifiable: 'bulk, figure, number, situation and motion', as Locke defines them.[29]

Corpuscular theory, mathematico-empirical method, and a general, explicit attack on scholastic metaphysics thus combine in a coherent fashion. And yet, as we see, the new philosophers did not always understand themselves as initiators of a 'method' along such lines and in such clearcut ways – just as the participants in a dance do not see the pattern they make. Consequently, the personal, extra-scientific metaphysics and theology of the scientists themselves can often seem simultaneously a means of concealing as well as (paradoxically) of making possible the main new line of their thought. On the one hand, they must have felt that they were immersed in a series of discoveries of real significance. On the other, they were anxious to keep a place in an increasingly mechanised universe, among the cosmic spaces, for the God of their fathers. In what sense, however (we may ask), does such a God providentially care for the fall of a sparrow and for every hair on our heads, if the laws by which sparrows fly and hair grows are determined by the interactions of the atomic particles of which these realities basically consist? The truth is that despite their anti-scholastic bias the new philosophers offered an often curious muddle of just enough of the old metaphysics (for instance, the idea of spiritual and material substances),[30] or of a more recently fashionable Neo-Platonist metaphysics, to enable them to proceed without catastrophic offence to the canons of received Christian belief. And, of course, even classical science carries its own (tacit) metaphysical assumptions, which coalesce with tradition in varying degrees: for instance, that the physical world is real, that it is intelligible, that it exists apart from the mind, that events have causes.[31] It was therefore no offence to the new method to posit God as first cause, even though such piety could also conveniently protect science from God by pointing out that this Supreme Cause was beyond investigation by human reason alone. Because of his 'extremely weak' created nature compared to God's infiniteness, Descartes concludes, 'this is enough by itself to show that what are called final causes are no use at all in Natural Philosophy'.[32] 'For certain it is', says Bacon, 'that God worketh nothing in nature but by second causes', and too ready an appeal to final causality has 'strangely defiled philosophy'.[33]

Insistence on God's utter transcendence and on the inscrutability of his will – the tenets of a thoroughgoing pious logic – therefore enabled science to get on with investigating nature unencumbered with theology or the kind of metaphysics which would raise the mind in a non-utilitarian fashion to the mystery of being. With respect to the relationship between the new science and traditional metaphysics E. A. Burtt has this to say:

> These founders of the philosophy of science were absorbed in the mathematical study of nature. *Metaphysics they tended more and more to avoid, so far as they could avoid it; so far as not, it became an instrument for their further mathematical conquest of the world.* Any solution to the ultimate questions which continued to pop up, however superficial and inconsistent, that served to quiet the situation, to give a tolerably plausible response to their questionings in the categories they were now familiar with, and above all to open before them a free field for their fuller mathematical exploitation of nature, tended to be readily tucked away in their minds with uncritical confidence.[34]

The successes of method indeed soon became so considerable, as Burtt says, that the philosophical and theological theories which accompanied them might seem to be mere palliatives, sops to orthodox opinion offered to preserve for method as much scope as possible. And yet Burtt's argument ignores the fact that not all the philosophers were so cynical nor so deliberate. Some of them, indeed most, were sincere as metaphysicians and theologians. They were, it seems, merely unable to grasp fully the metaphysical and theological implications of the ideas they were helping into the world. Their thinking is consequently often confused, and a modern philosopher can readily point to the logical imperfection of Descartes's *cogito*, or to the inconsistencies in Locke's treatment of ideas, not to mention the peculiar farragos of Henry More.[35] It is not, as I pointed out at the start, uneducative to demonstrate how these old theories are wrong, but it is less than fully educative to avoid the question of what they were getting at, and in that light to assess their value among the repertoire of ingenuities and cunning devices by which the human mind has explored its predicament.

As an example of the indirections by which, in the history of ideas, directions are so often found out, the anti-metaphysical bias of Calvinism is at this point relevant. For Calvin, like Luther, held reason to be futile when applied to the search for righteousness, and taught that we deserve only God's hatred. The theory of double predestination is put with a quiet lucidity designed (by the grace of God) to stultify reason's pretensions to any reliable insight into the creator's will. 'Blake's Urizen', writes A. D. Nuttall, 'is no harsh caricature of Calvin's God-the-Father, but is if anything a more sympathetic figure than the original.'[36] It is inviting to attempt some softening of Calvin's rigour by tracing the emergence of his fearsome God back, say, through Ockhamist distinctions between absolute and ordained power to a Scotist insistence on the inscrutability of the divine will, and so on to Augustine's anti-Pelagian polemics (to which the Reformers themselves looked), and beyond, no doubt, towards more generalised feelings of terror and awe, the *mysterium tremendum et fascinans* itself, before which we are all at hazard, at the whim of a savage God.[37] But Calvin's originality would be the cost, for his distinctiveness lies in the very clarity of his insistence on unmediated grace imputed to individual souls in an otherwise profane and secular world. His argument thus has the effect of separating in a novel way the inscrutable economy of the first cause, the divine will, from whatever concern reason may otherwise have with the world of secondary causes.

I stop short, here, of explaining the rise of science unilaterally in terms of Puritan thinking along the lines of the 'Merton thesis',[38] but wish rather to indicate merely the similarity between Calvin's anti-metaphysical stress on divine transcendence and certain equally anti-metaphysical tendencies of the new method. Calvinists, that is, could insist on a transcendent

God in the name of Christian piety with the same kind of confidence as scientists who asserted (for fear of offending piety) that God was really none of their business. Nor was the cool logic of Calvinist argument lost on proponents of the new method. Descartes and Bacon both drew on a version of it, being careful to display their Christian credentials, while stressing the inaccessibility of the first cause to human reason.

I have tried thus to be mindful of how complex was the discovery of method by acknowledging its implications – both conscious and unconscious – with the past, while insisting also on its novel contribution of objectivity to science. In tracing some consequences of an initial, fundamental assumption of responsibility for studying nature in a new way, I hope also to have suggested that the discovery of method intimates, however covertly, a twin determinism, which increases in proportion to our identification of objective scientific knowledge with the whole of valid human knowledge. In so far, that is, as certain knowledge of nature is determined from below, so to speak, by the laws of impact and motion and the mathematical means of their quantification, the world picture becomes inevitably mechanised, and man within it becomes increasingly a machine.[39] And in so far as certain knowledge of God is determined from above, by the fiat of an inscrutable will, we are dependent on unmerited grace for righteousness, an effect on which *scientia* has no direct bearing whatever.

IV   THE CONTRIBUTION OF LITERATURE

What, then, are the connections between literature of the seventeenth century and these remarks about method? Just as we have seen it is difficult to say of Plato that he is simply right or wrong, because he so successfully incorporates into his arguments a sense of the subjective life of ideas, so the poets of the English Renaissance expressed something of the necessary interpenetrations between old-fashioned culture and new scientific theory. They could, for instance, appreciate the sense in which certain abstracting and artificial procedures of the new method were in fact hostile to experience. In reaffirming the density and texture of our most immediate dealings with the world, the poets therefore in a sense deliberately reinstated the human significance of the old-fashioned secondary qualities in an intellectual climate which explicitly stressed their irrelevance. At the same time, however, in so far as literature was also invited to deal with questions such as the status of knowledge in a Copernican universe and the relation of language to the truths of faith, it participated in the revolutionary upheaval itself. In doing so it shared that fresh intensity of self-consciousness which accompanied the development of experimental–mathematical method, so that one major function which literature serves with respect to the new science, we might conclude, is to act as a kind of monitor. Poets, that is, in so far as they are constrained to know themselves with new clarity as neither theologians nor scientists, express the condition of man's middle state, able neither to usurp God nor wholly to vindicate him; neither to reject the world nor be completely at home in it. Theirs is a most compelling evidence of how humanly unacceptable is the calculus of determinism, that twofold tyranny of grace and of mechanism with which the discovery of method implicitly – and sometimes explicitly – challenges us. The poets do not provide solutions to theological and philosophical problems, but test the consequences of whatever solutions, whatever beliefs (elevated to certainties) the leading minds propose (or imply), by submitting such certainties to the test of imagined experience. In a sense, poetry has always stood in some such relation to ideas, but its self-reflexiveness is, in the Renaissance, experienced with novel intensity, as new a thing to literature as is the voice of Hamlet, as new as the discovery of method itself, with which it exists (for the reasons this chapter suggests) symbiotically. As method progresses, in short, poetry becomes aware of a curtailed scope, but also of a new responsibility.

And this brings me to a final point which I hope to develop in the particular cases with which the following chapters deal. With the rise of science, as we see, traditional metaphysics falls into disrepute. But poetry which would deal with matters of religious faith still requires some metaphysical structure to express the mystery of being, of God's ordering the world towards the higher perfections. Otherwise, poets can express only the anguish of their own powerlessness to deal with the world in religious terms at all, the transcendent God being divorced from his material creation, his will inaccessible to poets as to anyone else.[40] We find this kind of anguish, for example, in Donne's

Holy Sonnets and a good deal of Herbert. The discovery of method does not, therefore, inoculate poets from metaphysics; poets, rather, are forced to a new sense that literature is required to deploy *symbols which themselves indicate the difficulty* of mediating between the world poets experience and the God of their faith.

Obviously, not everyone who wrote English literature during the Renaissance felt compelled to engage such issues, any more than twentieth-century authors are compelled, say, to deal with Marxism. But some did choose the engagement (some, even, entered into it inadvertently), and this study deals with five examples: Thomas More, Ben Jonson, John Donne, Thomas Browne and William Law. Initially, I intend to establish some relationship between each of these writers and the new method, and then to ask about some consequences of the relationship for their literature, with special attention to two main issues which I have outlined in the previous pages: first, literature's responsibility for monitoring the twin determinisms (of grace and mechanism) which the discovery of method carries at its heart; second, the discontinuity between metaphysical ideas and poetic symbols engendered by the new intellectual climate which accompanied the scientific revolution. At the root of my argument and its various applications, however, there lies after all a plain-enough prejudice – namely, that a fully poetic expression of faith cannot well endure a God who is not in and through the world, any more than it can endure the vision of an utterly materialised humanity.

CHAPTER TWO

Thomas More's *Richard III*: Moral Narration and Humanist Method

I MORE'S HUMANISM

When Sir Thomas More mounted the scaffold where his head was to be struck off, he said to a lieutenant conveying him, 'praye you . . . see me safe up, and for my comming downe lett me shifte for my selfe'. The lieutenant's attention is directed, humorously, to the poor workmanship of the scaffold – 'so weake that it was redy to fall', Harpsfield tells us – and the remark was, we are assured, 'saide merily'.[1] How, More wants to know, can you get me onto this thing without it falling down? The tone is magnanimous, the victim is whimsically co-operative with the instruments of his destruction, and he seems unafraid. Once he is up there, his worries are over: his head will fall down of its own weight, his body might struggle, but 'shifte for my selfe' means also 'take care of myself': the dead man's concerns are no longer with the rickety structures of this world. And yet the remark is not so benignly compliant as it first appears, for it vibrates with a sinister energy quite typical of More, and especially astringent because of its apparent levity. The lieutenant is reminded of the shoddy and makeshift structure upon which this execution is mounted, and he is asked to consider that, although More's troubles will soon be over, his own will not. The lieutenant must make do, among such makeshift structures, and bear the burden elsewhere, disposing as he can of the consequences of his part in the action.

More, of course, was careful not to antagonise too directly those empowered to inflict physical pain, and he exercised a lifetime's habit of evasion especially during his sojourn in the

Tower; his letters to Margaret from prison are masterly combinations of private sentiment and public prudence. The author
well knew his words would be scrutinised for evidence against
him, and he became well-practised in the art of providing none,
while refusing also to betray his principles.[2] So with his merry
jests on the way to execution there is an apparent winning lack of
contentiousness, but we feel also at the centre some crystal-hard
assurance of the integrity of his own position, which he allows
his hearers to detect without stating it plainly. The merry jests,
we begin to see, are free as is the gracious movement of a limb:
pleasing to observe because underneath anchored to bone by
ligaments.

Again, More's half-jesting remark to the importunate woman
who accosted him on the way to the scaffold is instructive: 'take
patience a litle while, for the king is so good and gratious to me,
that even within this halfe howre he will disburden me of all
worldly busines, and helpe thee himselfe'.[3] There is no reason to
suspect that More was insincere in thinking of the King as good
and gracious for ridding him of the world's burdens: More's
contemplative, otherworldly and ascetic side had always provided sufficient assurance of the world's vanity, so that he had no
desire to extend his tenure unduly. From the early *Life of Picus*,
which praises contempt of worldly glory and embraces the way
of the cross,[4] to the *Dialogue of Comfort* and the letter to Dr
Wilson from the Tower, More's opinion is consistent: 'I put my
truste in God and in the meryttis of his bytter passyon, and I
beseche hym to geve me and kepe me the mynd to long to be owt
of this worlde and to be with hym.'[5]

Such an opinion is quite consistent with the words spoken to
the woman; Henry VIII's judgement against his life is God's
means of bringing More to heaven, and he is sincerely glad to be
on his way. And yet his remark also drips sarcasm. More, after
all, was no unilateral world-hater: 'Praying is better than
drynking', he writes, 'and much more plesaunt to God and yet
will god that we drynke.'[6] Indulgence of the world is admittedly
provisional, but it is provisionally admitted none the less, and
More was neither so stoical nor so sentimental as to ignore the
fact that the King's judgement against him had spoiled his earthly
good. A knowledge of just this fact salts his words; they are dark
with implied hostility, and no doubt the woman herself found
them disconcerting. The King in his mercy will attend to you if

you are patient, More tells her, and I recommend him to you, for, obviously, I cannot help you myself. But, says the undermeaning, this king executes people, such as I, who *could* have helped you, and you may have to be patient in a more extreme and literal fashion than you think, if you are to get any benefit from him. That is the way with tyrants. Besides, you should have more tact than to bother me at a time like this.

Nor did More come to such a caustic sense of the world's violence and cruelty late in life. His remark to the woman, even, has a sort of resignation about it, as of a man who has known all along this is what the temptations of power are likely to do to kings. Tyranny, indeed, was More's favourite preoccupation; his early epigrams deal conspicuously with conquerors and military despots,[7] and he had some sufficiently bracing experience of such power in action. As a young man, newly elected to the House of Commons, he successfully opposed (to his own considerable jeopardy and actual discomfort) Henry VII's plans to raise money for a royal dowry. In 1517 he successfully defended the Pope's cause in an attempted seizure by Henry VIII of a ship at Southampton.[8] A few years later, he reacted against Luther on grounds that a wholly private conviction of God's will as distinct from the consensus of the Church would lead to anarchy, and so to the rule of tyrants and the ruin of law and order.[9] On similar grounds he refused to advocate an all-powerful Papacy, fearing it, too, could readily become tyrannical: 'yit never thowght I the Pope above the generall counsaile', he writes to Cromwell, 'nor never have in eny boke of myn put forth among the Kyngis subgietis in our vulgare tunge advanced greatly the Popeis authorite'.[10] God alone is all-powerful; among humans of whatever station and at whatever point in history, power becomes the instrument of pride, and the checks and balances provided by a public consensus are necessary to prevent its abuse.

More knew all this as a matter of fact well before his execution, and, because he felt Henry VIII's demands concerning the marriage (and subsequent revisions concerning the law) were so dangerously unilateral as to be close to tyranny, he refused to co-operate. The metaphor of the tyrannical Turk, introduced for polemical purposes in the *Dialogue Concerning Tyndale*, finds increasingly wide application in the *Debellation of Salem and Bizance* and the *Dialogue of Comfort*. The Turks are of course traditional enemies of Christendom, and under Suleiman I posed an actual military threat in Eastern Europe as More wrote. But a Turk is, by extension, any tyrant whose designs thwart Christian unity, so that Luther is a Turk, and also Henry VIII.[11] And, as More became increasingly vigorous in his polemics against heresy and intransigent in his resistance to the King, he became increasingly emphatic about his opinion being that of 'the catholyke churche of Christ' and 'the olde holye vertuous fathers': the public consensus, that is, of universal custom and 'al the corps of christendome'.[12] For More, spiritual tyranny and physical tyranny – the enforcement of one's will on others, as it were, from above and below by an absolute spiritual authority or by a mere secularised, physical force – seemed equally horrifying and unacceptable. Finding a balance in the interests of peace (the *pax ecclesiae*, based on a spiritual Christendom and ensured by the solidarity of princes) was one of his main aims as a Humanist. Indeed, during the brief period when Humanism flourished in Europe, such a peace had appeared possible, and to More it had seemed eminently so under the new, enlightened king Henry VIII.

But how is one to combat a good king who becomes a tyrant? Is the answer to oppose one's singular will, one's combative vehemence to the other's strength, and, if so, to what degree? Although More satirised and deplored the futility of war, in practice as the King's good servant he made pro-war speeches to Parliament in support of Henry's invasion of France in 1522–3, and helped to collect the taxes.[13] He was, we may say, realistic: the degree of resistance to or compliance with established power is perennially a matter of tact and judgement, and More knew that too much self-righteousness may easily taint one with the very same prideful disease one would expunge. The clear line of opposition, in short, between tyrannical Turk and orthodox Christian becomes blurred when subjected to the test of experience. Given his acute sense of irony, More's appreciation of this fact is scarcely surprising.

On the one hand, therefore, More wants to say that Church councils, universal custom, and common belief are objectively reliable; on the other, he exploits with wonderful ingenuity the manifold refractions of language and intricacies of circumstance as a means of showing how unclear and ambiguous is our human condition with respect to our claims for certainty. The two positions are not, theoretically, irreconcilable, because they apply to different areas of discourse, but they are perpetually in collision, and thereby a very old, complex philosophical matter assumes a particular, Humanist form: More seems at once a realist (claiming a body of objectively true and publicly shared universals which become the measure of orthodoxy), and also a nominalist (showing the infinitely refracted play of language and its oblique, unstable relationship to things). It is not just that More became reactionary in his later career when he took to defending orthodoxy; he came also to see the tensions inherent in Humanism itself, including some unsettling consequences of Humanist linguistic theory for the traditional, metaphysically rooted values Humanists espoused.

Something of the resultant equilibrium of tensions characteristic of More at his best, combining muscular, objective judgement with astute pragmatism and almost sinister pleasure in the ambiguity of language, marks his comments *en route* to execution. It is hard to describe his exact poise, but the elusiveness is that of Humanism itself, faced with the encroaching shadow of a modern secularism,[14] and yet, without quite appreciating its position, representative of an old ideal of Christendom. And in some such context it is appropriate to discuss More's relationship to method, for, despite the fact that Humanism's contribution to the new philosophy is usually acknowledged to be indirect,[15] several major issues outlined in the previous chapter quite clearly press upon him. He is, for instance, faced with the prospect of a new secular power offset and complemented by a revolutionary Reform theology stressing God's transcendence and dispensing with traditional sacramental authority; he is faced with a new ideal of linguistic discourse (based on Humanist grammar and *bonae litterae*), subject to self-critical reflexiveness and aware of the ironic discontinuities between words and things; he must deal with a traditional metaphysics under fire from a new common-sense epistemology concerned with empirical affairs; and he is everywhere preoccupied with a twofold absolutism which he perceives with special acuteness as being a product of the times. On one side is the tyranny of sheer material power, a kind of institutionalised godlessness, as it were; on the other, the abstract tyranny of certain scholastic theologians (equally godless) whose obscurantist theories and jargon encouraged superstition and permitted exploitation, just as, by overreaction, did the disembodied spiritual determinism of the Reformers. For More,

Humanism was, simply, the most effective means for combating tyranny without falling prey to it one's self, and to get a further idea of what this implies let us turn to *The History of King Richard III*, More's full-blown study of a tyrant, written in the heyday of his literary productivity as a Humanist, though unpublished until after his death.

II *THE HISTORY OF KING RICHARD III*

Richard III is, in part, a medieval morality, an exemplum against tyranny, a story of the rise and fall of a prince on fortune's wheel. It is also a Humanist history, eclectically modelled on Sallust, Tacitus and Suetonius, from whom More learned how to represent the shaping force of character upon historical events through dramatic presentation and strong psychological portraiture.[16] It is also a unique document in the history of modern prose: More, claims R. W. Chambers, was the originator and master of a school of historical writing, the first Englishman to have an 'effective prose, sufficient for all the purposes of his time' to record contemporary events through a living, dramatic narrator.[17] Although, for religious reasons, most of More's works were unread in England after his death, *Richard III* was immediately acknowledged a masterpiece, and continually reprinted in the chronicles of Grafton, Holinshed and Stow. With revolutionary effectiveness, More brings native eloquence from the cloister to the political needs of sixteenth-century England.[18] And yet the work is unfinished; it exists in Latin and English versions (which stop at different places); it is peppered with historical inaccuracies, both in detail and, probably, in the general conception of Richard;[19] it is not quite a drama (though the long, formal speeches of the principals are given to us in direct speech); it is not quite a biography either, nor an old-fashioned morality (except in an inverse way).[20] It is, instead, an unusually successful period piece (if we view it against Shakespeare's mature drama), and a work of peculiar originality (if we view it against its precedents). But it is unmistakably Humanist in its rhetorical methods and its exploration of the political theme. Just as in the remarks recorded pending execution, More's irony and moralising remain here, too, in precarious equilibrium – an unsteady state, so to speak, characteristic not

only of More, but of Humanism itself. And in *Richard III* this
unsteadiness can be especially well described in terms of a certain
vacillating relationship between narrator and reader.

First, More's moral lesson against tyrants is plain. Richard III,
we are told at the start, in downright terms, is the worst kind of
criminal. By nature uncle to the princes, by office their protector
and bound by oath, he none the less 'al the bandes broken that
binden manne and manne together, withoute anye respecte of
Godde or the worlde, unnaturallye contrived to bereve them, not
onelye their dignitie, but also their lives'.[21] He was, moreover,
born 'unnaturallye', feet first, and with teeth. He grew up
crook-backed, ill-featured and dwarfish, and from even before
his birth he was 'malicious, wrathfull, envious' (p. 7). The
analogy More draws between Richard's physical and spiritual
deformity is complete and unsparing. Richard's general policy of
murderous dissimulation is clearly outlined (p. 10), and his death
suitably lurid, 'hacked and hewed of his enemies handes, haryed
on horsebacke dead, his here in despite torn and togged lyke a cur
dogge' (p. 87). His associates, Buckingham and Tyrrel, likewise
came to a bad end, and Dr Shaa, who preached a sermon in
complicity with Richard's ill designs, we are assured was so
overcome with shame that within a few days 'he withered and
consumed away' (p. 68). In Richard himself, we are asked to
reflect, God 'never gave this world a more notable example'
(p. 86). All that is quite plain, and the intent is unquestionable:
here we must meet the narrator head on, and take his message.

So far, then, we have a lesson but not literature, and to discover
the true distinction of *Richard III* we must ask how More's text
complicates his moral. In one respect it does so simply by
creating such a density of circumstances that the lesson cannot be
adjusted comfortably to the facts. The world is more peculiar and
wayward, more strangely full of perplexities ensuring our
complicity with evil, than we are likely to think, or to find
reassuring. Some of the participants, for instance, were still alive
as More wrote, as the text itself reminds us. These include King
Edward IV's daughter Katherine (p. 3), Mistress Shore (p. 56)
and even the murderer Deighton (p. 87). Others, such as
Thomas Howard, who had fought for Richard and now served
under Henry VIII, would evidently not wish to be reminded of
their past allegiances, and More's oral informants – none of them
named – would very likely have doctored their stories to protect

themselves against suspicion of disloyalty. For all his Humanist love of ancient models, More seems bent on showing us that the immediate past lives in and through the present in complex ways. When the narrator interjects scathingly, for instance, of Richard's murdering the princes, 'Loe the honourable corage of a kynge' (p. 86), the remark is transferable in principle to any king: he does not say, 'Richard is craven and wicked', but 'Any king may be craven and wicked in this fashion.' Given that Henry VIII, who had no male heir, executed Edward IV's nephew Edmund de la Pole in 1513, such an observation could be uncomfortably close to current affairs. Indeed, Richard Sylvester, among others, suggests that More did not have his work published because of the wide variety of politically sensitive issues on which it touches.[22]

The point here, I agree, is still not quite literary, but, in so far as such matters complicate the moral, they do have literary consequences.[23] The more fully rendered in actual, particular dealings, it seems, the less clearcut is the lesson, and More capitalises on this fact by rendering artfully perplexing the position of some of the principals with respect to Richard's nefarious activities. Hastings, for instance, in quieting the Lords' fears in Richard's favour, is in two minds: 'part hym selfe believed, of part he wist the contrarye' (p. 23). Although he is a dupe, to some degree he is a willing dupe. At the conclusion of Buckingham's hortatory speech to the Assembly at the Guildhall (he repeats it, because the first recital fell flat), the responsible burghers 'thought that they never had in their lives heard so evill a tale so well tolde', but they all remain 'styl as ye midnight' (p. 75) and none speaks out against the usurper. Some, of course, such as Rivers, *are* entirely duped (p. 18), and in the case of Stanley's dream of the boar, which he takes as a warning against Richard, intuition sends a message which common sense overrules (pp. 45–6). And there is the painful case of the council thinking, in a state of mind at least close to good faith, that no hurt is intended against the prince, and therefore siding with Richard's decision to remove the child from sanctuary by force: honest men operating in good conscience can be dangerously wrong.

With surprising economy, More manages to create, as Alistair Fox argues, a sense of how the sheer complexity of circumstances[24] can be morally compromising, and the single character who understands these facts just as fully as More, and who is a master at turning them to sinister advantage, is Richard himself. The narrator, however, allows us also to appreciate the tyrant's frightening success by showing us how certain irregular or anomalous patterns of experience can render us vulnerable to men such as Richard, even when we have good reason to think our defences are firm. Such a sense of things 'comming togither partly by chaunce, partly of purpose' (p. 45) to make and mar simultaneously is, in turn, one of the major achievements of *Richard III* as literature.

A case in point is the treatment of Edward IV's marriage to Elizabeth Grey (herself formerly married to Edward's enemy), in the context of his liaison with Elizabeth Lucy, in the teeth of his mother's opposition, and against a more general background of rumour about his generally libidinous habits (pp. 60–4). Despite the legitimacy of the marriage and of its offspring, the circumstances are fertile with morally compromising and suggestive possibilities, so that Richard can plant his rumours of illegitimacy with high hopes that they will produce fruit rapidly. The result he desires is not just wholesale discrediting of the late king, but disorientation and ambivalence; not the entire blackness of defamation, but a half-light appropriate for shady dealings, and sufficient to provide a purchase for his specious claims. Edward's circumstances, as More shows, are all compact of strength and weakness; the marriage is legally firm, but it is circumstanced, and we can see how shrewdly Richard appreciates the ironies of Edward's situation. Even as the King lay dying, giving voice to an ideal of political unity to which he may have seemed, indeed, at last to have given some physical shape, Richard already detects behind that momentary achievement the divisive antecedents which would ensure its dissolution.[25]

Or consider the account of the Queen's flight to sanctuary. She, we recall, sees through Richard's designs before the others, and, knowing the danger to her children, takes to sanctuary 'in all the haste possible' (p. 20). As she departs, the Archbishop visits her:

Aboute whome he found muche heavinesse, rumble, haste and businesse, carriage and conveyaunce of her stuffe into Sainctuary, chestes, coffers, packes, fardelles, trusses, all on mennes backes, no manne unoccupyed, somme lading, somme goynge, somme descharging, somme commynge for more, somme breakinge downe the walles to bring in the nexte waye, and somme yet drewe to them that holpe to carrye a wronge waye. The Quene her self satte alone on the rishes all desolate and dismayde.   (p. 21)

Far from flying in haste, the Queen in fact is immobile and dismayed, as all the details indicate, so that 'all the haste possible' turns out to generate very little speed. The scene is one of impractical energy and burdensome, even comic inefficiency. But that, More implies, is the nature of circumstances: we are more firmly tied than we think, more burdened and less free to manoeuvre than we ought to be, more compromised than we imagine. And, when the Queen does get to sanctuary, it turns out to offer, in effect, no protection at all. Buckingham's speech against it (p. 30) is based, not surprisingly, on an appeal to circumstances, to how sanctuary is *actually* used to harbour criminals (and women who run off with their husbands' goods). The oratory is persuasively detailed, and the result is a resolution to take the Prince whether the Queen releases him or not.

The Queen's decision to give herself up therefore takes account of a multiplicity of considerations. The cardinal who stakes his body and soul on Richard's honest intent (p. 40) is obviously persuasive; Richard's men in any case have moved swiftly to secure the building against the Prince's escape with friends, and the Queen recognises that some of the lords are well disposed to her. The situation is suspenseful, many-faceted, and the decision is far from simple. It is an example of how moral intuitions and actual judgements can be opposed, yet interwoven.

More seems pleased to pique us when he can with this kind of perception of life's anomalies: Clarence for instance is executed by drowning in a butt of malmsey (p. 7); Richard orders strawberries from the Bishop of Ely's garden to preface his grotesque accusations of sorcery against the Queen and Shore's wife, and his arraignment of Hastings. Despite the basis in tradition for the malmsey story, and the possible symbolic dimensions of strawberries, these details stand out as both odd and fascinating, somehow unsettling, and yet just the kind of peculiar thing that would happen: the ingenuities of cruelty lie exactly in the surprising and perverse uses of familiar comforts, and the very detachment of such effects from their predictable uses is both convincing and disturbing to our equilibrium. Richard, of course, knows all about life's anomalous dimensions: after all, he *chooses* to order strawberries. It is a demonstration of his control, of his capacity totally to mismatch the visible signs with actual intent, and to relish the shocking effects. He is deliberately theatrical: for instance, when he greets the Prince with a kiss, the action is at once poignant and cruel. The boy's mother has just parted from him with a kiss, and stands weeping as Richard, whose malign intent she all too deeply suspects, mimics her action – reassuringly, no doubt, for the onlookers, but mercilessly emphasising to her the finality of her deprivation. As the margin note 'O dissimulation' suggests, we should appreciate the theatricals; Richard is able totally to dislocate a conventional public gesture from private motivation, and at the same time to communicate his pleasure at doing so. This is the Richard who dresses up in old armour to suggest that he must have been suddenly put under duress by Hastings (p. 52), who struts on the gallery voicing mock refusals of the kingship, who parades Shore's wife through the streets as a public penitent, who prepares an elaborate coronation (p. 44) to distract attention from his own designs to terminate the kingship he pretends to celebrate, and so on. It has even been suggested that More's originality in *Richard III* to a large extent lies in his adaptation of theatrical metaphors to the purposes of history. For instance, he contrives a series of audiences.[26] At the centre is the main illusionist, Richard himself, who draws people into his performance. The Queen, however, and some others soon see through his act. Gradually, so also do the people, who are a kind of audience within the play, so that there are various degrees of credulous participation in, and knowing observation of, Richard's performance as the story unfolds, reaching out at last to the reader, who is treated also as an audience at a play. As Richard's performance becomes increasingly shoddy, so his credibility increasingly fails. The narrator, like a morality actor, accordingly steps on stage to clarify the didactic intent, and to keep our vision clear.

All this is terribly helpful, and does capture More's design, but there is a refinement also worth mentioning because it is of the sort wherein More's genius especially resides. Richard, from the start, is *not* a convincing actor:[27] he fools some of the people some of the time, and at critical moments effects confidence tricks, but when he attempts to put on a show to cover up his misdeeds he inevitably does it badly. Indeed, he is such a bad actor that it almost requires a kind of obtuseness *not* to hold him gravely in suspicion. More's history becomes, therefore, substantially an examination of just this kind of obtuseness: the sort by which, as Alistair Fox argues convincingly, ordinary people can allow free rein to such men as Richard. When he reaches London with the Prince (recently taken by force from the dukes and Lord Rivers), Richard makes a show of the 'barelles of harneys' which, he claims, Rivers and the other traitors had 'privelye convayd in theyr carryage to destroye the noble lordes with all'. The narrator then tells us that this device is easy to see through, and even 'made the matter to wise men more unlykely', but that the people were in 'muche part' (p. 24) satisfied with it. Already, Richard rouses more than a little suspicion. Among the Mayor, the sheriffs and aldermen, and the five hundred horse of the citizens who welcomed him with their own display of scarlet and violet, there must have been some sufficiently wise men, and More's words imply, as well, that not all of the people were satisfied; 'muche part' were. Among the dignitaries, we know that Edmonde Shaa falls readily into complicity with Richard's wishes; to what degree this complicity was already a fact, and to what extent other citizens were tacitly in compliance, remains unanswered, but not unasked.

Again, Richard's case against sanctuaries is a successful ploy for getting his hands on the Prince. It is not, however, just a theatrical trick: Buckingham's speech lists actual abuses of sanctuary, convincing because true. But the argument for wanting to take the Prince in the first place (namely, that young Edward had no royal playfellow, and therefore needed young Richard) is the merest equivocation, which scarcely can withstand a moment's scrutiny. The Queen sees through it immediately, and pronounces upon Richard's 'goodly gloze', his 'painted processe' and his 'trifling pretext' (p. 38). To her it is all, plainly, a piece of bad acting, though others do not see this so unequivocally, even though some, such as Hastings, half see and go along anyway. The episode demonstrates again how easily people will swallow camels. Richard's pretext is bad, and ill conceals a monstrous intent, but it is convenient to aquiesce, and the speeches on sanctuary provide a kernel of public-minded concern to distract attention from a whole granary of personal malignity. Even the crowd-pleasing preparations for the coronation are not a successful distraction: 'yet began there here and there about, some maner of muttering amonge the people . . . though they neither wist what thei feared nor wherfore' (p. 44). Perhaps, says the narrator, someone detected the truth and filled others with suspicion. But, once more, though Richard's charade is easily enough discovered, no serious objections are raised.

Again, poor acting is Richard's hallmark as he mistimes his entrance during Shaa's sermon, so that the preacher is forced to repeat the words for Richard to take his cue: the congregation, far from being fooled, 'bene turned into stones, for wonder of this shamefull sermon' (p. 68). At the end, all the people know quite well that they are observing 'a stage play'. But it is not just Richard's play: it is but a version of the universal political game. 'And so they said that these matters bee Kynges games, as it were stage playes, and for the more part plaied upon scafoldes. In which pore men be but ye lokers on' (p. 81).

The History of King Richard III, as Alistair Fox says, is full of people who know or suspect tyranny but who are too burdened by circumstances, or too half-hearted, or too much in complicity, or afraid, or compromised, or who think it is not their business, to do anything about it. There is thus a sheer empirical tyranny of circumstances, which, by neutralising the will, indirectly feeds the more blatant tyranny of a singular will to power. The fascination of Richard is not, after all, that of Iago, whom everyone thinks honest. Richard cares not to be thought honest, only sufficiently credible, or interesting, to take advantage of the ordinary man's moral ambivalence. He knows the immense gulf between rhetorical structures and moral intent, between words and action, and he knows that action alone counts. It is not so much that he is increasingly a poor performer; rather that he cares less about appearances (or words) as his power is increasingly assured. Appropriately, the terms 'colour' and 'frame' are used consistently to describe his devisings: he presents 'colorable proofe' (p. 24) that Rivers and the dukes are guilty, he puts 'some colour' (p. 52) on the matter of Hastings's arrest, he accuses Shore's wife when he cannot 'colour' (p. 54) matters otherwise, he uses 'colour' (pp. 59, 66) craftily to suggest the illegitimacy, and the Queen is worried because the princes are put 'in duresse with out colour' (p. 36) and may likewise be killed

without cause. Shaa undertakes to 'frame' (p. 58) the city to
accommodate Richard's plan, things are 'oute of al frame' (p. 68)
when the sermon goes wrong, Buckingham expects a response
from an audience that 'the Mayer had framed before' (p. 75), and
Hastings advises the lords not to raise objections that might put
things out of joint so that they 'shold never be brought in frame
agayne' (p. 23). All this suggests painterly illusion and perspective, which Richard knows how to manipulate, not so much in
order to simulate a real world as to raise questions – as in the
various experiments in curious perspective among Humanist
painters – about the peculiarities of our own point of view.[28]
Richard provides just sufficient colour, a just sufficiently oblique
angle, to raise a doubt in the mind of observers about the
structure and identity of the things observed. He disturbs their
equilibrium just sufficiently to make their day-to-day passivity
seem positively tempting.

Richard III is full of details which exploit in some such manner
the ironic and unsettling consequences of actions admitting a
variety of perspectives, and by which More creates for his readers
a striking sense of the equivocal nature of events. When Hastings,
for instance, on his way to the Tower to confer with Richard,
talks to a priest, the knight sent by Richard to escort Hastings
remarks on the conversation, 'you have no nede of a prist yet',
and then laughs 'as though he would say, ye shal have sone'
(p. 51). Hastings, unwitting of the fact that Richard plans to kill
him, joins in the joke. The knight thus appreciates how ironically
appropriate is the priest, and relishes his own, privileged point of
view, speaking duplicitously to protect it. Hastings's position is
the reverse: he takes the knight's statement at face value, and
thinks it ironically pleasing that the priest is *not* appropriate.
Finally, the narrator moralises on the scene, providing yet
another way of looking at it.

Likewise, when Richard at 'Baynardes Castell' greets the
delegation coming to offer him the kingship, his reaction is
partly cautious and distrustful (p. 77). More's syntax in describing the episode is complex to a fault, but the sense seems to be
that Richard is to some degree genuinely startled by such a large
group coming upon him suddenly, even though he sees that they
are coming for reasons that suit his purpose. Ironically, his initial
flinching moment of apprehension is appropriate, because the
plan calls for him not to seem too anxious to see them, and so he

works to keep up the initial appearance of reluctance and agitation. Buckingham then takes advantage of the situation, and there follows the charade of Richard's mock refusals. More isolates the volatile interplay of intent and circumstance, observes it precisely, and asks us to appreciate that it is the texture of experience itself.

Or consider the humiliation of Mistress Shore, forced to walk the London streets 'out of al array save her kyrtle only' (p. 54), with a taper in her hand, and walking before a cross. The people (and other observers) are titillated – voyeuristic and prurient, 'more amorous of her body then curious of her soule' (p. 55). Richard of course counts on this, for he is devising and exploitative, arranging the spectacle because his previous accusations of sorcery are so badly received. The narrator is at once full of sympathy for Mistress Shore (admiring her beauty, wit and graciousness), and also severe, moralising against concupiscence and the transitoriness of physical beauty (look at her now, he says, old, lean, withered and dried up). It is hard to know where the reader stands; the event invites his participation from three perspectives simultaneously, and the result is to complicate the moralising element of the narrator's speech, not to clarify it.

An interesting article on More's use of litotes in *Utopia* suggests that the use of double negatives (making a statement, that is, by denying its opposite) has an unsettling effect on the reader, which is part of More's purpose.[29] Litotes confuses the point being made, so that the reader is forced to do a double take, as it were, in order to reconstruct the speaker's perspective. Part of Elizabeth McCutcheon's argument has to do with the fact that More's Latin is full of litotes, which English translations often fail to render. In the English version of *Richard III*, however, litotes is everywhere, a fact which confirms More's practice as a habit of mind (as McCutcheon claims) and not just a device of his Latin style. Edward IV, we learn, is 'nathelesse not uncomelye' (p. 4); the Queen 'not unwisely devised' (p. 14); 'none of us I beleve is so unwyse' (p. 15), argues Richard; Rivers perceives that the closing of the gates is 'not begun for noughte' (p. 18); 'no manne' is 'unoccupied' (p. 21) as the Queen prepares to fly; 'never' was there 'so undevouwte a Kinge' as to violate sanctuary, argues the Archbishop of York (p. 28); 'neither none he nedeth, nor also none can have' (p. 32), says Buckingham of the Prince in sanctuary; 'I neither am so unwise to mistrust your wittes' (p.41), remarks the Queen in yielding; Rivers and the dukes are beheaded 'not without his [Richard's] assent' (p. 57); Edward IV asks advice about his marriage in such a fashion that his advisers understand 'it boted not greatly to say nay' (p. 61); the obstinate silence of the crowd reassures the Mayor and the Duke on the grounds that they hear 'no manne sayeng nay' (p. 76). The accumulation of such instances has the effect of forcing us to come at meaning indirectly, and of causing us to interpret undercurrents of implication, and to appreciate that life is not a clearly moral affair, but often rum, quirky and ambivalent: framed and coloured, we might say.

At this point we return perforce to the narrator, for some of the litotes is his. The more we look, the more obvious it becomes that he, also, is oblique, disturbed, and not quite morally the master of all the circumstances he describes, ostensibly, with clear didactic intent. About Richard's complicity in Clarence's death, he tells us, for instance, 'is there no certaintie' (pp. 8–9), and we are just as likely to shoot too far as to shoot short. He will recount the story of the princes, not after the various ways he has heard of their death, but according to an account 'as me thinketh it wer hard but it should be true' (p. 83); in fact the narrator never claims certainty with respect to Richard's responsibility for the murders. There is of course a consistent appeal to what 'wise men say' on various matters; we recall that More's sources were largely oral, and that, as his narrative makes clear in other ways, he well knew there was good reason for men such as his informants to tailor their stories.[30]

The position of Morton in *Richard III* is, at this point, especially interesting to consider, for as Richard's opposite he stands closest to the narrator. Morton is clear-headed, yet subtle; he is distanced from events, yet ready to influence them at the crucial moment. In his opposition to Richard, he upholds the plain moral, and in his clever indirection he exemplifies the witty vigilance also necessary to combat tyranny. The narrator, we feel, can point to him as exemplary. And yet, by inciting Buckingham to rebellion, Morton performs a political action which More must have seen as dangerous to recommend, the specific historical circumstances of Richard's reign notwithstanding. More, we conjecture, had two lines of interpretation open to him: either to see Morton's interference in events as tainted because contributing to a further series of events in the eign of Henry VIII wherein the tyrannies of Richard's reign were being re-enacted;[31] or to attempt, as author, to act as prudently as the exemplary Morton, and therefore to desist from publishing *Richard III*. Both ways, the narrator's moral certainty is compromised – either because the exemplary Morton cannot remain free from complicity in ill-doing by the very fact of his engagement in politics, as Fox maintains, or because the exemplary Morton would not approve such a piece of writing for publication in the circumstances.

Here, at the start of More's literary career, it may now appear, we are not too far removed from the temper of his remarks on his way to the scaffold. There, too, unshakable moral certainty accompanies the skilful indirection and ironic poise and ability to shift the perspectives of his interlocutors in surprising ways to reveal their complicity in evil beyond their expectation. In both circumstances, More remains a Humanist: his subject is the world of affairs and the responsibilities of rulers; his models are the classics adapted to current circumstances; his intent is educative and moral. *Richard III* remains a typically Humanist warning against tyrants, and the work provides a terrifying negative example about which, on the surface, it is comfortably easy to moralise. But the vigilance we need to preserve our freedom must bear upon the means by which the tyrant finds his way to power through the perplexities of circumstance, the double play of language, the ambiguities of perspective, the ironic incongruities between the sign proffered and the interior intent, and upon all the devices of wilful misinterpretation and foolish indifference.[32] Bringing alive this side of the interpenetrations between personal and political life is one of the major achievements of Humanist literature, and to show how it is implicated with the question of method we should turn briefly to Erasmus, doyen of the northern Humanists and More's admired model.

III MORE AND THE ERASMIAN MANIFESTO

The brief autobiographical document *Compendium Vitae* shows us something of Erasmus's elegant but touchy personality. The account of his parentage and of his entry into the monastery of Steyn is full of that combination of hypochondria, delicacy and waspishness which are so often held to characterise him.³³ But the defensive tone disappears entirely in the last page, when Erasmus provides a brief description of his scholarly work. The change is marked by a switch from references to himself in the third person to the first person: 'I will enlarge the catalogue of my works' (p. 30), he says, and the statement is prefaced by the plain assertion, 'In promoting scholarship no one accomplished more' (p. 29). Erasmus never doubts the integrity and value of his work, and his central positions remain consistent. They are based on his concern for 'grammar' and *bonae litterae*: for the exact study, that is, of the ancient languages, especially with a view to providing scholarly texts of the Bible and the Fathers. Philology, Erasmus held, in providing insight into the precise meaning (and, therefore, the spirit) of Christ's message, permits a true *philosophia Christi* based on the practice of a Christ-like life rather than on explicit doctrine or rules, on morality rather than argument, and calling for the reform of the interior life. True followers of Christ are tolerant, peace-loving and charitable; they hate violence and pursue openness, clarity and co-operation. The study of *bonae litterae* educates them in the expression both of exact meaning, and in the tact and refinement necessary to deal undogmatically and sympathetically with those whose perspectives are different. Underlying all this is a conviction that, if people think about language and literature in Erasmus's fashion, and if they could manage to imitate his style (or at any rate his advice about style), society would be better off; certainly, less prey to tyranny and the disasters of war.³⁴

Part of Erasmus's thinking therefore calls simply for large-mindedness and common sense. Truth, he argues in *The Paraclesis*,³⁵ is more powerful when simple and plain (p. 94); be without guile, he advises, and have a 'pious and an open mind' (p. 96); 'Christ wishes his mysteries published as openly as possible' (p. 97); a true philosophy calls for co-operation (ibid.), so that even 'a common labourer or weaver' (p. 98) can be considered a theologian. According to Beatus Rhenanus (his contemporary biographer), Erasmus's own 'great openness' (p. 47) occasioned the rebuke of certain scholars who accused him of 'divulging our secrets', but Erasmus desired to make truth accessible to all.

Erasmus therefore combines a certain optimistic belief in progress with a democratic attitude to knowledge such as might remind us of Francis Bacon. And yet we must read Erasmus's advice in context: unlike Bacon, he makes no attempt to separate theology and other branches of knowledge, but sees the main end of *bonae litterae* as the nurture of his labourer theologians.[36] Like More, he retains an allegiance to the general ideal of Christendom, and does not countenance (however much his thought anticipates) progress as embracing either secularism or Protestantism. Rather, he holds the main enemy to be scholasticism (or what he, and a great squad of Humanists, considered scholasticism to be).

The degeneration of Christianity from an original purity, Erasmus argues, can be blamed on the substitution of Aristotle's authority for Christ's, which has caused men to forget that Christ's teachings are directed primarily at practice, not theory.[37] For a genuine Christian life, he states in *The Paraclesis*, 'there is no need for . . . syllogisms' (p. 94). The aridness and formalism of the technical scholastic arguments are of course endlessly the butt of Humanist reproof and contempt, and Erasmus in England would have heard Colet's denunciation of scholasticism's pedantic and sterile procedures directly in context of a revolutionary attempt to preach sermons based on a historical and philological approach to Scripture.[38] In Colet's spirit, Erasmus never hesitates to equate scholasticism with the kind of formal abstraction which impedes the *philosophia Christi*: 'they still boast that they can see ideas, universals, separate forms, prime matters, quiddities, ecceities . . . And how they despise the vulgar crowd'.[39] The scholastics are obscurantist, that is, and their carefully harboured secrets are, in truth, insubstantial and meaningless.

All this is commonplace enough, but Erasmus's case against scholastic .metaphysicians takes a distinctive twist when he associates their love of abstraction and their obscurantism with war and tyranny. If priests and schoolmasters, Erasmus flatly argues, would inculcate the 'vulgar doctrine' instead of 'that erudition which they draw from the fonts of Aristotle and Averroës, Christendom would not be so disturbed on all sides by almost continuous war' (*Paraclesis*, p. 99). The philosophy of Christ should be made as 'simple as possible and accessible to all' (p. 112), instead of having the 'joined shields' of the 'most subtle and seraphic doctors, some speaking as nominalists, others as realists' promote their intricate arguments. In the wars against the Turks, such prescriptive and arid procedures will only show forth our ambition and 'our loud, tyrannical clamouring'; clearly, the attitude inculcated by such habits leads us to kill, not to save by example (p. 113).

The line of thinking here, again, is fairly clearcut: because scholastic formalism is technical and difficult, it is elitist, and its major utility is the preservation of power based on elitism and, therefore, on pride and arrogance. The scholastics 'fear good scholarship merely because they are apprehensive for their absolute power' (p. 82) and so 'they toss their heads in pride' (p. 68); 'They bring everyone to task; they condemn; they pontificate; they are never in doubt; they have no hesitations; they know everything' (p. 69). In a splendid piece of satire in *The Praise of Folly*, the narrator suggests sending 'these argumentative Scotists and pigheaded Ockhamists and undefeated Albertists along with the whole regiment of Sophists to fight the Turks and Saracens instead of sending those armies of dull-witted soldiers with whom they've long been carrying on war with no result' (p. 161). This at once suggests the causal relationship between scholastic obscurantism and war (it would be appropriate for the philosophers to take responsibility for what they have started), while denouncing the brutality of actual war (the barbarities of the dull-witted) and, of course, satirising the real impotency of the philosophers: if they were sent to fight with *their* weapons nothing very grave would happen. The tragedy of war is, therefore, that the barbarities and the destruction of social order actually promote the obscurantist elite in their superstitious ignorance and intolerant power by making impossible the pursuit of *bonae litterae*, for which peace is necessary and in which alone lies the hope of its continuation.[40]

True learning, Erasmus therefore argues, is the best antidote to war and political tyranny; Christ taught the same doctrine as Socrates, Diogenes and Epictetus, though more fully (*Paraclesis*, p. 101), and knowledge of the ancient languages makes available not only the moral teaching of the ancients but also their relationship with true Christianity as distinct from 'instances, relations, quiddities' and an 'obscure and irksome confusion of words' (ibid.). But studies, Erasmus says, must be 'transmuted into morals' (p. 105), for the philosophy of Christ is not to be learned off like a doctrine or formula: it depends on a 'disposition of mind', communicated by a quality of life, 'by the very expression and the eyes' (p. 98). What is important is not proved logically, not defined, but is an attitude of the whole being, a kind of personal tact; the true philosopher, he argues, can avoid discord and violence only by 'what I might call a holy artfulness'.[41]

Erasmus thus combines a radical faith in Humanist secular learning, especially philology, with an ideal 'plain man's' straight-forwardness, based on co-operation and the open communication of knowledge, and opposed to elitism and the powerful interests it protects. His anti-scholasticism, his sense of progress directed at the betterment of human society, and his egalitarian open-mindedness are forward-looking, modern attitudes, and yet Erasmus (like More) was himself anything but the plain and straightforward man of his own prescription.[42] The education of a truly Christian disposition, 'the holy artfulness' of true diplomacy and learning, as he well knew, was indirect and subtle. The Christian philosopher especially must monitor and carefully adjudicate the degree of truth and falsehood contained in 'venomous language' and 'poisonous defamation', because tyranny arises from just such 'false accusation'[43] rooted in powerful interests, and given to the manipulation of words. In *The Praise of Folly* we encounter the argument of 'a grim old man whose arrogance made it clear he was a theologian' on whether heretics should be burned instead of being refuted in argument. The theologian cites St Paul – 'A man who is a heretic, after the second admonition, reject (*devita*)' (p. 195) – and explains that Paul means the heretic to be removed from life (*de vita*). Folly tells us that some laughed at his ignorant abuse of the Latin, but others found the argument acceptable. Besides being dangerously arrogant, however, the theologian is irascible, and angrily roars out the verse from Scripture; such a combination of obscurantism with a vindictively self-righteous disposition constitutes for Erasmus the most dangerous human type.

Erasmus's thinking about morality is, therefore, deeply rooted in his sense of what language is and is not, with respect to its objects. On the one hand he calls for clarity, directness and simplicity; on the other, for subtlety and learning. We need to be artful simply because the masks of language are so deceptive, because there is no simple correlation between a person's disposition and the language in which he dresses it up, or between language and the things it seems to describe. In teaching us how to achieve the discrimination he recommends, Erasmus combines, in his own writing, the simple and complex in a manner we can describe only as literary. Not surprisingly, in such works as *The Praise of Folly* and the *Colloquies*, irony is his favourite figure, for it lives in that very difference between meaning and saying, disposition and expression to which his theory so keenly draws our attention. Through irony, Erasmus is free to explore the manifold misconstructions (whether the result of wilfulness or ignorance) through which people pursue their ideals, framed by a variety of arbitrary or curious perspectives, vulnerable in myriad ways, indulging one or other of an endless variety of follies, both benign and otherwise.[44]

The fact that what we today call 'literature' best expresses the main teachings of Erasmian Humanism was very well understood by Thomas More, and this is especially clear in his *Letter to Dorp*,[45] in which More defends Erasmus's practice in *The Praise of Folly*, as well as Erasmus's major ideas. More's letter duplicates the main points of Erasmus's own letter to Dorp in defence of *The Praise of Folly* – except that More's is longer, frequently more tedious, and distinctly more combative. Otherwise, the main points recur. More, for instance, vigorously defends the study of 'grammar', arguing that exactness of knowledge is necessary for apprehending the meaning of texts, especially of sacred texts (p. 14): 'Grammar teaches correct speech' and 'advises those who are unskilled in speech not to violate the customs of language' (p. 23). Grammar, in short, protects the 'normal meaning' of words against distortion and misinterpretation, and those who have studied the scriptural languages most closely are 'most deserving of having their names placed on the list of theologians', rather than those who spend a hundred years on the 'trivial quibbles' of scholasticism.

More also makes a strong case for textual criticism, arguing, basically, that the literal sense of the original languages is often difficult to grasp, and he demands humility, hard study, and open-mindedness (p. 34). Jerome and Augustine emended texts to clarify meaning, and such a process of clarification, More suggests, is potentially interminable (p. 44). The act of translation, it seems, does not cease, and the dialogue between meaning and style, calling for attention to the reader's perspective and to the demands of grammatical rigour and customary usage, is perpetually renewed.

In contrast to the humility and learning required for pursuit of exact philological knowledge, More, predictably, places the scholastic quibbles and formalised nonsense which he holds are perversions of ordinary language and clear meaning: 'sheer nightmares and wild imaginings' (p. 20). He isolates especially for criticism Peter of Spain's *Little Logicals*, the principal handbook of arts scholasticism, routinely pilloried by Humanists. He cites examples of 'enunciations . . . so silly, they have practically no meaning' (p. 21), and opposes them to 'customs of the language . . . ordinarily observed' and rooted in the 'nature of things', that is, as 'a common possession' (p. 23). These arguments of the scholastic pseudo-dialecticians, More claims, are entirely futile, and he shares Erasmus's fears that such obscurantism aids those who desire illegitimate power by enabling them to assert their egotistical wills under the guise of true authority. He cites the example of a theologian at a dinner party who reacts to any piece of conversation by at once tearing it apart with a syllogism (p. 30). The host, an Italian merchant, eventually takes to baiting the theologian with fake biblical quotations, a ploy which not only reveals the theologian's ignorance of Scripture, but also the extreme arbitrariness of his arguments. They are based on 'petty quibbles' directed not at all at the truth, but at gratifying his own power and superior authority. 'Sophists', More argues (meaning scholastics), use words deceptively, but theirs is 'a dull-witted form of cleverness and a stupid kind of ingenuity', because they base their victory on a sense of the words 'secretly agreed' among themselves, and 'contrary to universal acceptance' (p. 24). Again, elitism and obscurantism combine to assure the hegemony of those in power. More then proceeds to accuse Dorp of joining in this scholastic habit of mind by deliberately misquoting (p. 26) Erasmus. Does Dorp not see that 'there is nothing so insignificant that calumny cannot find a place for itself therein' (p. 27), including Dorp's own words (pp. 26, 27)? A 'malicious interpreter' (p. 26) can always cause trouble if not disposed to read with a kindly eye (p. 27), seeking common truth in the clear light of day, rather than pursuing his own self-will, consumed by pride, and bent on the distortion of words.

Like Erasmus, therefore, More insists on the centrality of disposition, convinced that morality is distinct from argument, and fully aware of the discontinuity between language and action. More concedes that his own arguments are not likely to persuade Dorp to change his mind about the significance of grammar, but he hopes that 'in the not too distant future, you will stop your arguments on this subject – your endless triumphs in them make it difficult for you to want to retreat – and that you will convince yourself of this point of view, for, as I see it, no one else can do that for you' (p. 50). As a means of pressing home the point, More attempts to accuse Dorp in the end not so much of bad argument as of bad taste, and to shake his confidence by undermining the security of his point of view. Concerning people's reactions to Dorp's criticism More writes, 'I wish you could watch through a window and see the facial expression, the tone of voice, the emotion with which those matters are read' (p. 13). The ploy admittedly is cheap, and amounts to assuring Dorp that people malign him behind his back. But the idea is also to shift Dorp's perspective ('through a window'), and to have him appreciate thereby the various dispositions of others, the kind of thing that shows for instance in facial expression and tone of voice. Dorp's sensibility is simply too unrefined, insufficiently artful in dealing with the world, too unilateral, dogmatic and intolerant. With certain relish, More picks upon Dorp's recommendation that Erasmus should write a praise of wisdom; 'that suggestion really brought a slight smile to my lips' (p. 62); how dull, and ironically self-condemning of Dorp not to see that *The Praise of Folly* really *is* a praise of wisdom.

If we now reconsider *The History of King Richard III*, we can see the degree to which it, too, is a Humanist document in an Erasmian sense. The plain moral, as we see, is against tyrants, and the implied moral is that good rulers are plain-spoken, open and co-operative, fostering a political climate wherein 'good plain wayes prosper' (p. 12). In Richard's ferocious malignity, which comes alive amidst the massive double-play of language, shifting perspectives, contradictory arguments, wilful misconceptions, and all the red herrings and decoys which his interlocutors argue and debate, we catch the drift of a tyrant's progress. The narrator as moralist thus instructs us clearly, and as ironist he offers us some practical training in the world's ambiguities, appreciative of how easy it is to fall victim to the distorted perspectives and intentions of others. And, in thus discovering a way to combine simplicity and complexity, More achieves, for his curious piece, a true literary distinction, amounting, even, to a discovery, a new thing for English letters.

And yet, as we now begin to see, *Richard III* is built upon a deep contradiction, on which this discussion has been touching all along, for More, like Erasmus, was attracted simultaneously to two contrary impulses with respect to language. On the one hand he argues for plainness, openness and co-operation, based on ordinary speech and common meaning. The study of 'grammar' he believes will help to reveal the spirit of Scripture plainly and openly, and thereby make life more Christian by showing the importance of reform from within. We are to cultivate the kind of language that keeps us in touch with things, and with common usage, open to plain discussion. The scientific study of philology, as a means to this end, thus is offered as a tool for the improvement of society, for in the *philosophia Christi* lie the true desire and principal means for peace, the best defence against tyranny, and the most fruitful incentive to co-operation. The chief enemy of such a philologically based programme is scholasticism, whose formal, arcane jargon is not at all the language such as men do use, but wilfully obscurantist, merely protecting the interests of a powerful and intolerant ruling elite.

On the other hand, More also argues that clarity and plainness are never sufficient, because their abuses can only be corrected and guarded against by those who know the unreliability of language, its inherent distance from things, its endlessly translatable meaning, its unrelatedness to disposition, and its impotency to effect reform from within. The language such as men do use is itself no clear guide to the secret direction of the individual will, as *Richard III* shows. More, like other Humanists, genuinely desired to bring the God of Christian tradition closer to the centre of individual lives, but his chief satiric weapon, irony (based on a sense of the division between words and meanings), was in fact hugely successful in demonstrating how language is not transparent to intent, and how the inner life of the spirit remains secret and mysterious. It may be argued that More, like Erasmus, thereby prepared for the very separation of theology from worldly affairs which neither of them desired. Only when Luther made explicit a conclusion which had all the time lain latent in the 'Erasmian manifesto' (namely, that the inner life is inaccessible to mediation by words) were Erasmus and More forced to take stock of, and correct, an unsuspected consequence of their own theories.

IV   METAPHYSICS AND TRADITION

Some implications of these developments for the larger history
of Humanism and its relationship with method become clear if
we consider for a moment Juan Luis Vives' *Against the
Pseudodialecticians*,[46] which repeats many of the arguments of
More's *Letter to Dorp*. Vives mainly attacks scholasticism, and,
again, the intent is to repudiate elitist jargon and to replace it by
rhetoric which is morally instructive. He recites the key positions
we have noticed also in More and Erasmus: he complains about
'monstrous' abuses of language, which act like ulcers and pests
on the mind to corrupt 'all good things' (p. 95); he complains
about the wild, insane clamour and inflexible arbitrariness of the
logicians, of their dangerously garrulous ignorance (p. 113), of
their secrecy (p. 95) and corruption (p. 49). He calls instead for
'common sense and normal human speech' (p. 79), and he
appeals to the adjudication of 'the whole crowd of workmen'
(p. 55). But Vives develops his position a step farther by taking
an extra look at the question of metaphysics. The scholastics, he
claims, apply logic immoderately to metaphysics, but do not
realise that certain secrets of nature cannot be known except
through sense experience (p. 113). The result is a riot of
nonsensical statements about universal nature (p. 115); such
people are not content with natural problems, and aspire, vainly,
to supernatural (p. 119). As Vives' commentator points out, he
holds here that first causes are beyond our reach because we do
not grasp even the laws governing secondary causes, and his
thinking thus belongs with the method of Ramus and Bacon.[47]

More, like Erasmus, was, of course, not interested specifically
in this kind of question, but the bias they both share with Vives in
other respects clearly disposes them to the same conclusions.
More, however, did not fully appreciate the implications of such
a bias; how, for instance, his typically Humanist deployment of
irony, satire, and the multiple perspectives of rhetorical discourse, would contribute to the dissociation (for everyday and
utilitarian purposes) between the language such as men do use
and the life of the spirit. Yet something of this dissociation, I
suggest, is already present in *Richard III*. The King's career, we
recall, is God's exemplum, and reverses the traditional hagio-
graphical tale. But More's appreciation of the conditions which
enabled Richard's outrageous progress have to do with the

incongruities between sign and signified, circumstances and truth, ordinary affairs and the providence directing them. For all its moralising confidence, *Richard III* is, in fact, a largely secular study of the deceptiveness of appearances, and of life's incurable ironies.[48]

More, however, scarcely suspected that Humanism would help to divorce theology from secular affairs in such a fashion, and, as soon as the Reformers made clear the prospect of such a development, his response was immediately reactionary. The spiritual unity of Christendom – the public consensus of tradition, the councils and the Fathers on which More, like Erasmus and Vives, had fairly tritely relied as a basis for universal public meaning – now becomes a cornerstone for More's resistance to Luther, Tyndale and Henry VIII. To defend Christendom, More ironically falls back on the intuitions (and to some extent the language) of scholasticism itself; not, admittedly, the Terminist vocabulary of Peter of Spain and the College of Montaigu, but the realist principles of the theologians who turned logic towards metaphysics in the defence of theology. More's polemical works, in short, powered by his fear of anarchy and tyranny, to which he thought revolutionary Protestantism would surely give rise, centre consistently on his defence of the Real Presence in the Eucharist, and on arguments which would confirm the real participation of sign and signified which that doctrine entails.

In the letter to John Frith[49] (who had written against the doctrine of the Real Presence), for instance, More deplores the 'evyll', 'canker' and 'contagyon' of lurking heresy (p. 441), and argues against Frith's 'allegorye' (pp. 444, 449, 451) – an interpretation, that is, whereby the bread and wine signify but do not really contain the body and blood of Christ. More then appeals to 'the hole trew catholyke fayth' (p. 444), to the 'commune Catholyle Church' (p. 446), to 'all good Chrysten folke' (p. 459), to the 'olde holy Doctours' (p. 458), as well as to Christ's plain words to confirm the mystery, which, admittedly, the human mind cannot fathom, but which it is imperative to believe: the Eucharist really contains what it signifies. The 'wurste kynde' (p. 457) of alternative interpretation, More avers, is the kind offered by Frith, for everyone will then end up believing what he wants (p. 457), and religious truth will, in that case, have no real place in everyday life.

In the *Treatise on the Passion*[50] (and elsewhere), More repeats and develops these positions. There are two elements in the sacrament, he claims: the bodily substance and the accidents of bread and wine (p. 140), which are also Christ's body and blood. This fact is basic to faith (p. 141); the sacrament not only betokens, but also contains (p. 152), and the language of substance and accident, matter and form, by which this unity is conventionally described, is both metaphysical and traditional.[51] Louis Martz has argued, even, that More's doctrine of the Eucharist is the heart of his spirituality,[52] and this is so not least because metaphysical realism guaranteed, for More, meaning to the world and to human experience by maintaining a true, rather than a merely token relationship between signs and things, words and reality, events and meaning. The potential tyranny of the elitism which caused More in the first place to suspect the language of metaphysicians he now modifies, as the opposite kind of tyranny threatens – that of a world from which God, for all practical purposes, is absent. God, we recall, is not much mentioned in *Richard III*, presumably because More assumed his presence in events, but a major achievement of the work is, rather, to show us how ironically and in what disturbing ways ordinary unregenerate people going about their everyday business behave godlessly. And it might then easily appear that such an ordinary, unregenerate world must take its own course – anarchic, disoriented, confused, violent – in a realm for all practical purposes separate from the world of traditional religious values, with which (for linguistic reasons) it can have no effective discourse. This prospect was frightening to More, but the fact remains that he helped to introduce just such a development; at his hand, a certain modern view of the world begins to take shape, filled with uncertainty, ironic, anti-metaphysical, expedient, secular, hard-edged.

A commentator on More's execution wondered how the condemned man could joke at such a time.[53] Part of the answer is simply that he had the confidence to do so; confidence born of an awareness that the true play of language depends at once on the binding of words to meanings, and on a sense of their freedom, their evasive distance from things. Too rigid a binding, or, equally, too much volatility, has a way of becoming tyrannous. More's language as a literary man, as we see in *Richard III*, is (like his jokes), most fully human, finding a place between. So, we may say (as with Humanism at large) that More's thought at once promotes those aspects of method which have to do with a self-critical attitude to language and its referents, with its suspicion of secrecy and intellectual elitism and with its desire for knowledge based on common sense and plain speech, pursued by an increasingly accurate scholarship, co-operatively developed, and with a strong secular orientation. This kind of Humanism was not primarily interested in experimentation or mathematics, and remains, consequently, at the edges of the revolutionary movement I have described in Chapter 1.[54] But More's place at the beginning of modern English letters is important not least because he provided, with such distinction, a version of the continental Humanism which not only created the climate in which the discovery of method was nurtured, but also gave shape to certain of its main preoccupations. That these entailed a division between material, secular power and disembodied spiritual authority (the two faces of tyranny) is a principal reason for including More here, for he deals self-consciously with a version of the very determinism with which method in its developed form challenges us. Thus *The History of King Richard III* gives striking expression to the problems of reconciling secular behaviour with religious morality. As he felt a chasm increasingly opening between these realms, More looked increasingly, and with increasing urgency, to the intuitions of traditional metaphysics. There he found a vocabulary for reconciliation, as it were, between the world and God, but it was a vocabulary More did not feel himself to be inventing. It had always been there, and he argued that he merely returned to the language of Christendom itself, the corporate myth, traditionally and self-evidently true. And yet the note of anxiety remains not only in More's imaginings of an imminent dissolution of Christendom, but in the polemical violence of his defence of tradition against the radical reforms of Luther and Tyndale. In his later career More is increasingly the defender of a tradition which has hardened behind him,[55] and, in so far as the discovery of method in its modern sense starts to become clear in his writings (as in the Humanist enterprise at large), to an equivalent degree the traditional metaphysics to which he reverts is less a self-evident matter of fact than a matter of fact which people must be persuaded again to acknowledge.

CHAPTER THREE
Ben Jonson's *Bartholomew Fair:* Physiological Determinism and Balanced Judgement

I JONSON'S VALUES AND *EVERY MAN IN HIS HUMOUR*

Jonson's *Discoveries*, like his masques and much of his poetry, leaves little doubt about his didactic intent or his Humanist premises.[1] The epigraph tells us that the collection is a kind of commonplace book 'made upon men and matter: as they have flowed out of his daily readings',[2] and the profuse marginal references, quotations and redactions make clear that such daily readings drew heavily upon classical authors. But classical scholarship for Jonson typically nourished an interest in current affairs: a 'reflux', as he says, 'to his peculiar notion of the times'. He warns specifically against academicism ('For never no Imitator, ever grew up to his *Author*' – ll. 885–6), and advises us instead to 'convert the substance, or Riches of an other *Poet*' to our 'owne use' (ll. 2468–9). Doctrine, that is, needs nature to come alive (l. 677), even though a lively style must be acquired by close observation of the masters (l. 1698): 'without Art, Nature can ne're bee perfect; and, without Nature, Art can clayme no being' (ll. 2503–4).

Jonson does not hesitate to make clear the moral implications of this theory. True imitation, he claims, produces 'Elegance and Propriety' (l. 1886), qualities which apply not only to literary style but also to human behaviour. '*Language* most shewes a man', he says in a famous phrase, 'speake that I may see thee' (ll. 2031–2). And elsewhere: 'A good life is a maine Argument' (ll. 91–2). Language, that is, expresses disposition, the wellspring of moral

48

action which, in turn, is the highest kind of eloquence. Literature
and morality are thus co-implicated, and Jonson assures us that
fitness of language to situation is the ground not only of decorum
and self-government, but of government in general: '*A Prince
without Letters, is a Pilot without eyes*' (l. 1234). Indeed, being a
man of letters is itself a kind of public office, so that Jonson as
critic and poetic practitioner sees himself as an arbiter not only of
style, but also of the public morality which style embodies.[3] He
writes poems instructing his reader, his bookseller, the 'learned
Critic' and 'Mere English Censurer'.[4] He writes in high praise of
people and things he values for the grace and humanity they
bring to civilised life, whether the Horatian invitation to supper,
with its combined formality and ease, sturdy individualism and
conviviality, or the complimentary verses to his old teacher
William Camden, or to Lucy, Countess of Bedford, or to the
Sidney country house at Penshurst, or to the musician Ferrabosco who composed for the court masques, or to King James
I, before whom they were performed.[5] Jonson's own masques
are strikingly elaborate celebrations of public order and the value
of monarchy; as Stephen Orgel points out, spectators at a masque
did not so much watch a play as watch a monarch at a play, the
action of which, at the end, passed beyond the proscenium stage
to embrace the aristocratic audience, so affirming the direct
relevance of art's idealised fictions to the actual social order.[6] The
court masque is, thus, essentially a Platonist entertainment
depicting and celebrating the direct participation of individuals
in the ideals which the heightened images of art represent.[7]
Jonson's special brand of Humanism, therefore, we might say,
attempts to reconcile a certain empirical, secular public-
mindedness, such as we find in *Discoveries*, with the gloriously
artificial metaphysical mythology of the masques. And in this
side of his work Jonson remains a direct heir to the tradition
developed in England by Erasmus, Colet, Vives and More. His
tendencies here, in short, confirm a certain optimistic assumption that *bonae litterae* can have an improving effect on human
morality, and that education can enhance the quality of civilised
life.

All this, however, leaves out the Jonson many of us know best:
the author of the famous comedies, the vicious condemner of
a multitude of human aberrancies. Admittedly, there is no reason
why the masques and plays should be irreconcilable, for a man

who upholds certain values must be permitted to condemn those who offend against them. 'By discrediting falsehood,' Jonson says in *Discoveries*, 'Truth growes in request' (ll. 2105–6), and we can perhaps regard the comedies as antimasques[8] designed mainly to show up falsehood and thereby compel us to such true values as the masques present directly. But there is, none the less, an immediately felt difference between the comedies and court entertainments, which has to do with the sheer, unmitigated ferocity of Jonson's comic depiction of human nature, a ferocity which threatens not only to 'discredit falsehood', but by its very unremitting completeness to numb us out of hope that such an array of humankind as these plays depict can be educated into good sense by any means whatever. As T. S. Eliot says, the characters of the comedies fit together with machine-like efficiency, developing very little, if at all.[9] Such characters cannot help themselves: they are victims, we come to feel, of their bodies and temperaments, lurching and colliding at random. They are examples of how completely human motivations can be reduced to blind material processes ('Lust it comes out, that gluttony went in'[10]), and the result is a distinctive Jonsonian ethos – cramped, violent, scatological and comic.[11]

The issue therefore reduces to an antithesis which can be put in the form of a question: how does Jonson the optimist (the Humanist, writer of masques, satirist who would laugh us into virtue) stand in relation to Jonson the pessimist (recorder of the failure of Humanism, playwright, comedian who would laugh us into accepting human aberrations we can do nothing to change)? Basically, we are faced here with the very old issue of freedom and determinism, which can serve now to bring us back to *Discoveries*, and especially to Jonson's praise of Francis Bacon, which is, considering Jonson's habitual asperity, remarkably positive: 'His hearers could not cough', we are assured, 'without losse' (ll. 893–4). The *Novum Organum*, Jonson goes on to say, 'really openeth all defects of Learning, whatsoever' (ll. 935–6), and a page is copied from *The Advancement of Learning* to affirm the Baconian edict against mere 'study of words' (ll. 2090–1) divorced from practical concerns.[12] It seems unlikely, given his receptiveness to this kind of opinion, that when Jonson turned to his first comedy of humours he would have been unaware of the kinds of attack mounted by empiricists, such as Bacon, on traditional Galenic theory, denouncing it for just such empty 'study of words'. Indeed, questions bearing on the relationships of temperament (in the Galenic sense, a human quality), to the body machine were, in Jonson's day, extremely vexed.[13] Certainly, the widespread attack on 'qualities' by partisans of the new method, as I have suggested, was closely associated with scepticism concerning real, formal relationships between words and things. But, if Humanism itself encouraged just such a scepticism, it stopped short of concluding that words have no effect on human action or that man is an automaton merely at the mercy of the blind machinery of his passions. In so far as mechanisation of the world picture extends to the revolutionary development of a modern science of anatomy (and I shall have more to say on this), we can therefore conclude that it stands opposed not only to traditional medical practice, but also to the metaphysically confident vocabulary in which the doctrine of humours and their 'qualities' is expressed. Jonson's comedies delight in exploring this kind of opposition, and they ask us to consider especially those areas of human behaviour where our actions appear as an uncertain amalgam of mechanical compulsion and free choice. Jonson, in short, could not help but be influenced by a contemporary climate of opinion whereby a traditional, humoral theory finds itself richly and provocatively disturbed by procedures and assumptions growing directly from the discovery of method. In *Every Man in his Humour* – the work in which, Jonson tells us, he began his 'studies of this kind'[14] – we can see something of his particular pleasure in exploring such an issue.

Jonson's main subject, in *Every Man in his Humour*, is the conventional notion that true gentility consists of a balance between inherited nature (blood) and acquired behaviour (virtue), even though the play presents us with no positive example at all of a true gentleman. We deduce Jonson's position mainly through the consistency with which he shows his characters trying to be gentlemen, but failing because their gentlemanly theories are so grotesquely at odds with their behaviour.[15] Also, the terms 'gentility' and 'gentleman' are constantly before us, and are played upon with a kind of quizzical insistence:

SERVANT. Sir, there's a gentleman, i'the court without, desires
    to speake with your worship.
CLEMENT. A gentleman? what's he   (v.i.42–4)

Clement's remark means at once 'Who is he?' and (speaking for the play at large) 'What kind of thing is that?' Moreover, there are insistent reflections on 'noble blood', and how lineage and virtue ought to combine.[16] Know'well, for instance, advises his foolish nephew Stephen in terms which Roger Ascham would approve:[17]

> Nor, stand so much on your gentilitie,
> Which is an airie, and meere borrow'd thing,
> From dead men's dust, and bones: and none of yours
> Except you make, or hold it.   (i.i.86–9)

Stephen, however, hopelessly confuses the outward forms of gentility with the real substance: 'I have bought me a hawke, and a hood, and bells, and all; I lacke nothing but a booke to keepe it by' (ll. 37–8). Know'well, on the other hand, as his name indicates, has a firmer theoretical grasp than Stephen of what is required for good behaviour, but his knowledge turns out to be an elaborate rationalisation of his mean-minded actions. To know what it takes to be a gentleman and to be one, Jonson reminds us, are two different things.

Again offsetting Stephen's emphasis on external forms, is the poor water-carrier, Cob's, fantastic, garbled recitation of his lineage:

> Why sir, an ancient linage, and a princely. Mine ance'trie came from a King's belly, no worse man: and yet no man neither (by your worships leave, I did lie in that) but *Herring* the King of fish (from his belly, I proceed) one o' the Monarchs o' the world, I assure you. The first red herring, that was broil'd in ADAM, and EVE's kitchin, do I fetch my pedigree from, by the Harrots bookes. His COB, was my great-great-mighty-great Grand-father. (i.iv.9–16)

Here Jonson parodies a widespread contemporary desire for pedigree on the part of the baseborn. With a small degree of ingenuity, anybody can discover a remarkable ancestry, but the facts of daily behaviour are as little changed for the better as they are by Stephen's acquisition of a hawk, a hood and a book.

Much of the entertainment in this example, as in the others, comes from Jonson's pleasure in revealing the sheer incommensurability between natural endowment and proscribed forms of conduct. Theory can be twisted all too readily to gratify the blood's ignoble urges, and the way is thus open for a variety of permutations on a theme. Paralleling Know'well's relationship to Stephen the country gull, for instance, is that of the wonderful Bobadill to Matthew the town gull. Full of his own idea of himself as a soldier, Bobadill has all the knowledge of what it takes to fight a duel: 'absolute knowledge i' the mysterie' (i.v.116–7), as Matthew avows. But the elaborate technical advice ('save your *retricato* with his left legge, come to the *assalto* with the right' – iv.ix.14–16), is wholly ineffective in making a duellist of Matthew, who is disarmed immediately by the 'tall man', Downright, while Bobadill (like Know'well) rationalises his own failure even to fight: 'sure I was strooke with a plannet thence, for I had no power to touch my weapon' (iv.vii.141–2).

The further violent contrast between the vigorous 'plain squire' Downright and his effete half-brother Wellbred (whom he is determined to make behave like a gentleman, by force if necessary) also shows how little is guaranteed by such a theoretical affinity as family relationship.

> He values me, at a crackt three-farthings, for ought I see: it will never out o, the flesh that's bred i' the bone! I have told him inough, one would thinke, if that would serve: But, counsell to him, is as good, as a shoulder of mutton to a sicke horse. (ii.i.72–4)

Though the harassed Kitely at this point pleads that Downright has natural authority over Wellbred, being 'his elder brother', Downright draws attention to nature's quirky ways, and to the futility of trying to make nature conform to theory.

In counterpoint, Jonson then presents us with Kitely's relationship to his trusted servant, Cash:

> He is a iewell, brother.
> I tooke him of a child, up, at my dore,
> And christned him, gave him mine owne name, THOMAS.
> (ll.15–17)

Cash's origins are unknown, but his worth, in Kitely's estimation, lies in what Kitely has raised him to be. Cash the foundling, it turns out, has more real affinity with Kitely than Downright with his blood relation Wellbred.

At this point it is easy to see how Jonson's concern for gentility fits his title, *Every Man in his Humour*: the quality of blood flowing from the liver and heart determines the body's humours, or temperament, which, as we see, often bears little correspondence to the mind's construction of how the body ought to behave. Certainly, the language of humours is as frequently present in the play as are allusions to gentility. On approaching Downright to ask if he will reprove Wellbred, for instance, Kitely explains why he has not reproved Wellbred himself:

> Nay, more then this, brother, if I should speake
> He would be readie from his heate of humor,
> And over-flowing of the vapour, in him,
> To blow the eares of his familiars,
> With the false breath . . .
>
> That I were iealous.   (ll.101–17)

The emphasis here is predominantly moral (though admitting the influence of passion upon moral judgement): Kitely fears that Wellbred would be affronted, and disposed ('ready') to mollify his bruised feelings by slander. By contrast, when Brainworm, disguised as an unfortunate soldier, offers to sell his sword to the idiotic Stephen, he explains his ill fortune as 'the humour of necessitie' (ii.iv.52). 'Humour' here seems to mean fortune's whim, and is used in such close connection with necessity as to imply a kind of fatalism. 'Humour' is used again in this sense in the explanation by Wellbred of Downright's anger as 'one of my brothers ancient humours' (iv.iii.8–9), for Wellbred seems reconciled to the fact that his brother's disposition is not likely to alter.

Throughout *Every Man in his Humour*, Jonson rings various changes on this theme: Stephen deliberately affects melancholy to put himself in the mood to write poetry. Immovable in his conviction that appropriate material circumstances will engender the desired humour, he asks, 'have you a stoole, there, to be melancholy' upon?' (iii.i.100). No amount of self-induced melancholy, however, will produce poetry from him, despite humoral theories about the somatic bases of imagination. But, at the same time, Stephen may well indeed induce in himself a melancholy mood. Our humours, as Cash reminds us, can be fed: 'Oh I, humour is nothing, if it bee not fed. Didst thou never heare that? it's a common phrase, *"Feed my humour"* ' (III.iv.24–6). Cash's advice comes upon Cob's complaint about fast days, and Cob goes on to express a desire for 'vinegar and mustard revenge' (III.vi.51); the body's temperament, the phrase implies, is determined by what it feeds upon. Such also is Kitely's assumption when, suffering the pangs of jealousy, he feels so physically ill that he believes himself literally poisoned:

> My wife drunk to me, last; and chang'd the cup: . . .
> I feele me ill; give me some *mithridate*.
>
> (IV.viii.21–4)

'Oh, strange humour!' says Wellbred (ll. 28–9), but Dame Kitely puts the contrary case: 'If you be sicke, youre owne thoughts make you sicke' (ll. 40–1). The humour here is fed, not literally, but metaphorically, though the effects are none the less physical. Jonson, it seems, is well aware of how obscurely *psyche* and *soma* interpenetrate, and how relative an explanation 'humours' really is. In all this, his writing reflects, as I have suggested, a widespread contemporary uncertainty in the fields of anatomy and physiology about how exactly the humours affect behaviour.

II PHYSIOLOGICAL THEORY

The main commonplaces of traditional humoral theory are quite straightforward.[18] The ancient Hippocratic scheme, developed by Galen, held that physical health is regulated by a balance within the body of the four humours – blood, phlegm, yellow and black bile. Being a little world, man comprises within himself the four elements of the large world (earth, water, air and fire), each of which has special qualities. Earth is cold and dry, water is cold and moist, air is hot and moist, and fire is hot and dry. Galen held that these elemental qualities are distributed in the body through the action of natural, animal and vital spirits, and that imbalance in the distribution of qualities produces a person's characteristic humour: the choleric man has a predominance of hot and dry, the sanguine of hot and moist, the phlegmatic of cold and moist, the melancholic of cold and dry.

Hippocrates also connected the humours with seasons of the year, and (despite Galen's disapproval of Hippocrates' theory on this point) popular handbooks of the Renaissance, such as John Jones's *Galen's Bookes of Elements* (1574) took delight in charting elaborate correspondences between humours and the seasons, or the times of day, or the ages of man. Since the humours are fed by what we eat, drink and breathe, this theory was especially concerned to preserve health through diet and the adjustment of an individual to the physical environment – with 'quality of life', one might say – rather than with disease as pathological anatomy.

The foremost example in English of Galenist regimen is Sir Thomas Elyot's *The Castel of Helth* (1541). Replete with advice on purging, bleeding and puking, it is based on the idea that nature is cured by what is contrary ('as cold by heate, heate by cold, drythe by moysture, moysture by drythe' – p. 42), and provides elaborate advice and tabulated schemes on the humoral consequences of different kinds of food, weather and seasonal change. The temperate man, for Elyot, is one whose life is balanced, and whose passions are not permitted to engender excessive bodily needs or desires. Behaving decorously – in a gentlemanly way – according to this programme, is therefore a moral matter: intemperance is less a physical compulsion or illness causing one to act destructively, than the result of free will abused by irresponsible action which consequently harms the body.

Admittedly, it is hard to believe that any thoughtful medical practitioner could long maintain such a thoroughgoing moral attitude as to hold individuals justly punished by sickness for their sins. Doctors faced with the array of human afflictions seem more likely to want to cure an illness than moralise about how the patient deserves to suffer, and in *The Methode of Physicke* (1583) Philip Barrough makes this point with reassuring explicitness: 'I have bene more curious in prescribing the sundrie curations and waies to helpe the diseases, then in explaining the nature of them . . . the former being more necessarie' (Preface). Still, traditional humoral theory is sufficiently susceptible of moral extrapolation to permit physicians who were naturalistically inclined in practice readily to reaffirm their orthodoxy in theory if called upon to do so. But during the Renaissance, and as part of that general upheaval which I am describing as the discovery of method, the naturalistic side of medical practice developed so considerably that a serious gap opened between those who would see illness mainly as a mechanical malfunction of the body machine, and those who continued to think about it, on the old model, as a qualitative disorder, theoretically implicated with moral indecorum.

The widespread attack on Galenism during the period reflects at every turn (and sometimes not without irony) the course of such a development.[19] The discovery and publication, for instance, of Galen's Greek text (1525) served to liberate the master from various scholastic, Arabic and assorted superstitious accretions which had gathered upon his ideas over the centuries, so that Galen himself ironically joined the ranks of the anti-Galenists. He was, it became clear, decidedly more ambiguous on the moral implications of medical practice than his scholastic, metaphysically oriented interpreters had held. Although, for instance, he does not actually say the soul is mortal, he does not say either that it is immortal, and he insists that it is a bodily temperament. It was therefore seductively easy for the likes of Pomponazzi to declare that Galen thought the soul is, in fact, mortal. The Humanist recovery of Galen thus became a weapon of attack against traditional Galenism just as the original Aristotle was used against Aristotelianism, and the intricacies of the debate were soon confusing. Paracelsus, for instance, vigorously attacked Galen, but he did so in terms which Galen himself had used against the physicians of his own time – that they sought wealth, not truth. And although Paracelsus was opposed primarily to the hidebound medical orthodoxy of his own day, which he associated with Galenism, his own elaborate theories of correspondence and influence retained a good deal of Galenic theory, even despite Paracelsus's explicit denunciations.

Significant also is the remarkable progress made during the Renaissance in anatomy. With Vesalius's *Seven Books on the Fabric of the Human Body* (1543), as Owsei Temkin puts it, 'the method of human dissection had gained methodological awareness'.[20] Vesalius, in short, had discovered that Galen's anatomising was based on animals, and that applications to the human body were therefore speculative. Thanks largely to Vesalius's actual dissection of human corpses, pathological anatomy became recognised in a novel, even revolutionary, way as the root of much human disease.

Not surprisingly, such a switch of attention to the body's 'Fabric' led to a further general reassessment of the relevance for medical practice of the traditional, metaphysically based 'qualities'. There were some predictable attempts (for instance, by Telesius and Campanella[21]) to materialise the humoral spirits, so that traditional descriptions could appear more machine-like. But such cosmetic treatments could not conceal the main problem, which had to do with how the physical body and non-physical spirits interact. Whether a lively sense of God would be best preserved by concretising spirit, or by insisting on its immateriality, was not generally clear, and the difficulties gave rise to, among other things, an acute sense of just how problematic was the relationship of physical passion to moral behaviour.[22] Montaigne and his followers, for instance, were prepared to stress how relative was morality – how much affected by such things as climate and geography – and the great Shakespearean tragedies can be seen as examples of how difficult it is in practice to extricate moral responsibility from passionate reactions compelled by physical circumstances.[23] The widespread concern about witchcraft and magic was likewise stimulated by uncertainty about the legitimate domains of spirit and matter, providence and mechanically determined physical structures – questions on which, as we have seen, the rise of science placed such crucial emphasis. Doctors were thus all too easily suspected of conjuring,[24] and their craft was often confused with the illicit arts of cunning men and wise women; Francis Bacon was prepared even to argue that 'empirics and old women are more happy many times in their cures than learned physicians'.[25] Nor were accusations of charlatanism always wrong. Keith Thomas records the case of a physician curing an abdominal pain in a man who thought himself possessed by demons. The cure consisted of letting a bat out of a bag at the moment when the incision was made, and then claiming that the incision had freed a malignant spirit.[26]

Such complexities have never quite left medical practice, even though, as scientific method in general attained to increasingly objective procedures, the claims of medicine to be an art based on occult qualities were subjected to scrutiny within an increasingly self-conscious and strenuously self-critical scholarly community concerned to describe and classify the operations of the body machine. And yet during the Renaissance such a community was still in process of formulation, so that the line between the domain of religion (the soul's welfare) and that of physiology (the body's welfare) was particularly uncertain. There was, for instance, recurrent debate on whether natural or supernatural causes (such as demonic possession) were responsible for certain kinds of derangements, as in the case of Elizabeth Jackson, tried before the Royal College of Physicians in 1602 (they found her guilty of causing fits in Mary Glover, a teenage girl, though the defence argued that the fits were owing to natural causes), or of Marthe Brossier, tried in France a half-century later, and found by a panel of ecclesiastics to be possessed, but subsequently acquitted by a panel of doctors who found her ill.[27] One result is that even conventional treatises on the humours, such as Timothy Bright's *A Treatise on Melancholy* (1586), show a distinctive uneasiness as they broach the question of the body's influence on soul.

Bright assures us that no essential alteration can occur to the soul (p. 39), and yet that the soul is not quite free while in the body (p. 41). He holds that passion can affect the spirits to such a degree that soul easily gives itself over to the 'grosse, and mechanicall actions of the bodie' (p. 39). The effects of 'straunge vapours' (p. 48) can thus cross 'the soules absolute intention', and such things as climate and diet seem to 'turne the mind about' (p. 51). What stability, he asks, can the mind have, affected by such change (p. 54)? The spirits, in relation to body, he concludes, are as a hand to a dead instrument (p. 62), and the operation of spirit is mechanical, even though body and spirit are under the soul's direction, and so are not to be explained wholly in mechanistic terms. Although Bright denies that soul is *essentially* affected by body, the very elaborateness of his circumspection makes clear that he knew the point was perplexed.

Similar attitudes and subterfuges are evident in numerous other contemporary physiological treatises.[28] Thomas Wright, for instance, in *The Passions of the Minde in Generall* (1604), has a chapter on how 'Passions blinde the Iudgement' (ii.l. 48ff.), and asserts roundly that 'reason and discourse, are bound . . . to represse and resist . . . unreasonable and beastly motions' (p. 49). But he responds, resentfully, also to contemporary intellectual fashion: 'yet I know some subtill witte would gladly understand how . . . vehement passions . . . undermine the judgement' (ibid.). Wright concludes uncertainly, claiming that the soul is 'a determinate power' (p. 52) which cannot attend to opposite impulses at once, so that the degree to which it is master of or subject to the body's agitations is variable. Wright is well aware, in these pages, of how forceful are the arguments of the 'subtill wittes' (presumably the modern, mechanistic sceptics) upon traditional, moral and metaphysically based theories.

In a similar fashion, Peter Lowe in *The Optick Glasse of Humours* (1607) argues that the soul follows the 'crafts and temperature of the body' (p. 9). But Lowe, like Timothy Bright, is clearly worried by the implications of this position, and hastens to reassure us: 'Wee must not imagine the mind to be passible, being altogether immaterial, that it selfe is affected with any of these, corporall thinges, but onely in respect of the instruments which are hand-maids of the soule' (pp. 12–13). The relationship, however, between 'instruments' and 'soule' is conveniently blurred in the metaphor of handmaids (and in the muddled description of spirits which then follows), so that the direct pressure exerted by mechanism upon morality is deflected. Lowe's evasion of the issue therefore only causes us to feel how unsettling are the questions he has raised.

When placed in this context, Francis Bacon's well-known engagement of similar issues will seem less exceptional, and more a particular (if unusually forceful) treatment of ideas which were in the air. On the one hand, Bacon is a mechanist who berates physicians for neglecting anatomy.[29] Doctors 'quarrel many times with the humours, which are not in fault, the fault being in the very mechanical frame of the part', and medical practice can be best improved by a 'silent and long experience' based on, among other things, comparative anatomy.[30] He attacks Galen especially for being non-empirical and non-progressive ('Is that Galen I see there, the narrow-minded Galen, who deserted the path of experience and took to spinning idle theories of causation?'.)[31] But worse even than the Galenists, he says, are the Paracelsians: their doctrines of sympathies and correspondences are slothful and even further removed from the patient inquisition of material facts.[32]

On the other hand Bacon is also full of pious reassurances: the effects of body on human temperament and action must not derogate from the sovereignty of soul, 'For Providence no doubt directs all kinds of death alike.'³³ The very explicitness of the caveat, as with so many contemporary writers on this subject, shows Bacon's sensitivity to the fact that a predominantly 'methodical' approach to the human body – based, that is, on patient experimentation, on detailed attention to anatomy, and divorced from the traditional, metaphysically oriented Galenism – could all too readily entail a thoroughgoing materialism.

To summarise: the mechanisation of spirit, the development of comparative anatomy, determinist theories of the passions, the relativity of morals, the empirical enterprises of apothecaries, barber surgeons, cunning men and wise women combined during Bacon's century to undermine the metaphysical bases of traditional Galenism. The root challenge offered by the discovery of method to Galen (as to Aristotle) was, therefore, basically straightforward, and lay in certain assumptions about what was most real in physical bodies. Galen had opposed the atomists outright, and his medieval commentators followed him on this point. He thought that qualities are real, and inhere in a material substrate, the *ousia*, called *soma* or *hyle* ('wood', body). For Galen, the primary qualities (hot and cold, dry and moist) have independent, objective existence; density, rarity, smoothness and hardness are therefore secondary. This interpretation, of course, is precisely opposite to that held by Galileo, Bacon and Hobbes, who, like the ancient Atomists, declared those aspects of matter to be primary which are pre-eminently measurable.

Debate about the humours and passions, therefore, even in conventionally based treatises on physiology during the Renaissance, takes its place in the larger history of the emergence of scientific method, in so far as the latter is linked to an assumption that the most dependable knowledge results from the measurement of corpuscular bodies. Writing in 1702, John Purcell recalls how the old doctors used to talk in terms of occult qualities, which showed they knew nothing of 'the true mechanism of Man's Body'. 'Nothing', he adds, 'is now acceptable but what is explain'd Mechanically by Figure and Motion'³⁴ – that is, by the mathematical quantification of mass in space. A hundred years earlier, this issue had not been so clearly decided, and Ben Jonson's comedies, I suggest, draw much of their energy from this very irresolution. Jonson was fully conscious of the claims of both sides of the argument with respect to the effects of body upon soul, and of the multitude of ironies and complexities which made the interpretation of humours – such as we see in *Every Man in his Humour* – at once so theoretically satisfying and so darkly comic.[35]

Jonson therefore remains a traditionalist, even a metaphysician, but one in whom resonates a certain disillusionment with a morality based on old-fashioned Humanist ideals; men *are* more mechanical and absurd than they are ever likely to admit. Their moralising might even seem, depressingly, a mere epiphenomenon bearing no certain relationship to action at all. At the same time, however, the quality of good judgement is necessary to preserve civilised order, and should be educated. Jonson, that is, could not entirely disavow his Humanist prejudice that men can attempt to conform themselves to ideals through virtuous action, a vision of things which, in good faith, he celebrated in public before the King. But the fact remains, as we have seen, that Jonson's mature comedies present the departures from virtue with such astounding vigour that readers and audiences can be forgiven for mistaking his negative examples for the human condition itself. In this respect, however, Jonson's late comedy *Bartholomew Fair* is unusual because it shows us with special completeness the author's sense of how the mechanical operation of spirit is indeed an ineradicable human fact, but also how humanity is not, for all that, merely automatic.

III PUPPETS AND VAPOURS IN *BARTHOLOMEW FAIR*

In broad terms, *Bartholomew Fair* belongs comfortably within the canon of Jonson's best-known plays, and we may even be struck by how much it resembles *Every Man in his Humour*. Both works have an ingeniously constructed but similarly decentralised action; both (alone among Jonson's major comedies) are concerned with family relationships; both are preoccupied with the dubious efficacy of legal warrants for correcting abuses; both contain a satire on tobacco; both show that justice is a matter of luck (and perhaps art), better obtained by the relaxation of strictures than by their rigorous imposition; and in both the principal officer of justice invites everyone home for a feast.

Bartholomew Fair, however, is more mellow[36] than *Every Man in his Humour,* and the action is more profuse: there are more speaking parts, and there is a more complex commingling of the various groups and sub-groups of characters. This in part suggests the randomness of ordinary human exchange – the complex, restless, aimless cross-currents of social intercourse. But the play never becomes just a series of events, for there is a difference between representing randomness and just being random; the first, we might say, is the achievement of art, the second its failure, and, as artist, Jonson therefore manages both to communicate a sense of the incorrigibly diverse and unpredictable in human behaviour while also sustaining a satisfying narrative design. His aim in doing this is to depict how readily human behaviour can veer off to rigid determinism on the one hand, and empty indetermination on the other. The structure of *Bartholomew Fair* itself helps to establish the point. The *dramatis personae* can be divided into three distinct groups: the Littlewit family, the Overdo family, and the fairdwellers.[37] Busy, Quarlous and Winwife are associated initially with the first group, and Cokes and Wasp with the second. Quarlous's curiosity about Cokes causes the two families to come together, and they do so at the Fair. Their meeting thus provides opportunity for a contrast between the two families, and also a further major contrast between the fairdwellers and those who visit the Fair. The visitors, especially when they act from rigid principle, intending to change things or to reprove, are most likely to undergo change themselves; the unprincipled fairdwellers remain perennially the same.

As a visitor to the Fair, the audience also is challenged to come to terms with what it represents.[38] Most obviously, it is a place where people smoke tobacco, get drunk, pimp and pander, steal purses, eat pig, are taken up endlessly by distractions, vanities and hobbyhorses, where it is in the swing of things to be quarrelsome, vain, foolish, out for larks, selfish and generous by fits, noisy, dirty and boisterous as whim declares. The word 'enormity' recurs everywhere, and especially to Overdo (the justice of the peace who has come in disguise to discover law-breakers), for it is all he sees. Literally, 'enormity' means 'departure from the norm'. But, as Overdo comes to see at the play's end, the norm we reasonably require we mostly cannot observe; that is the liability of Adam's flesh. Leatherhead's reiterated hawker's cry, 'What do you lack?', therefore rings through the play with the force of an almost metaphysical question, drawing attention to that radical human insufficiency which Overdo at last is forced to acknowledge in himself. None of us is quite normal, and the Fair proves it. Adam's flesh 'lacks' Adam's unfallen nature: the garden has become a fair, the earthly city, and there is not much we can do to alter it, except to tolerate the muddle, and be patient in seeking through the configuration of life's confusions a touch of beauty, and in the lineaments of beauty the form of a truth, such as art provides.

It is not difficult to detect the moments at which Jonson contrives to promote such a heightened, metaphorical sense. The Fair is, Wasp tells Cokes, 'i' your braine' (I.v.92–3); Busy sees it as Satan's shop (III.ii.42), and at the 'heart o' the Fayre' (I.v.155) is Ursula, the pig woman, who is in some manner akin to the carnal, voracious, fecund, intelligent, overpowering animals she roasts. At one point she spills hot grease on her leg, basting herself, as it were, to emphasise the affinity. Busy proclaims that she is the world, the flesh and the devil – the triad of sins, that is, inherited by mankind at the Fall. She compares herself to Eve, but not in a spiritual way; rather, in directly anatomical terms: 'I am all fire, and fat, *Nightingale*; I shall e'en melt away to the first woman, a ribbe, againe, I am afraid' (II.ii.50–1). Her booth is a focal point, a place of relief for those (such as Dame Overdo and Win) who are shy about acknowledging the exigencies of their physical nature, as well as those who crave a variety of other physical comforts.[39] Ursula, in short, is the centre of the Fair, and she is larger than life. Without being allegorical, the play thus gives us the sense that in her, and in the Fair in general, we see writ large the typical condition of that glorious enormity of nature, God's human creature.

The law, then (in the person of Overdo) must to some extent leave the Fair to itself, because of the incommensurability between reason's prescription – the letter of the law, that is – and the incorrigible facts. Certainly, Jonson takes endless delight in presenting us with instances of how ineffective is argument in influencing events, of how relative is spoken meaning, and how impossible it is to keep to our words. Thus we encounter again that key preoccupation of *Every Man in his Humour*, having to do with how intractable is ordinary, unregenerate fallen human nature to improving theories. This is, basically, an Erasmian kind of insight, but *Bartholomew Fair* buzzes so fiercely with a swarm of inconsequential, contradictory, fatiguing, irrational and out-landish verbal exchanges that language itself often seems (in a quite un-Erasmian way) just another example of the random compulsions and accidental collisions of the Fair:

> Hang 'hem, rotten, roguy Cheaters, I hope to see 'hem plagu'd one day (pox'd they are already, I am sure) with leane playhouse poultry, that has the boany rumpe, sticking out like the Ace of Spades, or the point of a Partizan, that every rib of 'hem is like the tooth of a Saw: and will so grate 'hem with their hips, and shoulders, as (take 'hem altogether) they were as good lye with a hurdle.   (II.v.104–10)

Here, Ursula's invective against Quarlous and Knockem is both vivid and gratuitous, a flamboyant piece of colourful abuse which has no effect on anything whatever, and is as quickly forgotten as it is spoken. *Bartholomew Fair* is full of such language, sometimes protracted and dreary, or on the edge of nonsense:

> Yes, fait, dey shal all both be Ladies, and write Madame. I vill do't myselfe for dem. *Doe*, is the vord, and D is the middle letter of Madame, DD, put 'hem together and make deeds, without which, all words are alike, la.   (IV.v.87–90)

Whit is no monument to intelligence, but his point that words without deeds are all alike is close to Jonson's heart. Further to enforce the point, there is a good deal of silly wordplay wherein characters admire their own conceits – the disembodied design of their own words, as it were – while we remain amused at their vain and ineffectual behaviour. The petty-bourgeois Littlewit does it all the time: 'and make a *Iack* of thee, instead of a *Iohn*. (There I am againe, la!)' (I.i.17–18); 'that ever had the fortune to win him such a *Win*! (There I am againe!) I doe feele conceits comming upon mee' (ll.30–2); 'I have an affaire i' the *Fayre*' (I.v.145–6). In the same vein, the naïf, Bartholomew Cokes, latches upon the likeness of his name to the Fair: 'I call't my *Fayre*, because of *Bartholmew*: you know my name is *Bartholmew*, and *Bartholmew Fayre*' (ll. 65–7). Cokes – the play's silliest mortal – sees no difference at all between names and things; the play, however, assaults us everywhere with exactly the opposite view.

There is, simply, too much in events, too little consistency in language, and too little judgement in mankind to permit the regulation of human dealings by principle. The extreme example is Grace Wellborn, who writes on a tablet two names proposed by her suitors, and promises her hand to whichever name is preferred by the first person who comes along. That this person happens to be a madman makes no difference, and there is nothing in the play to suggest a more reliable way of making a match.

And yet Jonson does not allow this side of his play to triumph totally. *Bartholomew Fair* is not wholly pessimistic, and does not describe the human condition as entirely anarchic. The Fair, after all, has its pie-powders (courts for petty offences), and the fairdwellers threaten one another with legal retribution, as Leatherhead does Trash, whom he accuses of spoiling his market. Justice Overdo's name is held in respect, and it is clear that the Fair must have regulation, even though Overdo's attempt to measure the length of puddings (II.i.19) is absurdly rigorous.

The degree to which Jonson's satire here is topical has not been sufficiently acknowledged. Contemporary laws governing market practices were intricate, even though dependent to a high degree on pledges, common sense and good faith. Deals were made not by contracts, but by verbal agreement and shaking of hands. There were no scales, for instance, to weigh cattle, and traders had to be expert at assessing without measurement.[40] And yet, because annual fairs were crucial to the country's internal commerce, there was, even from earliest times, as one historian tells us, 'great anxiety to secure fair dealing'.[41] Consequently there developed an extraordinary body of unwritten laws and observances, the *Lex Mercatoria*, which defies explicit codification, though the job of pie-powder courts was to administer it equitably when disagreements arose in practice.

In the case of Bartholomew Fair, legislation in Jonson's day was even more complicated. On dissolving the monasteries, Henry VIII had granted the revenues of the market's 'stallage, piccage, toll and customs'[42] to Sir Richard Rich, who then, in 1596, dealt with the corporation of the City of London to draw up a detailed composition of tolls and rules governing the Fair, satisfactory to both parties.[43] The ensuing, byzantine legislation was further vexed when King James closed the Fair in 1603, pronouncing that it was not to reopen until licensed by him.[44] As Jonson no doubt well knew, James could happily take an impossible attitude to such an issue, a fact sufficiently demonstrated by the King's having written a charter for the Luton Fair, which is, we are told, 'six times as long as any of the older charters':

> King James thought he knew more than his Chief Justice, Sir Edward Coke, or any other lawyer, and in his legal documents decided that nothing was to be assumed, but all details must be fully set out. Sir Edward told him 'he might be King of England, but he did not know English law'.[45]

It is not clear if Jonson knew about the Luton Fair charter, but *Bartholomew Fair* gives a wonderfully full sense of the actual difficulties of regulating such an event. It seems that we cannot avoid the responsibilities of judgement simply by concluding the problem too complex to judge, but we must also understand that overlegislation itself can become an evasion. There is, consequently, a marked interest, throughout Jonson's play, in licences and conventions; the means, as it were, by which society (like a fairground) is regulated both externally and internally, by explicit legislation and by unwritten, time-honoured practice.

Bartholomew Fair opens, for instance, with the Stage-keeper discussing the actors, and which parts they will play. He then talks with the Bookholder, who sends him off, scolding him for presuming to offer judgement on the play: 'Away Rogue, it's come to a fine degree in these *spectacles* when such a youth as you pretend to a judgement' (Induction, ll. 53–4). The Scrivener then reads, at inordinate length, a series of articles of agreement, supposedly drawn up between author and audience. What follows combines legal boilerplate ('IMPRIMIS, It is convenanted and agreed, by and betweene the parties abovesaid . . .' – Induction, ll. 73–4) and futile prescription that members of the audience judge the play according to their wit and the amount of money they paid for admission.

All this has the effect of drawing attention both to how different is art from ordinary experience, and also how plays depend on certain 'agreements' between audience and players, so that art is not entirely discontinuous with life. It is impossible to draw clear lines between the two domains, between audience and author, between approval and censorship, between legal prescription and the facts to which it applies. Working to rule inhibits life; yet rules are necessary, and the play needs a licence. Thus the Epilogue appeals to the King's judgement as to 'whether wee to *rage*, or *licence* break' (Epilogue, l. 7), and within the play the marriage licence is a central plot device. The relationship, therefore, between what we might call humane judgement and the laws which enshrine it appears at once arbitrary and necessary. It is arbitrary in so far as human behaviour is so subject to the compulsions of the body machine that no amount of language has much effect. And here we can observe how Jonson's typical Humanist irony threatens to spill into a nightmarishly comic sense that there is no reliable continuity whatever between words and deeds. But it does not quite spill all the way: judgement and law remain necessary, not just because we require order, but because, under certain conditions, they work successfully.

We must now ask what such conditions are, and this question brings us back to Jonson's response to contemporary physiological theory. For in *Bartholomew Fair* it seems that departures from judgement take place in either one of two polarised directions, each of which is describable in physiological terms, and good judgement is possible only when the poles are in equilibrium. Jonson's chief means of exploring this idea is the opposition between 'puppets' and 'vapours', those conspicuous devices which commentators on this play have been at pains to explain. Bad judgement, we learn, causes people to behave either like wooden dummies ('wood', we recall, is *hyle*, the material substance of which bodies are made), or as creatures volatilised under the influence of spirits, those thin substances which, when they rise to affect the brain in an unruly manner, are called 'vapours'. As Lemnius puts it in *The Touchstone of Complexions* (1576), 'the Spirite is a certayne vapour, effluence or expyration, proceding out of the humours' (p. 8). In both cases, departure from the ideal renders one subject to the body's determinism. Or perhaps the body's determinism causes bad judgement in the first place; the issue, again, is not clearly decided.

Puppet shows, in Jonson's England, were a favourite form of fairground entertainment, often associated with mountebanks, or quack doctors:[46] the 'miserable get-penny of a gang of rude, ignorant, and sordid mountebanks', writes Guastalla Baldi in 1589,[47] and John Evelyn's *Diary* comments on English fairgrounds as the haunt of 'Montebankes, Operators, and Puppet Players'.[48] Puppet shows were also known as 'motions', a word which describes mechanical movement, and in *Bartholomew Fair* the words are used interchangeably: 'a Puppet-play of mine owne making . . . that I writ for the *motion* man' (I.v.146–7). It seems likely that an audience would associate the puppets' mechanical 'motion' with the body's automatism, and Jonson elsewhere repeats the association between vapours and puppets (or motions) as if relying on a stock response. In *A Tale of a Tub* (1633) he writes, 'the very vapour of the Candle, / Drive all the motions of our matter about' (v.vii.33–4); and in *Every Man out of his Humour* Sagliardo, the would-be gentleman, 'comes up every Term to learne to take Tabacco, and see new Motions'.[49] In the first instance, 'motions' means a shadow show, driven by the hot air rising from a candle; in the second (as in *Bartholomew Fair*), tobacco smoke provides the 'vapour'. We may recall here Timothy Bright's description of the body (*hyle*, or 'wood') being moved by spirits as a hand works upon an instrument. Since Jonson's puppets in *Bartholomew Fair* were probably glove puppets, operated by hand, such a conjunction of ideas is suggestive.[50] I do not claim that Jonson deliberately reproduces Bright's metaphor; only that there is reason to suggest that puppets and vapours belong together cogently, as a figure for the body's mechanical operation. Indeed the theory of a complementary opposition of the body's rigid and fluid principles seems to have been commonplace in medical treatises of the time. Helkiah Crooke; for instance, in *Microcosmographia. A Description of the Body of Man* (1615), describes human bones as 'like the frame of a ship', hard and dry, and 'by siccity as wood' (p. 926). By contrast, the heart enlivens the frame by manufacturing vital spirits, 'ayrie and bloudy mingled together' (p. 373). Batman's well-known commentary on *De Proprietatibus Rerum* (1582) also talks of the bones as 'the hardest and dryest parte of the body', needing to 'receive temperance of kind heat of flesh and bloud' (p. 65), which are moist and airy. And in *The Touchstone of Complexions* Lemnius describes how, from the mind's affliction by 'vapours . . . proceedeth . . . slownes to understand', whereas a too 'dry' constitution makes for weak memory because excessive hardness will not 'admit anye impression' (p. 120). In the satirical, physiologically based *The Hospital of Incurable Fooles* (1600), Tommazo Garzoni likewise claims that folly proceeds on the one hand from 'an emptie soacked head' which 'whirleth about a thousand fopperies' (p. 1), and on the other from a temperament too 'blockish, and insensate' (p. 2); that is, either from 'fume and vapour' (p. 26) or from being 'as stiffe as a stake' (p. 117). Interestingly, *The Hospital of Incurable Fooles* is inspired by Erasmus ('the olde Dutch-man, he of *Roterodam*' acknowledged in the Epistle Dedicatory), and thus combines physiology with Erasmian satire in a manner recalling Jonson's own practice. Moreover, Garzoni's book is effective as satire precisely because it forces us to acknowledge the limits of traditional humoral theory in explaining the compulsive behaviour of the world's sick fools. In the context of the present discussion, *The Hospital of Incurable Fooles* therefore bears an affinity with works apparently unlike it, such as Crooke's *Microcosmographia*, where we also find an intriguing mixture of old-fashioned language and new method. Crooke, for instance, combines sophisticated, post-Vesalian anatomical drawing and detailed descriptive analysis with a great deal of Galenic language and presupposition. Both books, in short, like so many others in the period, record a pervasive, dynamic sense of questions raised by the new anatomists for traditional humoral theory.

The relationship between puppets and vapours in *Bartholomew Fair*, I suggest, is therfore one of complementary opposition, such as that between the body's hard and soft members. These opposites are not exclusive: the puppets after all have vaporous fits, and the Fair's volatile pickpocket, Edgeworth, is very likely compulsive, a kleptomaniac. But we are, none the less, presented with a distinct opposition which we can take to represent two sides of the human enormity: how judgement is dehumanised when we are made wooden by becoming mere spokesmen, mere imitators of abstract ideals, mere parodies of ourselves, and how judgement is dehumanised by our having no principles at all, acting just by impulse.

The characters in the play who behave most like puppets are Overdo, Busy and Troubleall. Overdo, who visits the Fair in disguise to reprove enormities, is ready to 'defie all the world' (II.i.2) in the name of strict regulation: he would 'measure the length of puddings, take the gage of blacke pots and cannes, I, and custards, with a sticke; and their circumference, with a thrid; weigh the loaves of bread on his middle-finger . . .' (ll. 19–22). Of course, this excess is as impossible to implement as the Scrivener's 'Articles of Agreement', and insisting upon it drives Overdo only towards distraction, while guaranteeing a failure of judgement.

In Troubleall, Overdo's one-time deputy, a similar imbalance has tipped all the way into insanity: Troubleall 'haunts the *Fayre*' (IV.ii.8), demanding of the world Justice Overdo's warrant for any action whatsoever. 'Warrant, for what, Sir?' asks Edgeworth. 'For what you goe about, you know how fit it is' (ll. 3–4), replies Troubleall, with remorseless, demented logic. His mind, as we say, is gone. It is not just that he is wrong to ask for a warrant; indeed he is sometimes exactly right, as when he comes upon the disguised Overdo sitting in the stocks, where he has been (wrongly) put on suspicion of being a pickpocket. 'Had they warrant for it?' asks Troubleall, 'shew'd they *Justice Overdoo's* hand? if they had no warrant, they shall answer it' (IV.vi.125). Troubleall, alone, speaks to the point, but he does not know that he does, for he speaks without judgement, as an automaton.[51] Slot machines sometimes do, gratifyingly, come up with the right combination: they are none the less mechanical for that.

Zeal-of-the-Land-Busy is the third main puppet character, and, appropriately, he receives his come-uppance at the motion man's booth, where the real puppet Dionysius argues him into acceptance of the Fair which Busy was secretly pleased to visit, under the hypocritical pretence of condemning it. 'So, walke on,' Busy advises, 'fore-right, turne neyther to the right hand, nor to the left: let not your eyes be drawne aside with vanity, nor your eare with noyses' (III.ii.30–2), and, as he proceeds, Leatherhead's cry 'What do you lack?' echoes in his ears. Here, as throughout, Busy's Puritan cant expresses a mind inflexibly fixed, though amusingly at odds with the man's voracious appetites in other respects: 'I found him', Littlewit explains to Purecraft, 'fast by the teeth i' the cold Turkey-pye, i' the cupbord, with a great white loafe on his left hand, and a glasse of Malmesey on his right' (I.vi.34–6). But at the puppet booth Leatherhead's question turns up again as part of the show – 'By and by, you shall see what *Leander* doth lacke' (V.iv.127). What is it, we ask, that the puppets lack, to distinguish them from Busy?

As a way of getting to an answer, we should notice that, when Busy breaks into the puppet theatre, he is himself like a marionette, and becomes part of the show. The spectators enjoy this, as Puritan and puppet argue about the legitimacy of theatrical entertainment, until, finally, the puppet replies to Busy's (predictable) charge based on Deuteronomy 22:5 prohibiting the sexes from changing clothes. 'It is your old stale argument', says the puppet (spoken, he adds, with 'malicious purblinde zeale' – v.v.103–6), but it is confuted by the fact that puppets do not have sexual characteristics. Dionysius proves this by lifting up his garment, with the result that Busy is confounded and yields the argument. The puppet lacks rebellious members, whose excitation is not predictable nor subject to reason's rule, but rather subject to the body's fluid energies. In at last accepting the puppets, Busy therefore ironically distinguishes himself from them, and in so doing accepts the Fair, with its seething variety of rebellious energies and its refusal to be governed by principle. He accepts, that is, what is indicated by 'vapours', the random rising-up of spirits under the influence of the weather, or of food and drink, to cause the unpredictable range of our bodily whims and moods.[52]

Throughout *Bartholomew Fair*, the word 'vapours' is used (somebody has counted[53]) sixty-nine times, and culminates in the game of Act IV, which seems to consist in contradicting whatever anybody else says. 'Here they continue their game of *vapours*, which is non sense', reads the stage direction (IV.iv). 'I have no reason, nor will I heare of no reason, nor I will looke for no reason, and he is an Asse that either knowes any, or lookes for't from me' (ll. 42–4), says Wasp near the beginning of the exchange, as if laying down the rules. All this, clearly, belongs with the vigorous, inconsequential, irresponsible fountaining of language characteristic of Whit and Knockem and Ursula and the fairdwellers generally, and it is opposite to all that is represented by the rigid forms and demands for consistency of Overdo, Busy and Troubleall, the play's chief human automata.

In so far, therefore, as puppets and vapours claim our allegiance independently from one another, we can conclude that they impede judgement. Alternatively, all the moments of genuine revelation in *Bartholomew Fair* tend to come when puppets and vapours are most closely in conjunction: 'Two pence a piece, Gentlemen, an excellent Motion', cries the doorkeeper; 'Shall we have fine fire-works, and good vapours?' (v.iv.22–3) replies Knockem, as if asking for the complete picture. It is as if the two principles of bones and blood, tending to rigidity and fluidity, need to be held in equipoise to enable judgement itself to operate. Judgement does not, therefore, so much banish the rebellious body as neutralise its adverse effects, a fact of singular importance for that aspect of the play which, at the end, calls upon the King's judgement in a sense to neutralise the Fair by treating it as an antimasque. As one critic puts it, the King's judgement is called upon so that 'the play can end in the happiest of transformation scenes, in which the king turns the sunlight of his countenance on playwright and players, and the vapours disperse'.[54]

And yet I am not sure how wholehearted is Jonson's compliment to the royal countenance. The playwright does not, of course, insult the Court, but there is a complexity in his art which prevents him from concluding that men at Court and men at the Fair are entirely unlike. Thus the deliberate confusion of levels of reality at the beginning of the play (when the Stage-keeper and Bookholder and Scrivener speak), is reproduced at the end by a series of masque-like revelations which work, as it were, outward, towards the King. The first of these is the puppet show itself. It is, already, a play within a play (and parodies much of the main action), resulting in Busy's transformation, in which he dispels 'enormity' in a moment of true insight, or judgement. This is precisely the kind of thing that happens in a masque, and, indeed, the puppets are associated explicitly with a masque earlier, when Cokes engages them to 'furnish out the Masque' (III.iv.146–7) at his wedding. Revelation thus comes when Busy steps out of his inadvertently assumed actor's role as Puritan hypocrite, and discovers the relevance for real life of the values the motion man has led him to see. But no sooner is this emergence complete than Overdo in turn 'discovers himself', throwing off his disguise, much as the puppet and Busy had done, and making *his* judgement, turning *his* countenance on the action. 'It is time, to take Enormity by the fore head, and brand it; for, I have discover'd enough' (v.v.125–6).

Overdo's view of the proceedings is more comprehensive than Busy's in the argument with Dionysius, and his authority is superior. But his attitude remains much like Busy's before the debate with the puppet, and some further revelation is therefore required to dispel his illusion. This comes when the Justice's good wife, model of propriety, discloses her presence by throwing up on account of too much drink, and calling upon her Adam for a basin. The stage direction is wonderfully restrained: 'Mistresse Overdoo is sicke: and her husband is silenc'd.' Vapours again correct the puppet: as Busy admits rebellious members, so Overdo admits he is Adam's flesh, until, at last, the burden of final judgement is thrown upon the King, and the sequence of characters disclosing themselves, or stepping out of the flow of the action to pass judgement, comes to rest with him.

In this final step beyond the proscenium altogether different, however, from those which precede it? The play would seem to suggest, No, not altogether. The King cannot dispel the Fair any more than Justice Overdo or Busy. His judgement, like theirs, requires balance between puppets and vapours, between acquired knowledge and inherited temperament, between the body's inertness and the fluid operations of the spirits. This does not mean that judgement is impossible, or that soul is not free. But it presents in the richest form, among Jonson's works, the claims and counterclaims of the ameliorative Humanism he espoused, and the facts of human behaviour he knew by experience. His art, I suggest, takes energy not only from his genius – his natural inheritance, as it were – but also from the fact that the current state of thinking on relationships between moral behaviour and physiological compulsion provided him the opportunity to acquire, as he did, such complex insight into the demands of body upon soul, of mechanism upon morality, and into the uncertain domains of each. Although his characters so frequently behave with the lurid violence of the sub-human, and although, at different times and in different modes, Jonson seems to tip the balance towards mechanism (judgement determined by puppets or vapours) rather than towards free and sound judgement, he refuses complete certainty to one solution or the other. The greatness of his art resides, partly, in that refusal.

The discovery of method, therefore, impinges upon Jonson's art according to a certain mode, having to do specifically with how the body's mechanism determines our actions. In so far as Jonson's vision is comic, we may conclude that it is pessimistic, for we watch his assortment of helpless puppets career and lurch and crash into one another, each preserving an illusion of freedom (this combination the surest source of laughter, according to Bergson). Such characters are determined equally from 'above' and from 'below': driven no less, that is, to folly by disembodied ideals than by reasonless whim and desire, the twin determinisms of abstracting intellect and volatilised will.

Still, Jonson's literature would be a lesser thing were his vision only thus. He is also a satirist who would move us to virtue; who, despite his appreciation of our bodily compulsions, did not give up on the ideal that virtue was to some degree teachable by art. Such an ideal, I began by pointing out, declares itself most explicitly in his masques, those elaborate metaphysical statements about the reality of virtue and the hierarchy of values. Admittedly, contemporary records suggest that courtly appropriations of the masque were not always high-minded and formal, and performances could turn into uproarious affairs suggesting a kinship with popular revel and festival.[55] The fact remains, however, that Jonson's masques are explicit statements of the kind of metaphysical vision which the monarchy found theoretically sustaining.[56] And, as we see, his plays do not turn away from such ideals, though the plays are more complex and interesting than the masques precisely because they show us how problematic is the construction of a metaphysical vehicle to sustain those traditional values which Jonson wishes to inform all his writing, however tacitly.

We can conclude, therefore, that Jonson proceeds one step further than Thomas More in the direction of a free investigation of the relationship between metaphysics and art, and such a development, I suggest, follows upon Jonson's serious engagement with issues arising out of the contemporary discovery of method. Although not a philosopher of science, Jonson is none the less seriously concerned about the kinds of challenge extended by the new method to traditional morality in the form of deterministic materialism. A good deal of his satire makes fun of the old, dogmatic humoral theories. It does so, however, in terms directly reflecting a fact recorded even by traditionally based physiological treatises during the Renaissance: namely, that new, mechanistic models of human anatomy and physiology were raising difficult questions, in a fresh and pressing manner, about our freedom to direct our bodies' actions. Methodological developments in the sciences of anatomy and physiology consequently challenge, and are in turn questioned by, the traditional, metaphysically oriented humoral theory.

From the interplay between this challenge and refutation, grown provocatively intense in Jonson's day, his own writing draws, in part, its unusual energy.

CHAPTER FOUR

John Donne's *Anniversaries*: New Philosophy and the Act of the Heart

I THE POEMS AND THEIR PROBLEM

The trouble with the *Anniversaries* was clear from the start, as we know from Ben Jonson's trenchant and famous observation on *An Anatomy of the World* (*The First Anniversarie*) that the poetry was 'profane and full of Blasphemies', and 'if it had been written of ye Virgin Marie it had been something'.[1] Donne himself, in a letter, complains of 'many censures'[2] upon his book, and it seems likely that contemporary readers felt uneasy at the embarrassing extravagance of the poet's praise for a dead fifteen-year-old girl whom he had never seen. It is hard not to share something of this reaction; it is just as hard, however, not to feel the massive distinction and disturbing power of the poetry.

The *Anniversaries* therefore place a special burden on criticism having to do with a certain, evident flaw which, because it is a matter of taste, threatens to vitiate the whole. Consequently, it is insufficient to claim that the poems are good in patches; the hyperbole remains problematic, and we must try to explain it. One way to do this is to provide some formula for 'understanding' Donne's treatment of Elizabeth Drury: perhaps we should see in her Astraea, or Queen Elizabeth, or Wisdom, or a Protestant version of the restored Image of God.[3] Or perhaps we should remove her from the centre of the poems altogether, and allow the real subject – whether an Ignatian meditation on the soul, or a disquisition on scepticism or on the new science – to hold our attention.

These alternatives all require us, however, to take our eyes off the forlorn fifteen-year-old upon whose slight shoulders other-

wise is placed the burden of the whole world's corruption as well
as the significance of contemporary scientific discovery, and here
we may well be reminded of the old schoolboy question about
'Lycidas', concerning the poem's 'digressions' and the relationship of the theme to its occasion. Yet Milton so elaborately
formalises his subject that the particular friend, Edward King, all
but disappears, taken up by the tropes and figures of classical,
pastoral and elegaic conventions. The poem, in short, makes it
easy for us to forget about him. Not surprisingly, Donne made a
gesture at this kind of apology for his own practice when he said,
replying to Jonson, 'that he described the Idea of a woman and
not as she was'.[4] One critic calls this 'undoubtedly the most acute
defense of the poems ever made',[5] but I am inclined to doubt it.
Donne's reply is a predictable cliché: of course *The First
Anniversarie* transcends its occasion, otherwise it would be no
poem at all. But one very curious effect of the *Anniversaries*
(unlike 'Lycidas') is that the hyperbole remains obtrusive: the
poems refuse to allow us to free our minds from the fact that they
are occasional, and that the girl's particular, faceless ordinariness
is, somehow, what gives rise to the very disturbing energy we
admire.

The critic who has done most to accommodate ordinary girl to
high significance is Barbara Lewalski.[6] The essence, she claims,
of a Protestant approach to salvation lies in a special insight into
the way profound spiritual events occur in particular individuals
who are to all appearances unexceptional. Donne thus praises
Elizabeth Drury not as a Catholic saint might be praised, but
according to Calvinist principles, because she bears Christ's
image within by God's grace.[7] Lewalski's learned formulation of
the subjective character of Protestant devotional poetry and its
special deployment of traditional figures and meditative tech-
niques is painstaking and impressive. None the less, even she
allows at last that 'it is evident that Elizabeth Drury as image of
God functions in some sense as a Platonic symbol', even though,
it appears, 'the direction in which this symbolism works is in
important respects anti-Platonic'.[8]

The impasse again declares itself. On the one hand, to insist on
an extreme Calvinist position, claiming that the girl is not, to all
appearances, significant, and that God's invisible grace alone
matters, quickly annihilates the poetry. Donne, after all, cannot

know of her inner state, and so cannot undertake to praise her sanctity: for all he can judge from appearances – with which the poems must deal – she may be damned. To be authoritative according to their own principles, the poems therefore must be directly inspired by God – written by God, as it were, and not Donne, which is absurd, as a recent critic points out with engaging brilliance in a discussion of George Herbert's similar attempts to present a Calvinist doctrine of grace poetically.[9] On the other hand, explanations along the lines of Donne's 'Idea of a woman' fail to convince because the ordinary girl does, as the critics notice, remain so embarrassingly undistinguished, a fact to which the praise (so arbitrarily, it seems, heaped upon her) merely draws our attention.

There is, I think, no solution, no way in the end to readjust our thinking so that the poems will appear entirely satisfying. The main task of this chapter is, consequently, to provide some further account of the difficulties Donne faced, given his subject, his learning and his beliefs, and to suggest how the poetry is, in part, effective because of the very pressure we feel these difficulties exerting upon it. The *Anniversaries*, that is, communicate Donne's awareness that he must struggle to achieve significance for Elizabeth Drury, rather than depend upon the traditional, public content of his language to disclose allegorically the higher meaning of her life and death. The poems are, thus, partly about the difficulty itself of treating the girl as a symbol, and in this connection they can be especially well understood in terms of the human heart. Donne's claim that the world lost its heart with Elizabeth Drury's death indicates both a general human disorientation (which the poetry keenly records and links specifically with the rise of science), and also the human creature's peculiar, uncertain status as embodied spirit. Throughout his career, Donne's thinking about the heart is closely connected to his understanding of how the human being is, paradoxically, directed to a supernatural end while confined in a material body. In the *Anniversaries* his allusions to the heart consequently indicate a set of preoccupations which can help us to grasp what is most distinctive in his treatment of the dead girl.

II DONNE AND THE HEART

The word 'heart' occurs easily to Donne. In the *Songs and Sonnets*[10] it is the seat of the lover's emotions, and there is a conventional play of hearts given and lost, broken and mended, hardened and softened, devoted and cold. The heart thinks ('A naked thinking heart' – 'The Blossome', l. 27) and feels ('My ragges of heart can like, wish, and adore' – 'The Broken Heart', l. 31); it is private ('The ground, thy heart is mine' – 'Loves Infiniteness', l. 21), and its affections can be physically visible ('true plaine hearts doe in the faces rest' – 'The Good Morrow', l. 16). Its affairs are personal and interior, but the impersonal, outside world impinges on it ('Loves Infiniteness') both as seat of the soul ('in my heart, where my soule dwels' – Elegie v: 'His Picture', l. 2) and as bodily organ ('When I had ripp'd me, and search'd where hearts should lye' – 'The Legacie', l. 14). The heart is changeable ('And when I change my Love, I'll change my heart' – Elegie xii: 'His Parting from Her', l. 98), equally subject to dark impulses ('Thou art not so black, as my heart' – 'A Jeat Ring Sent', l. 1) and to bright ('The fire of these inflaming eyes, or of this loving heart' – 'Epithalamion at the Marriage of the Earl of Somerset', l. 115[11]), and its disequilibrium threatens the entire human organism ('Mad with much heart, then ideott with none' – Elegie x: 'Image and Dream', l. 26). Donne's profane poetry clearly shows his fascination with the heart, man's central organ, symbol of his psycho-physical nature, and (following a well-tried tradition) microcosm of man as man is microcosm of the world: 'As man is of the world, the heart of man, / Is an epitome of Gods great booke / Of creatures' ('Epithalamion', ll. 50–2). Donne likes to stress that, like man himself, the heart occupies a middle state between spirit and body: in the elegant language of 'The Dreame', it mediates between sense and understanding; in the ribald language of 'Loves Progress', between the non-physical love of 'barren Angels' (l. 23) and the instinctive physical urge for 'the Centrique part' (l. 36).

Much of this, of course, is conventional, but the quality of Donne's interest imparts to his descriptions a special concentration and relevance. The heart becomes a central, pervasive figure in his writing for that slightly nightmarish physicalism mixed with spiritual intuition which he saw as characteristic of the human predicament. So let us now look briefly at two well-known poems, the first of which deals explicitly, and the second implicitly, with the heart.

In 'The Legacie' a lover's ghost visits his mistress to deliver his heart to her, but the ghost finds nothing to take from the dead man's breast except the woman's own possessive heart, for he had given his to her long before. The hearts clearly represent their love. Hers has 'colours' and 'corners' (l. 18 – suggestive of deceit and hidden secrets); his is the symbol of consuming self-dedication, a vulnerability to her which renders him physically and spiritually powerless. The fact that she is haunted from beyond the grave suggests also that his love is under some non-material compulsion, and the beautiful line 'And Lovers houres be full eternity' (l. 4) directs our attention to this higher mystery. None the less, his love is, like his heart, irreparably carnal, as a certain unmistakably coarse vigour indicates: 'When I had ripp'd me, 'and search'd where hearts should lye' (l. 14).

The heart thus represents the body's turbulent relationships with spirit in human experience. In such a context, even the elevating, non-material component can become a kind of torment, because self-consciousness so readily creates out of a single painful event a potentially infinite series of anguished reflections. This is suggested in the poem's deliberately confused deploying of the first-person pronoun, used by the ghost to refer both to itself and to the dead lover: 'I can remember yet, that I' (l. 5); 'Though I be dead, which sent mee' (l. 7); 'I heard mee say' (l. 9). In addition, the simultaneous separateness yet identity the lover feels between himself and his beloved is expressed by the invasion of his breast by her heart, so that 'I' and 'you' interpenetrate and are at the same time painfully divorced: 'That my selfe, (that's you, not I')' (l. 10). These witty refractions of self-consciousness so multiply the separations of 'I' from its object (whether one's self or others), that the gift of human intelligence itself is seen to carry with it a liability to endlessly self-generated spiritual suffering.

The complexity of human love – sexual yet not just biological, a disturbing amalgam of haunting devotion and bewitched resentment – is Donne' subject in this poem, and the heart is his controlling symbol. We should beware, however, of identifying Donne too closely with his speakers in the *Songs and Sonnets*, and we should also hesitate to identify the speaker in 'The Legacie' too closely with the turmoil he so wittily describes. All that play with pronouns and the dexterity with which the figure of transposed hearts is developed towards the poem's dismissive conclusion poised between compliment and insult ('But oh, no man could hold it, for twas thine'), suggests a speaker half a step removed from the perplexity which is his ostensible condition. Or, at any rate, we should detect here at least some hint of an attempt to deflect whatever genuine anguish he does feel – 'Look, I am doing all this too cleverly really to mean it.' And yet such an attitude inevitably is haunted in turn by the further frisson of undermeaning – 'Yes, but I am having to be this witty because I have indeed been hurt': wit, after all, closes the coffin on an emotion, as Nietzsche says. This kind of perilously vigorous tone remains one of Donne's chief fascinations, but in this poem it does not so much detract from the suggestiveness of his controlling image of the heart as it adds to the series of possibilities, both beautiful and painful, to which the heart is so poignantly exposed.

My second example is 'The Exstasie'. It belongs in a tradition of poems which celebrate the awakening of spring, and then make an invitation to love.[12] But Donne's pastoral setting declares not so much his celebration (Donne is rarely a poet of nature), as his desire. In the opening lines, 'Where, like a pillow on a bed, / A pregnant banke swel'd up, to rest / The violets reclining head', we already feel a kind of human taint, not natural innocence. Calling her attention to the natural setting is, partly, his means of being improperly suggestive: pillows, beds and pregnant swellings pertain more to human sexuality than to nature's production of spring violets. But the lines also allow us to feel that perhaps he cannot help himself: like the violet (a symbol either of modesty or erotic love depending on what tradition we choose[13]), the human mind never ingenuously appreciates mere nature.

The poem then describes the ecstasy, or spiritual union, which they achieve and which becomes, for this strangely bewitching lover, a means of convincing her that they need a carnal component to make a properly human relationship. The poem is thus an elaborate seduction, but it is not just a seduction,[14] because the speaker has too keen a sense of how ridiculous is the human predicament to place much store on physical gratification alone. The spiritual ecstasy, however, likewise entails an amusing imbalance:

> And whil'st our soules negotiate there,
> Wee like sepulchrall statues lay;
> All day, the same our postures were,
> And wee said nothing, all the day.
>
> (ll. 17–20)

Like neglected children, the bodies are consoled by the exaggerated solicitude of something like baby talk (poor things, all, all alone . . .). The sound of 'All day' against 'lay', and then 'all the day', is sufficiently forlorn (albeit touched by mockery) to deprive the spiritual claim of total seriousness. Despite the sophisticated ideas that inform it, pure spiritual communion is not the human condition: 'This Extasie doth unperplex' (l. 29), says the lover, archly, before he proceeds with his description of 'mixt soules' (l. 35), which are then mixed again in a manner anything but unperplexed. Speculation thus having confounded itself ('O alas') we are advised that we do in fact need our bodies: 'Loves mysteries in soules doe grow, / But yet the body is his booke' (ll. 71–2). But it is not, again, a matter of *just* body, any more than just spirit; rather, of body as a condition of the human soul:

> As our blood labours to beget
> Spirits, as like soules as it can,
> Because such fingers need to knit
> That subtile knot, which makes us man.
>
> (ll. 61–4)

As every contemporary physiologist knew, blood begets vital spirits in the heart, seat of a man's soul.[15] The 'knot' remains of course tied, but we must maintain it so, and the poem therefore brings us back almost to the beginning, where the lover's hands are 'cimented / With a fast balme' (ll. 5–6), and their eyebeams twisted ('and did thred / Our eyes, upon one double string' – ll. 7–8). This is grotesque, yet such a mixture of physical with immaterial is, precisely, the human thing. The subtle knot moreover suggests man's heart, the place where the physical organ knits soul and body in one through the mysterious engendering of vital spirits. It is, as 'The Exstasie' demonstrates, comically odd, and a little frightening; we are driven to it because running away from it leaves us even worse off.[16] Admittedly, in this poem the heart is not Donne's principal subject, but my point is that he never does treat the heart just literally. He sees it rather as representing man's dual nature. And so in 'The Exstasie', which is mainly about that duality reduced to a unity, we not surprisingly find the imagery of the heart in a minor key, as it were, suggestively at work.

Donne's interest in the heart is evident also in the *Divine Poems* and *Sermons*. Its association with love and its status as seat of the soul remain constant, as it becomes the battleground of our struggle with God and the world. The Holy Sonnets,[17] being love poems converted to spiritual ends, combine these motifs: 'Marke in my heart, O Soule, where thou dost dwell' (xiii), says the meditator, who also calls upon God to 'draw mine iron heart' (i), and to turn him from his 'profane mistresses' (xiii). Yet, like 'The Exstasie', the Holy Sonnets are not escapist. They continually reassert tensions inherent in the human condition, especially expressing the anguish of faith that seeks understanding but never understands enough, so that it must fall back upon a sheer act of will, or love, a true act of the heart: 'Yet dearely' I love you, and would be lov'd faine' (xiv). We learn in 'The Crosse' that the heart alone of man's organs points downwards towards the earth, and we must therefore 'Crosse those dejections, when it downeward tends', just as we must also 'Crosse' it when it aspires 'to forbidden heights'. The Holy Sonnets would impart the same lesson.

In his *Sermons*[18] Donne is at leisure to be more explicitly instructive. The heart, we learn, is the soul ('the heart, that is, the soule'), and has 'thoughts', though these are inseparable 'from the colledge, from the fellowship of the body' (iv, 358). It is also vagabond (i, 180) and deceptive (ix, 180); we must correct it, file off its 'rust' (i, 199), and set it in tune (iv, 310). In so doing we are assured that the heart is not just sensual – '*cordis* and not *carnis*' (ii, 154) – nor, obviously, is it wholly immaterial (iv, 358). God's spirit from above must shine on it (iv, 109), but we are not to trust in irresistible grace, for we must endeavour to improve ourselves (x, 63). Yet purity of heart must not lead us to pride, for a fool trusts in his own heart (ix, 236) – that is, in human self-sufficiency. Rather, 'the flesh and the spirit' need to 'be reconciled' (iv, 301), as they are in Christ when we glorify him with all the faculties of our soul and body. The incarnate Christ and the heart are therefore closely linked, for Christ is our intermediary between heaven and earth: 'Thither have we sent our flesh, and hither hath he sent his Spirit' (IV, 62). In this sense, Christ dwells in our hearts so that through the 'Integritatem Christi' (V, 149) we may negotiate life's trials. Christ's blood, we are told, flows down from 'that head' (IV, 293) into our hearts (that is, our souls), and the blood is *'sedes animae'*, the 'seat of his soule, the matter of his spirits, the knot of his life' (IV, 294).

The close association of the heart with Christ's love returns us again to the mysterious 'knot'. We cannot, it seems, discover the spiritual secrets above us, but we must not give our hearts to worldliness, like vultures delighting on dead carcasses (I, 178). Man's heart, we are told, is incurable; after all, it palpitates ceaselessly (I, 179). It needs to be ploughed, planted with the seed of the word, and watered with the dew of grace (I, 241). Corrections and sufferings precede heavenly joy (IX, 407) because our memory is weak and sensual (V, 149) and our understanding is blind. Likewise, our will is perverse, and yet in the will (that is, the heart's blood – IV, 294) lies our love's direction, which is neither wholly in our power to choose, nor wholly out of our power to influence.

Much of this thinking is, I repeat, conventional. Indeed, using the heart to indicate the reconciliation of physical and spiritual is common to many cultures; it is one of the perennial ways, says a modern theologian, 'in which man, knowing himself, expresses the mystery of his existence without solving that mystery'.

> For when he speaks in this way of the heart . . . he is evoking what is original in the genuine sense of the word, that in which the manifold reality of human reality is still freshly one, that in which . . . the whole (concrete) being of man, as it is brought forth and unfolded and flows away in soul, body and spirit, is taken and grasped and remains as one, as though knotted and fastened at the midpoint.[19]

It is doubtful that the German Jesuit Karl Rahner, talking here of the heart as a knot, was thinking of the seventeenth-century English poet, but the general content of this passage no less than the particular phrase about the knot applies very well to Donne, no doubt because the idea itself is, as Rahner suggests, perennial. But in dealing with a literary text one must distinguish the perennial from its occasional dress, and in this respect we should notice a historical tendency among the great luminaries of Western tradition to interiorise the heart's significance; to see it, that is, less in terms of objective reason and thought and more in terms of private emotion.

In St Augustine, for instance, 'heart' (*cor*) is used indiscriminately to indicate *anima, mens, intellectus* and *ratio*,[20] as well as the affective side of spiritual life. This usage remains in Gregory, in Cassiodorus, Peter Lombard and Isidore of Seville, who thought *cor* derived from *cura* because the heart is the seat of all knowledge, indicating soul, intelligence, judgement, and zeal for holy devotion.[21] In the twelfth century, especially with St Bernard and the Cistercians, the development of affective devotion stressed the heart especially as the seat of our desire for God.[22] Hugh of St Victor proceeds on such grounds to classify the heart's sentiments,[23] and Richard of St Victor states that the highest love of which we are capable emanates from there. Richard, however, also retains the older idea that reason and affection join in the heart, which is the organ of judgement,[24] and in the thirteenth century St Bonaventure likewise insisted on the heart's intellectual capability, though at the same time giving special attention to its affective nature. In him, as in the Franciscan tradition generally, devotion to the heart accompanies a renewed interest in Christ's humanity, wherein the wound in the side of the crucified, which exposes the heart, is interpreted as a wound of love.[25] This Franciscan emphasis clearly retains, as we see, the Augustinian idea of the heart's 'reasons'; thus it stands in contrast to the opinion of Thomas Aquinas, who states categorically that the heart is the place of will, not of thought.[26]

It would be too simple to claim that the heart in Christian tradition becomes associated exclusively with feeling and not with thought, for the word is used too frequently and imprecisely to allow such generalisation unambiguous utility. As we see, Donne talks of the thinking heart and at the same time stresses its special association with will and love, and his use of the term is eclectic, not systematic. Moreover, Donne's poetry is influenced by the courtly-love tradition, where the tormented and longing heart both thinks and feels, as with Dante's *cor gentile*. The transmission of Petrarchan convention, for instance, into the *Songs and Sonnets* is sufficiently evident to suggest that Donne's sources are often poetic, rather than theoretical.[27] And yet, when we turn to Donne's devotional writing, the distinctive quality of this interest in the heart does seem part of the broad tendency I have outlined, to depict the heart's function as more predominantly affective than rational, and to associate it especially with grace and the will. This is not surprising, because the heart's secret interior, visited privately by God, was emphasised by Protestants. Depictions of the heart in Protestant emblem books, for instance, draw upon the traditional motifs – the ploughed heart, Christ within the heart, the heart burning with love's fire, the wounded heart, and so on. But, as Barbara Lewalski has shown, the tradition is subjected to special modifications which stress God's transcendence and his unmediated correction of the wayward heart, rather than the heart's deliberate and co-operative surrender.[28]

In general, sacred emblem books in the Renaissance are associated with the Jesuits, who adapted figures from the courtly-love emblem traditions: 'Thus Eros and Anteros from Otto Van Veen's book *Amorum Emblemata* (1608) became, by the expedient of added haloes and wings, Divine Love and Anima in the same author's *Amoris divini emblemata* (1615)' (Lewalski, p. 184). Within this tradition there developed a kind of book concentrating entirely on the heart, the earliest example of which is the *Schola Cordis* (1629) by the Jesuit Benedict van Haeften, which takes over the Anima and Divine Love figures and depicts a progress of Anima's heart along the mystical way, through stages of purgation, illumination and union. Christopher Harvey's English version of the *Schola Cordis* (1647) uses most of van Haeften's plates, but 'he wholly omits any division according to stages or planes of the spiritual life, so that, though there is clearly some progress shown in the renovation of the heart, there is no finality of achievement' (Lewalski, p. 194). The English, Protestant emphasis, as Lewalski shows us, is not upon steady spiritual development, but upon the heart's renovation by grace; not upon mystical union, but upon the heart's willingness to endure whatever further trials it encounters, patiently, and in Christ.

Although the *Schola Cordis* books are too late for Donne, they are of interest because they depict so clearly the means by which profane emblems were adapted to sacred ends, and how Protestants tended to stress the vacillations of the heart and its particular aloneness before God. Also, the principal contents of such books were available to Donne from assorted earlier sources. His fondness for St Bernard and his reading in Franciscan authors,[29] for instance, would enliven an affective devotion to the heart; his knowledge of Aquinas would highlight the distinction between will and intellect and sharpen his sense of the heart as a seat of love;[30] his Protestant profession would impress upon him a sense of the heart's powerlessness to love God worthily, and of its dependency on grace. Moreover, Donne had likely seen the French Protestant Georgette de Montenay's *Emblemes, ou Devises Chrestiennes* (1571).[31] As Lewalski points out, Montenay's emblem of the heart being drawn from above by adamant, and Donne's line 'And thou like Adamant draw mine iron heart' are strikingly similar (p. 202). Elsewhere, Montenay also depicts a man on his knees holding out his heart, with the devil, emerging from a walled town and armed with a lance, about to seize the offering. The man's eyes, however, are turned heavenward to a cloud bearing the tetragrammaton, situated in the sky above the walled town. The heart, poised thus between God and the devil and powerless to resist captivity within the town except God intervene, resembles closely the predicament described in Holy Sonnet XIV. Also, in *The Second Anniversarie*, Donne's 'dangerous apostem' (l. 479) recalls to mind Montenay's 'apostume', broken by a physician. Montenay's point is that the physical relief represents the ridding of vice 'Dedans le coeur', and that neither form of relief occurs without pain.[32] Donne's point is that mere physical cure is accidental, and he concentrates on the irony that a scab forming over the wound may itself prove fatal. Such, we might conclude, is the poet's freedom with words which a single graphic depiction cannot reproduce. Still, Donne's point is to compare the physical affliction of the breast with the essential joy mentioned a few lines earlier, having to do with the 'reparation' of the image of God within Elizabeth Drury's 'heart'. His point thus remains parallel to Montenay's. So also his injunction in the *Sermons* not to give our hearts to worldliness like vultures delighting on dead carcasses (I, 178) seems close to Montenay's depiction of vultures feeding on a dead horse, a scene which, as she says, is a 'beau miroir pour les coeurs'.

It would be rash to claim Montenay's *Emblemes* as Donne's source in these several instances, for it is difficult to assess the joint-stock elements on which the two authors independently draw. But the similarities – the coincidence of particular details and of general intent – allow the comparison value as an indication of how Protestants might typically think about the heart as a subject of Christian devotion. For, like Christopher Harvey, Montenay stresses the heart's powerlessness in a typically Protestant manner, and God's hand striking downwards upon the heart through a cloud is her characteristic device (pp. 34, 81, 82). We are warned, for instance, not to glory in ourselves: God does us the honour of choosing us for his temple (p. 64), and this point is illustrated by a soldier carrying a heart on which the tetragrammaton is engraved. The heart, though in the world, remains at war with the world, and its victories depend on spiritual power from above. Montenay's book shows us no mystical union, but ends with a sarcophacus, and the legend 'Patientia vincit omnia': the heart must resist pride and accept the body's corruption and pain. 'Scientia inflat' (p. 87), reads the inscription on one emblem; 'Ex corpore ruina' (p. 88) reads the next. Both deal with the heart, which must hold its place between illegitimate spiritual aspiration, and mere carnality.

III   THE ANNIVERSARIES

Such, I am claiming, is Donne's subject in the *Anniversaries*: they are poems about the human heart, which he feels compelled to understand. On the one hand, as we see, the heart remains, throughout Donne's writing, a primordial symbol of the human being as a mysterious unity of body and soul. But, on the other hand, Donne's treatment of the heart as a devotional subject reflects a contemporary bias to differentiate its function as the seat of will and affection, from its relationships with understanding and memory. The heart's secrecy, the failure of understanding to compass it, the mystery of the will's dependence on grace, we might conclude, are not affirmed just by Protestantism; in some sense, these truths themselves helped to engender Protestantism as their adequate expression. Yet to insist to an extreme degree on the heart's hiddenness would be to deny the integrity of the 'subtile knot' which combines outer and inner reality. Elizabeth Drury's ordinariness is, clearly, incommensurate with the actual, hidden, state of her heart in which Christ's image dwells. But if the relationship were wholly incommensurate the poems could not record it. The treatment of Elizabeth Drury as a symbol can therefore even seem a kind of protest against the apparent injustice of this ordinary, wonderful child's death:

> Shee, shee is dead; shee's dead: when thou knowst this,
> Thou knowst how lame a cripple this world is.
> And learnst thus much by our Anatomy,
> That this worlds generall sicknesse doth not lie
> In any humour, or one certaine part;
> But as thou saw'st it rotten at the hart . . .
>
> (*FA*, ll. 237–42)

This could very well seem to say that her death calls into question the meaning of creation itself, 'rotten at the hart'. Protest atheism of course is not Donne's explicit intent; none the less, he was peculiarly attracted to forbidden lines of thought and sentiment, letting us be touched by them, just as in the *Songs and Sonnets* and *Elegies* we are made to feel the morbid, obsessive, vindictive and gloating divagations of those thwarted male egos the poetry dramatises, and which are in some sense Donne, but with which we cannot identify him *tout court*. William Empson draws attention to Donne's 'secret largeness of outlook',[33] which consists, partly, of the poet's willingness (and ability) to communicate the weight of opinions he does not fully endorse. *Biathanatos*,[34] written just before the *Anniversarie* poems, is a conspicuous example, but it is so because the 'largeness of outlook' is less guarded there than usual.

In *Biathanatos*, Donne tells us straight out that he has often felt a 'sickely inclination' (p. 17) to suicide, and believes that insufficient charity and compassion are shown to those who kill themselves (pp. 19–22). The question, he argues, is complex, but there can be no healthy thinking about it until it is deliberately vexed, just as the pool at Bethesda brought no health until its waters were troubled. The author's deliberate pursuit of 'compassion' therefore depends on his ability to vex the question, as he does by providing some alarming insight into the ambivalence of human motivation and the fine points of distinction between commendation and condemnation. He thereby imparts to *Biathanatos* an unmistakable frisson of hypnotising doubt and existential terror, an effect immediately recognisable also in much of his best work.

Something of this effect certainly is present also in the

Anniversaries. It comes, partly, from the way the hyperbole itself vexes us, communicating by its very outlandish excess how difficult it is to detect a providential order based on the facts as we know them, the main fact being the death of an ordinary child. On the question, for instance, of whether she is restored to heaven, the poet replies, 'Heaven may say this, and joy in't, but can wee / Who live, and lacke her, here this vantage see?' ('A Funerall Elegie', ll. 47–8). To our chagrin, we face yet a further question, a further uncertainty, for the world has grown mute trying to explain God's higher purposes in the teeth of darkly perplexing evidence. Such are the facts, and *The First Anniversarie*, with all its protracted analysis of the body's suffering and the soul's anguish, is a lament, but a lament touched with protest, and protest then crossed in turn by fear lest it tip too far into unseemliness. Jonson was right, after all, to detect blasphemy, but not because Donne praises Elizabeth Drury unduly; rather because the hyperbole itself carries the flavour of a rebuke to the powers that be for providing no better evidence of their benign purposes.[35] And yet the hyperbole itself goes some distance towards neutralising its own protest because, simply, it so often strikes us as an extravagant game, a huge, witty display which can veer off, for instance, into odd moments of perplexing satire: 'One woman at one blow, then kill'd us all, / And singly, one by one, they kill us now' (*FA*, ll. 107–8). John Carey, indeed, thinks that the main point about the *Anniversaries* is their venal exaggeration, not their serious grappling with conceptual difficulties which Donne was trying to solve. And, although I find the poems more sincere than Carey, he is correct to point out that the complex tone has a way of deflecting us from any uniform high seriousness as distinct from a kind of unprincipled, dashing indulgence in exaggeration. The catalogue of the girl's perfections is, indeed, preposterous, a witty effort to make her more than we know her to be. But the very excess of wit none the less calls attention covertly to a kind of failure: to the fact that the poet here has his wheels spinning off the ground, as it were, because he cannot find purchase on a symbol adequate for teaching us about the girl's death: a symbol, in short, such as a poet could grasp and write about with confidence.

Of course, Donne does not say directly, This is a scandal, what kind of God is responsible? We should not exaggerate the 'atheist's protest', not just because the *Anniversaries* are at once so evidently Christian and so disconcertingly witty, but also because Donne knew the human psyche better than to think it could long be satisfied with such an attitude of protest, however pertinent. We are, on the contrary, specifically warned,

> except thou feed (not banquet) on
> The supernaturall food, Religion,
> Thy better Grouth growes withered, and scant;
> Be more than man, or thou'rt lesse than an Ant.
>
> (*FA*, ll. 187–90)

These lines are less a promise of illumination than an acknowledgement that man is incurably a self-transcending creature; he is, as it were, a metaphysical animal, and in order to preserve his humanity needs metaphysical satisfaction. The last line is an imperative which does not promise but threatens: to seek comfort by ignoring the higher side of one's nature is to destroy one's nature, increasing its anguish. The opening lines of *The First Anniversarie* alert us again to this point: 'He who doth not this [celebrate Elizabeth Drury] / May lodge an In-mate soule, but 'tis not his' (ll. 5–6). We refuse the challenge of transcendence, it seems, at our peril.

The poetry cannot, therefore, without presumption declare upon the mystery of grace which makes Elizabeth Drury's inner life so remarkable, for how does the poet know she is blessed? Yet neither can it take refuge in the despair of straightforward materialism. And, if Protestantism, we might say, made Donne's problem as artist more acute in the first respect by emphasising God's transcendence and the imputation of Christ's merits to the elect, contemporary science made it more acute in the second, by declaring the incommensurability of the phenomena with conventional beliefs about the hierarchical order of creation.

The *Anniversaries*, consequently, are remarkable because they state so cogently the problem of dealing at all with the subject matter they address.[36] In so doing, they raise once more the problem of the human heart, with its unified but dual allegiance to soul and body, to heaven and earth, to spirit and matter – a heart which is incurable, as Donne says, prone alike to spiritual pride and sensualist despair, never attaining final assurance, always to be tested, but capable of its own kind of heroism and honesty, and joy of itself in the midst of its own most terrible knowledge.

In some such fashion, Elizabeth Drury is the heart of *The First Anniversarie* just as she is, we are told explicitly, of the world, for, when mankind lost her, 'he lost his hart' (l. 174). His 'Carkas verses', Donne writes, would be sickly and short-lived 'whose soule is not shee' ('A Funerall Elegie', l. 14). Soon after, he develops the idea:

> But those fine spirits, which doe tune, and set
> This Organ, are those peeces which beget
> Wonder and love; And these were shee.
>
> (ll. 27–9)

The heart is both immaterial and the physical organ producing 'fine spirits' which vitalise the blood. His verse lives because, through her, it has a material subject of spiritual consequence.

But what are we to make of the fact that, on the one hand, the girl's death causes corruption of the world's body ('This world, in that great earth-quake languished' and its 'vitall spirits' are drawn out when she dies – *FA*, ll. 11, 13), and, on the other, that the world's corruption causes her death (when Adam fell to the incitements of Eve, 'that first mariage was our funerall' – l. 105)?[37] Harold Love deals with this problem specifically, again, in terms of the heart.[38] *The First Anniversarie*, he suggests, is like a double fugue, in which Elizabeth Drury is spiritually the soul of the world and physically the heart of its body. The hard lesson, therefore, which Donne asks us to face about the body is that even such a piece of perfection as Elizabeth's could not escape the grave. This is helpful, even though Love tends to equate heart with body as distinct from soul, whereas for Donne, as we see, heart is body and soul in one. Elizabeth Drury as the world's heart is the physical means by which the world makes concrete what it loves, and the same is true when she is regarded as mankind's heart, and the heart of Donne's verse.

At the beginning of *The First Anniversarie*, for instance, when her soul goes to heaven, the world languishes. It gets a fever, forgets its name and loses its form. The world was 'Nothing but she, and her thou hast o'repast' (l. 32). Here she is the world's soul. Soon after we learn that her death teaches the world 'that thou art / Corrupt and mortall in thy purest part' (ll. 61–2), and here, presumably, she is the purest part of its body, later identified as its heart. When mankind lost her, we recall, 'he lost his heart' – that is, her immaterial virtue ('so much refin'd' – l. 177) in the form of a physical body ('Shee tooke the weaker Sex' – l. 179). The poem assures us that 'The heart being perish'd, no part can be free' (l. 186): this goes for the world and for mankind and for verse, all of which require an interpenetration of confining form (the body) and a creative energy (spirit). The anatomy assures us that her significance is not just physical: the world's sickness 'doth not lie / In any humour, or one certaine part; / But as thou saw'st it rotten at the hart' (ll. 240–2). The 'hart' of the world clearly is not 'one certaine part' but a pervasive principle of the body's life. It is what 'she' stands for, she who 'should' (l. 220) reunite the parts in one, both as form (the 'first originall' – l. 227) and as physical being ('whose rich eyes, and brest / Guilt the West Indies' – ll. 229–30). But corruption of the 'inward' (l. 329) heart is not just spiritual either, for it poisons our 'actions' (l. 337) and puts us physically out of joint with the world. Thus the joys that possessed her 'hart' (l. 433) are alone worth our trouble and grief and perishing, for her body, as we learn in 'A Funerall Elegie', clearly encompassed her soul.

The Second Anniversarie begins by describing her as the lower world's and the 'Sunnes Sunne' (l. 4). Conventionally, sun is to cosmos what heart is to body, and here we find her again located so perfectly in the middle position, both physical and spiritual, that it is appropriate to say, 'her bodie thought' (l. 246). She was, after all, uniquely able (by divine grace, we are assured), to see God in nature itself, and in her heart she kept God's image. What this means, for practical purposes, is that the 'outward skin' (l. 505) as well as the 'mindes within' (l. 506) showed forth God's blessing.

We must not let go unconsidered, however, the implications of that crucially placed 'should' ('She that should all parts to reunion bow' – *FA*, l. 220). Elizabeth Drury should, but does not, in fact, hold 'the sundred parts in one' (l. 222). This of course is partly because as a symbol uniting heaven and earth she is hyperbolical and preposterous, and the poet who wrote those inflated descriptions of her perfectly elemented body, I suggest, knew himself to be having a hard time making her live up to what he conceived her to be – 'the Idea of a woman'. But, since she is the heart of his verse, as of everything else, the poetry becomes in one respect a lament for the passing of a certain kind of symbolic mode of writing whereby physical events could, indeed, happily convey 'higher' spiritual meaning through a multi-levelled allegory.[39] Elizabeth Drury is thus *allegory manqué*, and draws our attention alike to the limits of poetry's encroachment upon theology, and to the human difficulties of settling for a soulless world. In this she reflects, once more, the poet's fascination with the heart and the human predicament which it represents, even though it is a heart deeply troubled by the timely questions with which it must contend.

Indeed, throughout the *Anniversaries* Donne insists on timeliness: on how present circumstances have a crucial part to play in what we are to make of the dead girl. For instance, he repeatedly contrasts the world 'now' to what it was when mankind felt more at home in the universe, when he lived longer and in harmony with his surroundings, 'So spacious and large that every Soule / Did a faire Kingdome, and large Realme controule' (*FA*, l. 124). 'There is not now that mankinde, which was then' (l. 112); 'If man were any thing, he's nothing now' (l. 171). The world, it seems, even though fallen, was once a happier place; it had more vitality, it was closer to God, and the designs of heaven were more clearly perceived by men on earth. But 'Where is this mankind now?' (l. 127). It has dwindled, and, as the poem also tells us, it has lost its heart, its capacity to see itself as mediator between heaven and earth, to feel at home in the world, to see the larger significance of temporal events, to appreciate how the girl's death has meaning. 'Now', with his shrunken and devitalised heart, man has extreme difficulty writing about such a subject at all, as the poem itself shows: the symbolism by which poetry can present metaphysical reality is, now, conspicuously arbitrary and full of strain: 'Up, up, for in that squadron there doth live / Shee' (*SA*, ll. 356–7). The present times have, the poet complains, uniquely divided man from the heavens, body from spirit, corporeal images from informing ideas. We are assured on the one hand that the transcendent God operates by grace upon those he loves, but the operation has become hidden so that it threatens to elude poetry altogether; on the other hand, human knowledge – *scientia*, the advance of modern science – is sceptical about correspondences between physical fact and spiritual sense, and threatens poetry from precisely the opposite direction.

IV   THE NEW SCIENCE AND THE DISORIENTED HEART

It is a cliché that *The First Anniversarie* records Donne's knowledge of contemporary scientific discoveries and how he found them disorienting. As C. M. Coffin[40] has shown in detail, Donne was keenly sensitive to the discoveries of Kepler and Galileo in support of the Copernican thesis that the earth moved and that the heavenly bodies were both corruptible and irregular. In *Ignatius his Conclave*, for instance, Donne alludes twice to Galileo's *Siderius Nuncius*,[41] and Copernicus is interviewed for a place in hell for deriding Ptolemy, thus joining the company of those whose innovations induced doubts and anxieties by having 'turned the whole frame of the world'.[42] Kepler's name appears in Problem VIII of *Paradoxes and Problems*, as it does also in *Ignatius his Conclave*.[43] The passage in *The First Anniversarie* on 'New starres' (l. 260) likewise seems to draw upon Kepler's *De Stella Nova* (and perhaps on the further discoveries of Tycho Brahe, Kepler's disciple).[44] The *Anniversaries* allude besides to the earth's magnetism, as William Gilbert described it in *De Magnete* (1600) to account for the earth's diurnal movement (thereby undermining the old idea of the *primum mobile*): as world soul, Elizabeth Drury is thus able 'To draw, and fasten sundred parts in one' (*FA*, l. 222) like a 'magnetique force' (l. 221).[45] Speculation on the plurality of worlds, a subject of antique origin but championed provocatively during the Renaissance (as by the unfortunate Giordano Bruno), would also have been known to Donne through Kepler and perhaps Thomas Digges, or through Bruno himself.[46] Certainly, in Holy Sonnet V, Donne talks of 'new sphears' and 'new lands'[47] beyond the heavens, and in *The Second Anniversarie* the moon is alluded to as a 'new world' (l. 196). He does not dwell on the idea or its consequences for theology, but his knowledge of current interest in the theory is at one with his appreciation of how radically the new science had disturbed the traditional, providential conception of the universe by rendering (as William Empson suggests) Christ's incarnation perhaps not a unique event. Finally, Donne was an enthusiastic (though unsystematic) follower of Paracelsus,[48] whose 'new principles' he praises as superior to the humoral theory of Galen and Hippocrates.[49] Paracelsus is referred to in *Biathanatos* and, with Copernicus, makes an appearance in *Ignatius his Conclave*.[50]

Scholars interested in Donne's concern for the new science are at pains to point out,[51] however, that his treatment of such data is not systematic, but mainly expresses his sense of the instability of human knowledge. For instance, the lines in *The First Anniversarie* on the 'perplexed course' (l. 253) of the heavens constitute, according to Coffin, 'one of the most curious and significant utterances Donne ever made'. The poet's reaction to the new astronomy, Coffin explains, 'marks the birth of an idea in Donne's mind that a critical study of the new philosophy was bound to produce, that all systems of natural philosophy, traditional and new, are subject to modification and revision, and, therefore, will not suffice as a foundation for a satisfactory religious faith. The idea of the relativity of natural knowledge is essential to an understanding of the poem; but no less fundamental is an appreciation of the role of the new philosophy in bringing Donne to this conclusion. Donne is not merely echoing the medieval poet's contempt for the world.' In short, just as a Calvinist doctrine of imputed merit makes God inscrutably transcendent, so the extreme 'alterability' of the heavens destroys the sense of a world-order arranged by ascending degrees of perfection: "Tis all in pieces, all cohaerence gone;/ All just supply, and all Relation' (ll. 213–4). Man instead is thrown back upon the mystery of himself – 'For every man alone thinkes he hath got/ To be a Phoenix' (ll. 216–7) – and on the arbitrariness of his own imposition of significance upon the world as a creator, not just a receiver, of metaphysical truth:

> Man hath weav'd out a net, and this net throwne
> Upon the Heavens, and now they are his owne.
> Loth to goe up the hill, or labor thus
> To goe to heaven, we make heaven come to us.
>
> (ll. 279–82)

It seems that Donne very well knew his treatment of Elizabeth Drury reflected just this kind of arbitrariness, expressing the particular anguish of a mind constrained to *achieve* significance to satisfy its own metaphysical nature, rather than to disclose the *given* metaphysical significance of heaven and earth.

In light of these remarks, it is pertinent to look again at how, in *The Second Anniversarie*, Elizabeth Drury is the sun ('this lower worlds, and the Sunnes Sunne' – l. 4), and how the 'Eccentric

parts' and 'overthwarts' and 'New starres' (*FA*, l. 260) so distort
the heavens that this sun, disenfranchised, can no longer
'maintaine his way / One inche direct' (ll. 269–70) but is 'Serpen-
tine: And seeming weary with his reeling thus' (ll. 272–3). As I
have mentioned, it is a commonplace that the sun is to the
heavens as the heart is to man. The idea occurs, for instance,
frequently in blood-letting charts which divide the human body
according to signs of the zodiac and consistently present the heart
as Leo, pictured as a sun.[52] Discussing 'the signe Leo' Batman
says that it especially 'helpeth in a man the . . . heart',[53] and
Cornelius Agrippa states plainly, 'Hinc veteres physici Solem
ipsum cor coeli appellaverunt.'[54] Shakespeare draws on the idea
in *Henry V*: 'a good heart, Kate, is the sun and the moon, or
rather, the sun, and not the moon, for it shines bright, and never
changes, but keeps his course truly.'[55] Robert Burton talks of the
heart as 'the Sun of our body, the King and sole commander of
it',[56] and Samuel Purchas describes love's throne in 'the HEART,
the Sunne of this *Microcosme*'.[57] In physiological terms, the heart
was thought to produce body heat by a kind of combustion
analogous to heat provided by the sun. 'The basic principle of
life, "the divine spark",' a historian of the subject assures us, 'was
said to enter the foetal heart in the fourth month as an occult ray
via the sun',[58] and the air of the lungs worked as a kind of bellows
to fan and feed the heart's fire. As John Davies of Hereford
explains, the '*Lunges* (breath's-forge)' are 'First to receaue the
Aire that cooles the *Hart*'.[59] The fiery hearts of sacred-emblem
tradition are therefore not just metaphorical, but are depictions
also of an actual physiological function.[60] It thus seems clear that,
when Donne compares Elizabeth Drury to the sun, and also to
the world's heart, we are meant to see the relationship between
new scientific theory having thrown the sun into disorientation
in an eccentric universe, and the world having lost its heart
because of the girl's death. The conventional symbolism no
longer works as it ought to do to describe the relationship
(qualitatively) of the inner man to outer world. The private,
inner significance of Elizabeth Drury does not correspond in any
immediately compelling way to the course of her public life. Just
as, in the new science, the sun is materially (quantitatively) at the
centre, but spiritually (qualitatively) imponderable, so with the
girl herself in the poem: she like the sun is somehow out of place,
suddenly become also extravagantly large, dangerously prob-

lematic. In this respect, Donne's emphasis differs sharply, for instance, from that of Paracelsus, who insists that a person's external appearance does reveal the inner life and, specifically, the heart's disposition: 'Physiognomies is the art of discovering what is within and hidden in man. . . . It tells us in what relation his heart stands to God'; 'the shape of a man is formed in accordance with the manner of his heart'.[61] Donne's lament for the decay of the world is a lament for the loss of just this correspondence between the heart's condition and exterior appearances. In this sense man has indeed 'shrunk', for the extent of his discourse and the reality encompassed by his heart are confined and imprisoned increasingly within his own breast.

The hyperbole and sheer difficulty of the *Anniversaries* consequently derive partly from the fact that they are public poems. Donne is compelled to remake, if he can, a correlation between the world and God by way of the poem's chief symbol, the girl, 'Idea of a woman', the world's heart, at the same moment as he acknowledges the near-impossibility of doing so in the intellectual climate of his times. The *Anniversaries*, however, I repeat, are significant, less because of their obvious failure to make, as it were, a viable metaphysical symbol out of the girl's career, than for a kind of covert success, which comes from the sense they convey of why they cannot succeed, conveyed partly by a self-protective bravado and display of extravagance for its own sake. 'Nor could incomprehensiblenesse deterre / Mee, from thus trying to emprison her' (*FA*, ll. 469–70), Donne writes. This remarkable statement partly acknowledges the poem's limits, but it is no mere gesture of respect to the mystery; it is an insistence also that the poem (like *Biathanatos*) has tried a task beyond its scope and has taken its very life from that trial. 'Incomprehensiblenesse' in this case offers a kind of release, a licence for wit to fill the gap between heaven and earth, even though Donne's inordinate, gratuitous wittiness itself calls attention to the absence which makes it free.

Throughout his career, then, Donne's fascination with the heart is clearly a fascination with the central paradoxes of the human condition; with the fact that man is neither angel nor beast, spirit nor body. The heart thus conceived becomes, for a critic, a particular means of approach to the larger scope of Donne's poetry, and my claim is not so much that the heart is, literally, Donne's subject as that Donne's subject is the middle state that the heart represents. Donne himself, however, as I have pointed out, treats the heart always as a metaphor carefully developed to expand our understanding of this middle state, and I therefore wish to maintain that it is indeed a key motif in his writing. Certainly the *Anniversarie* poems allude to the heart in such a sense to define and represent man's differences from what is above and below him. The poetry does not acquiesce in the radical disenchantment of sheer materialism, one consequence of the discovery of method pushed to an extreme whereby human experience is reduced entirely to the quantifiable. The mere 'cutting up a man that's dead' (*FA*, l. 435) discovers only a stinking carcass. The human corpse, rather, clutches at its soul–life. Just as the decapitated body twitches 'And seemes to reach, and to step forth to meet / His soule' (*SA*, ll. 16–17), so the poet also turns our eyes upwards, towards the heavens, where Elizabeth Drury is enshrined with God's image in her heart. That image, we are told, is present by grace, the imputation of God's mercy. But neither does the poem fall silent, struck dumb, as it were, by God's inscrutable, unmediated power. For here lurks another kind of tyranny, bound up, likewise, as we have seen, with the discovery of method in so far as new philosophy found it expedient to separate theology from science by stressing the imponderable distance between the first, originating cause and the created world. Spiritual absolutes are no less dehumanising than the material sort, and Donne self-consciously finds his subject between the two, refusing the temptations of both.

In this respect, it is interesting to reflect on how frequently the descriptions of Elizabeth Drury establish her middle condition by distinguishing it from what is above and below, rather than by stressing participation: 'heaven keepes soules,' Donne writes, 'The grave keeps bodies' (*FA*, ll. 473–4), but the girl, like his verse, 'hath a middle nature' (l. 473) distinct from both. When her 'rich soule' (l. 1) climbs to heaven, the earth languishes. But the poem's real subject is not heaven or earth, but rather, 'a perplexed doubt / Whether the world did loose, or gaine in this' (ll. 14–15). Man, we are told, has 'lost his hart' (l. 174) as part of a more general catastrophe which began in heaven, and first 'seis'd the Angels' (l. 195) and later the 'beasts and plants' (l. 200). But the 'rotten . . . hart' (l. 242) of 'The noblest part, man' (l. 199), removed from angels and beasts alike, is the poem's preoccupation. 'What is't to us, alas,' the poet asks, 'if there have beene / An

Angell made a Throne, or Cherubin?' ('A Funerall Elegie', ll. 49–50). The subject is not the grave or the angel, but lies in the very question, what 'vantage' (ibid.) can we take of her? 'In Heaven thou straight know'st all' (*SA*, l. 299), the poet assures his soul, but the earth is 'Our prison's prison' (l. 249). Meanwhile, the question presses: 'Poor soule . . . what do'st thou know?' (l. 254).

On the physical side, concerning 'matters of fact' (l. 285), not much: 'Knowst thou how blood, which to the hart doth flow, / Doth from one ventricle to th'other go?' (ll. 271–2). On the spiritual side, even less: 'Thou art too narrow, wretch, to comprehend / Even thy selfe' (ll. 261–2). But in the girl, heart of his world, the physical blood is 'eloquent' (l. 244). The poet's real subject is here, in the human heart disenfranchised by science on the one hand and Calvinism on the other, the mysterious 'knot' which it is the task of literature to describe, in all its pathos and magnificence. Donne thus attempts, in his treatment of Elizabeth Drury, to make of the deal girl a symbol adequate to his hope and faith and knowledge. But his deliberate metaphysical fabrication succeeds less in assuaging the fears and uncertainties of the human condition than in enabling the poetry to find its true subject by expressing those very fears and uncertainties.

CHAPTER FIVE

Thomas Browne's *Religio Medici*: Baconian Method and the Metaphysical Cross

I   METAPHYSICS AND IMAGINATION

The first critic of Thomas Browne's *Religio Medici* was Sir Kenelm Digby[1] – virtuoso, duellist, renegade Catholic, swash-buckler, romantic lover, Fellow of the Royal Society, and *'Mirandula* of his Age' according to Aubrey.[2] In a sense, Browne's early reputation stood on Digby's shoulders: the *Religio Medici* had been written by an obscure country doctor, and the pirated printing which occasioned the critical *Observations* did not even include Browne's name. It took the attentions of a celebrity (Digby consorted with the likes of Descartes and Mersenne, and was a friend of Hobbes) to thrust the country doctor into the limelight.[3] And, yet, doing Browne a favour was not Digby's whole intent, for he did not entirely approve of what he read. The *Religio* was, he thought, too fanciful and airy, and without sufficient judgement (p. 37); however, he did admire Browne for making right use of that kind of religious zeal in which bigots lose themselves, and for his sense of mystery.

Today, we are likely to side with Coleridge's opinion that Browne's first critic 'ought to have considered the Religio Medici in a *dramatic* and not in a metaphysical View – as a sweet Exhibition of character and passion, and not as an Expression or Investigation of positive Truth'.[4] By failing to do this, Digby becomes, according to Coleridge, 'a pedant in his own system and opinion'. Following his own injunction, however, Coleridge goes on to notice Browne's humour, quiet subtlety, gravity and satisfying completeness, even confessing that he has never read a book 'in which I felt greater similarity to my own *make* of mind'. But he also adds a qualification: had he written the *Religio* himself, he would have attempted to 'tell the *whole* Truth', which Browne 'most assuredly . . . has not done'.

It is hard to know exactly what to make of this, for Coleridge does not develop the point, but he probably meant something closer to Digby's objection than we at first expect. Browne, Coleridge says elsewhere, is 'a useful enquirer into physical Truth and fundamental Science', but reads nature 'by the light of the faery Glory around his own Head' (p. 448). Digby also had said Browne was too fantastic, and both critics thus point to the same fault: Browne does not tell the whole truth because he is insufficiently rigorous in attending to the 'fundamental Science' of physical nature.

The fact remains, however, that people still read *Religio Medici* but attend to Digby scarcely at all; editions of Browne remain in print, but the *Two Treatises on body and soul* has fallen into oblivion. Tradition (democracy of the dead, as Chesterton says) has nicely reversed the original experience of the living, and Browne today is the celebrity who helps to redeem Digby from obscurity. Clearly, the imaginative achievement of the *Religio* does remain its major strength, and, although Browne is everywhere concerned with metaphysics, he treats that subject, too, imaginatively. But, if metaphysics is merely fanciful (Digby, for instance, held it was not), then it tells us nothing about the objective world and becomes another of the linguistic idols with which we amuse or deceive ourselves: a deliberate fabrication which an artist can deploy for his purposes, rather than a science based on definitions which can be examined logically.

To virtually all the major figures of the scientific revolution, in so far as their work contributed to what I am calling the discovery of method, metaphysics did indeed seem to be just such an idolatry. 'It may not be easy to say why such a thing should have happened,' writes Herbert Butterfield, 'but men unconsciously betray the fact that a certain Aristotelian thesis simply has no meaning for them any longer.'[5] Talk of quiddities and essences and first principles and formal causes seemed futile because useless and obscurantist. And, of course, the new thinkers were correct; the old metaphysics was, for their purposes, both muddled and beside the point. Nevertheless (we remind ourselves), value does not attach to the utilitarian alone: poetry and art and the works of imagination judged strictly by empirical standards are also useless, but they provide values by which our multiform experience of things can be most fully, most humanly, developed. To proceed as if this were not the case is like saying that nothing on the tree is useful but the fruit, and then digging out the roots.

Whereas poetry, however, expresses value by describing the links between human nature and the world through an affective appeal to concrete particulars, metaphysics, traditionally understood, does so by abstraction: its object is the unity of being, and its procedures are logical. As a consequence of the discovery of method, as we see, traditional metaphysics was widely regarded with suspicion, and often seemed just another kind of imagination. Consequently, a scientist with old-fashioned leanings, such as Browne, had to choose either to defend traditional metaphysics philosophically or, by deploying metaphysical language imaginatively, to run the risk of confirming its fictional status. As Digby and Coleridge detect, the second option best describes Browne's practice. Of angels he writes, 'there is not any creature that hath so neare a glympse of their nature as light in the Sunne and Elements . . . in briefe, conceive light invisible, and that is a Spirit'.[6] Metaphysical intuition here takes the form of imaginative insight; the aim is not an abstract and systematic analysis of light, or God, or of the limits of human intelligence (though all these impinge upon Browne's subject), but an invitation to concede how attractive and satisfying and agreeable it is to conceive the world in such terms. But, although he proceeds by an excited, imaginative extrapolation and not by deduction, Browne still engages with metaphysics in an old-fashioned way:

> There is but one first cause, and foure second causes of all things; some are without efficient, as God; others without matter, as Angels; some without forme, as the first matter; but every Essence, created or uncreated, hath its finall cause, and some positive end both of its Essence and operation; This is the cause I grope after in the workes of nature, on this hangs the providence of God; to raise so beauteous a structure, as the world and the creatures thereof, was but his Art; but their sundry and divided operations with their predestinated ends, are from the treasury of his wisdome.   (i.14)

This passage deals easily with causes, essences, first matter, angels, and the design of creation wherein the divine art is proper subject for human speculation and wonder. Browne cannot, indeed, consider nature without its first cause ('God the true and infallible cause of all' – 1.18). He delights in the hierarchical order of things ('for there is in this Universe a Staire, or manifest Scale of creatures, rising not disorderly, or in confusion, but with a comely method'). And "tis no bad method of the Schooles' (1.33), he tells us, to progress by analogy from what we know of perfection in ourselves to the higher perfections of pure spirits. He laments that 'so many learned heads should so farre forget their Metaphysicks' as to 'destroy the Ladder and scale of creatures, or to question the existence of Spirits' (1.30). He sees in nature a kind of 'stenography', for things (though equivocal) 'counterfeit some more reall substance in that invisible fabrick' (1.12). He adds that the characters in nature's book serve 'wiser reasons' as 'Luminaries in the abysse of knowledge', and are 'as scales and roundles to mount the pinnacles and highest pieces of Divinity' (ibid.).

In all this, Browne affirms that metaphysics leads us by natural reason to the mystery of being itself, while providing to the eyes of faith an approach to divinity. He passes easily from the visible world to invisible principles which sustain it, and delights in correspondences, analogies and mystical mathematics. But, although his practice here is imaginative, he is no iconoclastic rebel, and his metaphysical attitudes remain broadly traditional.[7]

Much of the rhetoric of *Religio Medici* expresses Browne's carefully poised position, at once sceptically modern and old-fashioned. As his title implies,[8] he is both a doctor and a religious man; ruefully, he notices that atheism is 'the generall scandall of my profession' (1.1). Then, with careful and elaborate gracious-ness, he assures us he is a Christian,[9] but not a narrow sort with proselytising designs, and the very carefulness of the circumlocu-tion with which this assurance is written helps to convince us of the fact.[10] It soon becomes clear, however, that despite being accounted by contemporaries as among the new thinkers, Browne really does not have their character at all. He is not a mathematician, nor is he much of an empiricist.[11] Instead, he likes to let his mind play on mysteries which humour his fancy, and to encounter them in 'an easie and Platonick description'. His emphasis, even, falls on 'easie', and he tells us he prefers an allegory before 'Metaphysicall definitions' (i.10). One result is that his imaginative use of metaphysics draws attention to the fascinating activity itself on the human psyche, and to how complex and unresolved (rather than 'metaphysically defined') is man's spiritual quest. Not surprisingly, he voices a low opinion of the systematic kind of metaphysics based, as he says, on 'definitions', and abjures Aristotle for attempting to label reality and reduce God's mysteries to an abstract scheme: '*Aristotle* whilst hee labours to refute the Idea's of *Plato* ', Browne concludes, 'fals upon one himselfe: for his *summum bonum* is a *Chimaera*, and there is no such thing as his Felicity' (ii.15). Reality always exceeds language, and we should beware of falling victim to our own terminology by taking words too literally: 'It was the ignorance of mans reason that begat this very name, and by a carelesse terme miscalled the providence of God' (i.18).[12]

Precisely this sense of the relativity of language and meaning constitutes the most distinctively modern side of Browne's mind. We are as ignorant of the 'Antipathies and occult qualities', he reminds us, by which the divine hand limns the design of nature, as we are of our destiny (i.43). True faith is necessary not only as 'a marke or token, but also a means of our Salvation, but where to find this, is as obscure to me, as my last end' (i.60). The complexity of experience, the multiplicity of ideas (i.55; ii.8), the fantastic divagations of the human mind, bemused 'whilst wee sleepe within the bosome of our causes' (i.39), correct the 'Insolent zeales' of religious dogmatists and the promulgators of pedantic certainty alike. Browne chastens both licentious empiricism and intolerant religion; metaphysics, used imaginatively, is his principal means (the 'method', even) of his doing so, and of discovering thereby a balance between extremes:

> we are onely that amphibious piece betweene a corporall and spirituall essence, that middle frame that linkes those two together, and makes good the method of God and nature, that jumps not from extreames, but unites the incompatible distances by some middle and participating natures.   (i.34).

Unself-consciously, the metaphysical vocabulary recurs – 'essence', 'participating nature' – to assure us that our place requires us to be amphibious, so that we do not recoil into either crass materialism or dull abstractions. And yet, as Digby was first to see, Browne's characteristic deployment of metaphysics remains problematical. Although he is serious about the real metaphysical truth attainable by natural reason, Browne's 'easie and Platonick description' (i.10) remains too closely allied with metaphor and allegory, and he is blithely undisturbed by the problems this raises.

Digby, by contrast, scrutinises the very points Browne ignores, and questions specifically the relationship of 'artificiall terms' to real existences. Notions of 'matter, forme, act, power, existence, and the like', Digby writes, though useful for our understandings 'are never the lesse, no where by themselves in nature' (p. 22). He warns against attributing to things the entities we create in our minds (p. 23), and accuses Browne of doing just this. Digby's position is thus indistinguishable from that of Hobbes or Bacon, except that Digby soon makes clear that he argues from traditional scholastic and Aristotelian premises. Although joining the chorus of moderns who denounce scholastic jargon as tautologous (pp. 14–15), he maintains a thoroughgoing realist attitude towards language, and desires even to build a system on Aristotle's foundation (p. 24). '*Truth*', he claims, in conventional scholastic terms, is the 'adequated and satisfying object of the understanding' (p. 65). With its inherent capacity for abstracting form from matter, the soul apprehends God's design reflected everywhere in created being, and thirsts for 'that infinite entity' (p. 66), the sole foundation of existence itself.

Digby's epistemology, though cautious about metaphysical oversimplifications, therefore remains just as old-fashioned as Browne's; more so, in one respect, for Digby corrects Browne's misapprehensions about the relations of matter to form (pp. 21, 83), and about angelic intelligence (p. 39). He is, in short, a more technical or 'scientific' metaphysician than Browne, and insists that the process of abstract knowledge is exacting and laborious. The scholastics had taught that by natural intelligence we do not understand the essence of a thing as God apprehends it. The work of human intelligence therefore does not exhaust the meaning of creation, though our partial apprehensions of that meaning remain objectively true. The careful organisation of knowledge, thus abstracted, Digby calls 'method', and he thinks Browne short of it. 'But were such things, scientifically, and methodically declared, they would bee of extreame satisfaction' (p. 15).

Browne, as we see, is indeed happily unconcerned with

problems of this order. Here, for instance, is a passage where he, like Digby, deals with the deficiencies and indirection of conceptual knowledge:

> God, who knowes mee truly, knowes that I am nothing; for hee onely beholds me, and all the world, who lookes not on us through a derived ray, or a trajection of a sensible species, but beholds the substance without the helpe of accidents, and the formes of things, as wee their operations. Further, no man can judge another, because no man knowes himselfe; for we censure others but as they disagree from that humour.   (II.4)

God alone fully apprehends the created essence; our information is partial, and is derived through sensible species by means of abstraction. Again, Browne easily deploys traditional metaphysical language ('sensible species', 'substance', 'accidents', 'formes'), but his reason for making the point is quite unlike Digby's, for Browne wants to show the obscurity of our self-knowledge and therefore to warn against making rash judgements of others. Digby, by contrast, wants us to sift our concepts methodically, so that we shall not make mistakes about how our language relates to things.

Not surprisingly, Browne's use of the word 'method' in *Religio Medici* is unsystematic: 'every Countrey proceeding in a peculiar Method' (I.4); 'my humble speculations have another Method' (I.13); ''tis no bad method of the Schooles' (I.33); 'It is the method of charity to suffer without reaction' (I.5); 'the mysticall method of *Moses*' (I.34); 'The method I should use in distributive justice' (II.13). The word applies with equal readiness to a number of subjects, and we are not invited to interrogate it too precisely, or to demand too much from it in terms of technical consistency. Similarly, when the question of relations between words and things is raised, Browne again is 'easie' rather than philosophically rigorous. For instance, in *Pseudodoxia Epidemica*, when he considers errors arising from mistaken relationships between verbal and real, he is mostly concerned with the misreading of metaphor and confusions resultant upon taking figurative language literally: 'herein may be comprised all Ironical mistakes for intended expressions receiving inverted significations; all deductions from Metaphors, Parables, Allegories, unto real and rigid interpretations' (*Works*, II, 34).

Although this may seem a version of Bacon's Idols of the Market Place, it is not nearly so Baconian as it first looks, for Browne is not concerned to disencumber the world of metaphysical reality nor (as one critic puts it) with the strictly philosophical consequences of the 'inadequate reference of abstract words to the things they are supposed to name'.[13] He does not really encounter the problem of scientific method at all. The philosophical difficulties of reconciling mechanism with spiritual reality, or body with mind – difficulties which are at the centre of empiricist and rationalist concern throughout the period of the scientific revolution – hardly touch him, and he had no interest in mathematics as distinct from numerology. He was, none the less, attracted to several enterprises which are plainly enough Baconian: he operated his own laboratory, was a curious investigator of nature, a medical doctor (who thought Harvey's theory of the circulation a great discovery) and the author of a monumental anti-encyclopaedia dedicated to the advancement of learning.[14]

Browne's predicament, as we have so far described it, is, therefore, something like this: he thinks of himself as a new philosopher, and in some respects behaves like one, for he is a curious empiricist and is judiciously sceptical about metaphysical definitions and the relationship of language to reality. But he remains an old-fashioned metaphysician, convinced that the things of this world are hieroglyphs of a higher, spiritual reality. Besides, his metaphysical practice is so informal and conducted in a style so personal (at once epistolary and meditative),[15] that he makes of the subject something subjectively pleasing and imaginatively coherent, rather than something rigorous and logical. While we may see him, then, in one sense as rescuing metaphysics from pedantry (by reaffirming it as creative), in another he threatens to reduce it to fiction by the very fact of his treating it imaginatively and without critical rigour.

II *RELIGIO MEDICI* AND THE METAPHYSICAL CROSS

Today, most readers of Browne do not pursue these kinds of distinctions because history has made clear that he is not an original thinker, and readers are sufficiently pleased by the tender, whimsical, melancholy and tolerant view of the world which his best-known writings characteristically express. But the fact remains that Browne's imagination to some degree depends upon what he was able to take seriously as a metaphysician. And, to clarify the structure of what I am calling his 'metaphysical imagination', I should like to suggest that the principal organising-motif of Browne's best-known work, the *Religio Medici*, is the traditional image of the cross, which he treats metaphysically. By this means, he keeps before us the paradoxes and antinomies of experience (the arms of the cross) as well as its transcendental unity (the circle which the glorified cross bears within its arms), so that the symbol becomes a way of directing us imaginatively (and not by way of definition) to the metaphysical foundations of human knowledge itself.

Browne's most explicit references to the 'metaphysical cross' occur in *The Garden of Cyrus*, where the ubiquitous quincunx is pictured as a 'decussation' (or crossing) of lines, with a circle at the centre. Near the end of *Hydriotaphia* (the companion piece bound together with *The Garden of Cyrus* for publication), Browne had stated that 'Circles and right lines limit and close all bodies and the mortall right-lined circle must conclude and shut up all' (*Works*, I, 166). This combination of 'right lines' and circles to indicate the fundamental design of created being is made clear repeatedly in *The Garden of Cyrus*. Browne begins, for instance, by admiring Cyrus's tree-planting, and then goes on to find the whole shape of nature in the five-pointed design Cyrus chose (consisting of two crossed lines, like a letter X). Cyrus is admired not just because his design is pleasant, but because it truly represents a basic principle of creation. Browne then points out that the crossed lines – 'the Emphaticall decussation, or fundamentall figure' (p. 181) – need not be in the form of the letter X, but can be a perfect square. Either way, we are reminded of the cross; Constantine's emblem used the Greek X for such a purpose: 'the crucigerous Ensigne carried this figure, not transversely or rectangularly intersected, but in a decussation, after the form of an *Andrean* or *Burgundian* cross' (p. 182). All this, says Browne, raises again 'the old Theme' 'of crosses and crucifixion' on which he will not dwell, though his dismissal of the subject entails a conspicuous summary of what is being omitted. For instance, he will not conduct a study of Egyptian crosses with circles on their heads, or the combination of circle and cross in the sign of Venus which was 'looked on by ancient Christians, with relation unto Christ'. This symbolism, Browne reminds us in passing, has to do with the relations of spiritual and elemental nature 'implied by a circle and right-lined intersection' (ibid.). Browne is concerned, that is, with a metaphysical rather than psychological or moral or theological interpretation.

Throughout *The Garden of Cyrus*, Browne continues to discover the quincunx everywhere in nature. 'Right lines and circles make out the bulk of plants' (p. 207), and we may discover, by study, all kinds of elegant 'analogies in the orderly book of nature' (p. 206). For instance, Granadilla is the 'flower of Christs passion' not only because of right lines and circles, but because it shows 'The Figures of nails and crucifying appurtenances', and the '*Barbado* pine' also gives us a 'handsome draught of crucifixion' (ibid.). Not surprisingly, such a pursuit of the quincunx 'mystically apprehended' (p. 220) leads to a variety of amusing speculations wherein consists a large part of the author's attractiveness and originality. Still, Browne attributes to Plato special credit for the basic idea because of an image in the *Timaeus* of two crossed strips bent into circles representing 'the motion of the soul, both of the world and man'. Browne explains,

> The circle declaring the motion of the indivisible soul, simple, according to the divinity of its nature, and returning into it self; the right lines respecting the motion pertaining unto sense, and vegetation, and the central decussation, the wondrous connexion of the severall faculties conjointly in one substance. And so conjoyned the unity and duality of the soul.   (Ibid.)

Cross and circle, again metaphysically considered, represent the very condition of the human soul in the world, both divine and self-divided. The next paragraph then claims that Justin Martyr applies Plato's figure to 'our blessed Saviour', borrowing from Plato the phrase '*Decussavit eum in universo*'. The fact that these words do not occur in the *Timaeus* serves less as evidence of Browne's inaccuracy than of his desire to find in the metaphysical speculations of a great philosopher an intuition of the truths revealed to faith; a means, that is, by which the chief sign of Christianity also symbolises our knowledge as rational creatures.

The *Religio Medici* does not deal so explicitly with right lines and circles and with nature's 'crucigerous Ensigns' as does the

Garden of Cyrus, but the metaphysical cross is none the less evident and, once we look at the earlier work in light of claims made in the later one, it seems obvious that Browne all along had some such symbolic and metaphysical view of human epistemology in mind.[16] The passage on Plato which I have just cited, for instance, claims that the circle represents the soul's divinity, and the right lines its several connections to the world through sense and vegetation, so that the soul is at once 'unity and duality', represented by the sign of the cross metaphysically understood. Though Coleridge does not develop the point, his admission that he found in Browne's thinking in general a resemblance to his own was likely based on just this sense of polarity, wherein both men find contraries paradoxically united: 'contraries,' says Browne, with unusual directness, 'though they destroy one another, are yet the life of one another' (*Religio Medici*, II.4). It follows that the metaphysical cross is, for Browne, an especially appropriate device for representing the mind's participation in, yet distinctness from, the world – the conjunction, that is, out of which human knowledge itself arises.

The *Religio Medici*, I suggest, develops this general approach to knowledge through a witty display of paradoxes, creating tension and opposition which are then tempered by elaborate circular arguments.[17] Browne, as Stanley Fish points out, has no designs on us: he does not want to persuade us of anything definite, but allows his arguments such leisurely and expansive elaboration that we get entangled in the complexities, and give up trying to follow them exactly.[18] We are left with an exercise in suspended judgement, as an encouragement to us to find a tolerant balance between positions which, if taken singly, would lead to undesirable extremes. The effect is deliberately contrived, and is not just a corollary of Browne's natural mode of expression. Here, for instance, is Browne to his son, Tom:

Honest Tom bee of good heart and followe thy buisinesse. I doubt not butt thou wilt doe well. God hath given thee parts to enable thee. If you practise to write you will have a good pen and style. It were not amisse to take the draught of the college or part thereof if you have time, butt however omitt no opportunitie in your studie. You shall not want while I have it. (*Works*, IV, 17)

If we did not know the author, we could not tell from this banal prose that the passage is from the same hand as *Religio Medici*,[19] for there is no hint here of the Browne we admire. Yet the letter advises the young man to practice in order to have a good style. It is as if Sir Thomas acknowledges that good style is an accomplishment, say, like singing; we sing when the occasion calls for it, but we do not sing every time we wish to talk. In the *Religio Medici*, we listen to a specially trained voice; an instrument deployed to raise us to an *o altitudo* (1.9) where the 'decussations' of our daily discourse are apprehended by the simple gaze of the soul 'according to the divinity of its nature'. Here is a characteristic passage:

> At the sight of a Crosse or Crucifix I can dispence with my hat, but scarce with the thought and memory of my Saviour; I cannot laugh at but rather pity the fruitlesse journeys of Pilgrims, or contemne the miserable condition of Friers; for though misplaced in circumstance, there is something in it of devotion: I could never heare the *Ave Maria* Bell without an elevation, or thinke it a sufficient warrant, because they erred in one circumstance, for me to erre in all: that is in silence and dumb contempt. Whilst therefore they directed their devotions to her, I offered mine to God, and rectified the errour of their prayers by rightly ordering mine owne. At a solemne Procession I have wept abundantly, while my consorts, blinde with opposition and prejudice, have fallen into an eccesse of scorne and laughter: There are questionless both in Greek, Roman, and African Churches, solemnities, and ceremonies, whereof the wiser zeales doe make a Christian use, and stand condemned by us; not as evill in themselves, but as allurements and baits of superstition to those vulgar heads that looke asquint on the face of truth, and those unstable judgements that cannot consist in the narrow point and centre of vertue without a reele or stagger to the circumference.   (1.3)

Browne attempts to describe his religious position, neither so strenuous as that of the Reformers who would dispense altogether with material aids to devotion, nor so indulgent as the Roman Catholics. He has just assured us he is 'not scrupulous', and now tries to communicate a sense of how he is drawn to a middle way between the poles of 'misguided zeale' and 'superstition' (ibid.). Although 'not scrupulous', however, his relaxed position is, paradoxically, the result of his being very scrupulous stylistically about weighing up his reactions, so much so that it is difficult to determine precisely where he stands. But we know his position is somewhere between the various pairs of extremes he mentions and rejects, and to the extent that we come to agree with him about the extremes we are learning to trust his judgement. When he dispenses with his hat, but not the thought of his saviour, for instance, he declares his willingness to respect the visible, outward sign, but only in so far as it assists true, inward devotion. The idea of dispensing and refusing to dispense initially establishes a contrast, but Browne really shows that there is no contrast here at all; rather a unified and properly pious attitude. So throughout the passage we are asked to discover the centre wherein the contraries vitalise one another: between laughter and pity, between one circumstance and all, between the errors of superstition and the blindness of prejudice, between 'silence and dumb contempt' and 'eccesse of scorne and laughter'. Though not above sentiment (weeping at the solemn procession), nor, even, free from a certain tone of self-congratulation, Browne contrives to avoid 'unstable judgements'. For instance, his sketchy gesture of approval which may intimate uncritical relativism ('there is something in it of devotion') is quickly firmed up by the sturdy affirmation, 'I offered mine to God'. Likewise, his compassion and willingness to participate are offset by unsentimental and objective vigour: 'blinde with opposition and prejudice', 'the miserable condition of Friers', 'baits of superstition to those vulgar heads'. Throughout the passage, weight balances counterweight, and the syntax is deliberately elaborate. Within this massive construction, the 'I' expresses a judgement inseparable from the manner of the discussion and thereby embodies a united attitude to experience at large, although dwelling in the midst of contraries.

Significantly, the passage begins with the cross and ends with a circle. This is not just a product of my own decision to excerpt the passage as I have done, for I have taken a unit of Browne's thought which really does begin and end in this way. Moreover, I should like to suggest that such a combination of cross and circle is basic to the entire structure of the *Religio*. The cross suggests a set of polarities, of 'decussations' which need to be reconciled; the circle, symbol of such reconciliation, is centred at the intersection of the crossed 'right lines'. Circle and cross are, for Browne, inseparable, representing the conditions of man's very being in the world as a rational animal. Characteristically, reason's antinomies lead Browne to circles, but the exercise of reason is necessary to human enquiry, and therefore has a positive side; likewise, the circle, though a symbol of wholeness, expanding knowledge and wise judgement, also represents the limits of knowledge by suggesting constriction. As A. Guibbory convincingly argues, Browne's use of the circle at first seems to indicate a Baconian attitude to the progress of learning, but the figure carries also an anti-Baconian sense.[20] The 'unity and duality of the soul' represented by Browne's treatment of the cross as a 'mystical decussation' therefore shows us simultaneously the poverty and glory of the human mind, as circles and right lines are held in an elaborate and varied counterpoint, which it is pleasing to follow through the text.

Thus we are assured that good judgement may 'expect an union in the poles of Heaven' (i.4), and the discussion then shifts 'into a lesser circle' with Browne maintaining that no church 'squares' (i.5) exactly with his conscience. In philosophy, we are told, truth seems 'double-faced' and in this respect Browne admits himself 'paradoxicall'; however, he submits to 'the great wheele of the Church', which he compares to the 'epicycle' (or limited circle) of his 'owne braine', from which he reserves no 'proper poles or motion' (i.6). Where reason and 'the arguments of our proper senses' fail, he admits an obscurity too deep for him, and appeals to the 'allegorical description of *Hermes*' of a circle with its centre everywhere and its circumference nowhere (i.10). Consultation and election are 'two motions in us', but one in God (i.13), and God's providence moves in a 'vast circle' (i.14). God is a geometrician who might 'divide a right line' or proceed 'in a circle or longer way' (i.16). All things in creation are 'founded on contrarieties', but God comprises 'all things' and is 'contrary unto nothing' (i.35). Faced with a 'Dilemma', Browne feels that he must 'take a full view and circle of my selfe' (i.38). Heaven and hell are contraries, but can be manifest 'within the circle of this sensible world' (i.49). In the 'compasse of my selfe' he finds contraries at war: 'passion against reason, reason against faith' (ii.7). His conversation, he claims, 'is like the Sunne's with all men', smiling alike on the opposites 'good and bad'; 'poysons', we are reminded, 'containe within themselves their own Antidote', but men must try to stay 'within the circle of those qualities, wherein they are good' (ɪɪ.10).

In each of these examples – and the list could be extended – Browne clearly juxtaposes 'decussations' and circles, and universalises their significance by deploying such a variety of instances that the result, as he says himself, is 'Metaphysicall' (ɪ.13). Indeed, he has remarkably little interest in the cross as a subject for meditation in the usual sense, calling for *compositio loci* and evocation of the physical suffering. He talks briefly of 'Crosse or Crucifix' (ɪ.3), but only as a church ornament; he mentions the true cross, supposedly found by St Helena, but only to wonder why it should have power to heal (ɪ.28); he reminds us that things which seem to others 'crosses' or 'afflictions' can often appear, on further enquiry, as 'secret and dissembled favours' (ɪ.53). The cross in these instances is either an object of curiosity, or a casual metaphor; not the occasion for anguish or soul-searching, nor for meditation upon personal guilt, sin, grace and atonement.

This is not to deny Browne's melancholy side, for his lucubrations on death and on the vanity of human wishes are sufficiently obvious. But he appeals to the cross not to develop directly this element of his sensibility; rather, to suggest a metaphysical truth, an interpretation of the status of human knowledge, its transcendent position not being reducible either to scepticism's 'extream of despaire' (ɪ.7), nor to false dogmatism's excessive certainty which leads to violence and self-righteousness (ɪ.1–6).

Just as, in the *Garden of Cyrus*, Browne first seems to describe some curious shapes in nature, but ends up discussing the metaphysical nature of shape itself, so in *Religio Medici* the epistolary and confessional meditation of one man on his religious beliefs becomes substantially a treatise about man's sense of the scope and limitations of reason in broaching such a subject at all. Browne's success in this, as I have said, resides largely in the triumph of his style and the distinction of his language, but he is less a rambling, antiquarian charmer and wool-gatherer than is sometimes supposed, and I have suggested that the symbol of the cross, metaphysically considered, provides a coherent structure for the work. It is the means by which the manifold turns of his mind – the effect of shot silk, as Coleridge has it[21] – are given unity, and thereby raised towards the contemplation of divinity, the end to which metaphysics is drawn. There *is* order here, even though it is not the kind of order which the book's first critic, Sir Kenelm Digby, desires. It is, however, the kind of order without which metaphysics becomes a mere inert rigmarole of abstractions. The seventeenth-century empiricists, who by and large regarded metaphysics as indeed an inert rigmarole, are therefore to some degree answered by Browne, who attests the creative energy at the heart of metaphysics at its best.

The extent to which Browne was 'metaphysically imaginative' for the express purpose of correcting the empiricists is, of course, debatable, and, as we see, the new thinkers could just as well take solace from the fact that in Browne's hands metaphysics shows itself so *clearly* an act of imagination, rather than of logic. To the extent, however, that Browne took metaphysics seriously, living its subject matter from within, as it were, we must in the end acknowledge him reactionary; a man of another age, thinking himself modern, but whose deepest feelings were not modern at all. And at this point a further look at Digby may be helpful, for he too was an old-fashioned metaphysician who thought himself part (indeed at the forefront of) the modern scientific movement, but whose position is in some respects so clearly the reverse of Browne's that his *Observations* on the *Religio Medici* are of special interest.

III   KENELM DIGBY'S ARGUMENT FROM METHOD

Digby thought highly of the moderns, both empiricists and rationalists. He agreed with his friend Hobbes on the radical importance of corpuscular philosophy,[22] and even introduced him to that key work of his other friend, Descartes – the *Discours de la Méthode*.[23] His own thinking followed Descartes in making a clear distinction between spirit and body, a distinction reproduced in the two-part structure of his central work, the *Two Treatises* on body and soul.[24] He recommended (and practised) experimentation as a way to understand the structure of bodies, and he thought mathematics the key to organising the results. In all this, he conforms very well to the major tenets of the new method.

Digby, however, is perhaps best known today for his odd treatise *Of the Sympathetic Powder*,[25] describing how wounds can be healed by remote control (for instance, by a blood-soaked bandage being dipped in vitriol). But it should be appreciated to what extent even this fantastic bit of lore is based on his 'modern' convictions about the affinities of atoms and their kinetic interactions. 'Bodies,' he tells us, 'which draw the atomes dispersed in the air, attract to themselves such as are of their own nature, with greater force and energy, than other heterogeneous and strange atoms.'[26] Thus blood atoms on the bandage are transmitted by light and heat to the wound, to which they are drawn by natural affinity. The blood atoms treated with vitriol, however, carry with them the vitriol's curative agency, and so relieve the wound. We should remember that Digby claims this theory is based on an actual cure; there is therefore no inconsistency between the author of *The Sympathetic Powder* and the Digby who describes atomic structures and ridicules magic.[27]

Descartes (who charmingly refers to a person called d'Igby) at one point observes, however, that his English acquaintance was too fond of Aristotle,[28] and, indeed, despite his Cartesian rationalism, his Hobbesian atomism and his Baconian experimentation, Digby did turn to Aristotle for metaphysics, and remained traditionally Thomist in his descriptions of the mind's grasp of formal essences by abstraction. There is, indeed, an unfortunate awkwardness in Digby's theory, on the one hand, that the world of bodies is a congregation of quantifiable and infinitely divisible atomic particles, and, on the other, that bodies are made up of Aristotelian qualities. But the problem is no more severe for Digby than for Descartes, or for the men of the new method in general, who wanted the physical world to be fundamentally quantifiable, and also needed to preserve the human soul. The least that can be said for Digby is that he stopped short of desperate devices, such as Descartes's pineal gland, for joining up what reason had put asunder. But he really has no theory at all of how spiritual 'apprehension' and atomic 'sensation' are interrelated.

In the Preface to his treatise on bodies, Digby explains how the book came to be written. He had set out to write just on the soul, but decided he needed a preface on bodies, which then grew to be more than twice as long as the eventual work on the principal subject. He blames a widespread 'current of doctrine' in certain philosophical schools, whose 'loose methode' he denounces for imposing on him this 'unavoidable necessity'. These schools are content to explain phenomena by appealing tautologically to 'powers' and 'sensible qualities' (for instance, 'white' is a sensible quality which has the power to make a thing white). Digby prefers a 'further searching into the physicall causes', and against 'loose methode' he places mathematics and a procedure based on 'quantitative and corporeall partes', which he reduces to the density and rarity of bodies (that is, their weight in relation to volume).

All this is clear enough, except that Digby then proceeds, at some length and with considerable intricacy, to deduce Aristotle's four elements, with their qualities (moist, dry, hot and cold), from the quantifiable, corporeal structure of bodies, and to declare the elements the basic building-blocks of the material world. A problem of course arises when Digby comes to account for elemental qualities according to the experimental and mathematical model which he has recommended, for, inevitably, it turns out that the traditional elements are just as 'hidden and unexplicable' as the entities Digby accuses the schools of inventing uncritically.

This problem surfaces most clearly when we are advised to proceed 'in imagination', construing what physical effects the various combinations of rarity, density and gravity are likely to produce. These effects Digby concludes to be the elements themselves, but, after questioning whether or not they can be found in pure form, Digby balks, and gives his answer a hundred pages later, saying that they are indeed found pure, but only in very small atoms, which are too subtle for our senses to discern. The elements, in short, end up being as notional as any of the scholastic qualities, and Digby's attempt to deduce them from his corpuscular theory falls before the very objections he himself raises against the naïve metaphysicians. To be a thoroughgoing atomist, we might conclude, Digby would have to abandon old-fashioned metaphysical jargon altogether.

But it is seductively easy to point to these kinds of lacunae as flaws, for in a sense Digby *wants* us to see the incommensurability of the metaphysical and corporeal. As he assures us in the Preface, his very long discussion of bodies is necessary because his major demonstration of the soul's spiritual power is precisely that it cannot be reduced to corporeal explanations. Body, in short, is irrelevant to soul, and Digby believes this is the strongest argument for the soul's immortality. He points out that any discussion of physical bodies must admit some metaphysical component (p. 24), because the act of understanding is itself not corporeal. Quantity and substance, he says, are different: milk can boil over and so occupy more space than before it was heated, but it is still milk (p. 25). The metaphysical and physical thus operate in some elusively synchronous way, and, with considerable patience and ingenuity, Digby investigates their mutual encroachment on the level of sensation.

At the end, however, Digby does remain a dualist, for the simple reason that he does not reduce spirit to extension. This of course could very well seem a classical anti-metaphysical gambit permitting Digby the empiricist to dispense with final (unmanifest) causes, except that Digby is not anti-metaphysical in this sense at all; his claim against the metaphysicians is not that they give a wrong account of things, and therefore impede science, but that their claims are too large. Indeed, he is quite happy to fall back on metaphysics when his own account of the material world reaches a limit beyond which his experience (and imagination) of corpuscular structure cannot reach. For details of how quantity and substance are divided, he tells us, he would need to 'make a greater inroade into the very bowels of Metaphysickes' than is possible in the present context (p. 26). In the discussion of light (which he thinks corporeal), the question of quality as a real entity arises, but, Digby says, it pertains to metaphysics, and so he will not go into it (p. 40). Whether or not the substantial forms of elements remain in mixed bodies, he decides, is a question for 'Metaphysicians (those spirituall Anatomistes)' (p. 143).

Far from dismissing metaphysics, therefore, Digby looks to it for an answer to basic scientific problems which are otherwise unsolvable. None the less, the metaphysician's legitimate province is determined negatively by encroachments made on it by the sciences, and this attitude accords well with Digby's Cartesian bias. But a predominantly logical approach, we conclude, will not solve Digby's problem, for logicians can only divide and distinguish further: the interpenetration, the unity of opposites which Digby intuits, can be experienced in the end only as a *quality of vision*, and on this Digby is decidedly short.

The inordinate length of the treatise on bodies indicates, at least, that Digby was deeply concerned with the new science, and how acutely he felt the problems raised for metaphysics by the discovery of method. At the same time, he remains an old-fashioned metaphysician; the soul for him is a 'pure substance' (p. 422) whose state is 'pure *being*' (p. 432), whose basic apprehension is 'the notion of *Being*' (p. 358) and whose knowledge is by the abstraction of universals. As we see, he wanted a system of philosophy based on the Aristotle[29] whom other moderns had largely rejected. But Digby saw no sense in throwing out the baby with the bath water, and thought that a well-scrubbed Aristotelian logic and metaphysics, cleansed of the accretions of nasty jargon, could make a fine contribution to the nursery of modern science. In this, he has some affinity with Browne, except that Browne rather liked the baby dirty. The *Religio Medici*, as I have suggested, is winsome, imaginatively coherent, unsystematic, and does not really grasp the key problem of modern method having to do with the quantification of corporeal reality as distinct from the metaphysical concern with quality. Digby clearly does grasp the importance of this problem, and insists on solving it rigorously. But he runs the risk, as a result, simply of juxtaposing one system of abstract metaphysical terms with another of mathematical terms, without being able to reconcile them.

The difference can be summarised as follows: Browne as a metaphysician operated imaginatively, and suggests that through the human soul's creative energies metaphysics can open up the world's intelligible order to the divine mysteries of faith. Digby, by contrast, operates systematically, and suggests that metaphysics can earn its way in the world when justified by contrast with the limited practices of science; metaphysics, however, in answering our need to organise what we know in terms of value, must also retain intimate contact with the world of science.[30] Both men, of course, are correct, and metaphysics must attempt to do what each of them says; yet modern metaphysics has been decidedly hard put to recover from the schism between body and spirit with which the discovery of method forced it so nakedly to contend.

In light of these remarks, the main impetus behind Digby's *Observations* on the *Religio Medici* is predictable, and, although his argument can scarcely be described as organised (being a series of hasty jottings), its logic is clear. He criticises Browne consistently for taking metaphysics up and away from the world of things, instead of down into it. Browne, claims Digby, is interested in the state of the soul after death, but this leads only to 'abstracted metaphysicall speculations' 'flying continually . . . in the Subtile ayre' (p. 8). The attempt to treat of the Trinity by way of analogy with the human soul is a 'wild discourse' (p. 19) clothed in negations, and without hope of 'positive examples' (p. 20). On similar grounds, he accuses Browne of giving too much authority to astrology (p. 32) and of being insufficiently sceptical about witches (a subject on which Digby reserves opinion, it being disagreeable to his 'philosophy', which keeps separate the realms of spirit and body). So also, Browne's thoughts on a 'universall *Spirit*' seem to Digby 'a wilde fancie' (p. 37); Browne rushes too quickly from 'naturall speculations' to subjects too far removed from nature to be verifiable (p. 38). Although Digby admires Browne's '*Iuditious* piety' (p. 6) and sense of mystery (p. 14), he wishes that 'such things' were 'scientifically, and methodically declared' (p. 15). He points out that even exact mathematicians (who have to deal with 'differences of quantity') seldom become good metaphysicians (p. 9), and Browne's wit (that of a physician who deals with corpses) is far from mathematical, and quite unfitted for 'so towring a *Game*' (p. 10). Basing himself on mathematical principles, Digby declares that light is not a 'bare quality' as Browne claims (p. 40) but a 'solid Substance and body' (p. 41). Such pseudo-spiritual events as murdered corpses bleeding afresh at the approach of the murderer ('frequently seen in *England*' – p. 47), Digby explains in terms of corpuscular physics, on the model of *The Sympathetic Powder*. Physics, he declares, may be as plain as mathematics, 'if men would but apply themselves to a right method of Study' (p. 100).

Clearly, as far as the natural sciences are concerned, Digby wants the regulative principles to derive from mathematics and not from metaphysics, and in this he is entirely modern. But he also wants to reserve for traditional metaphysics the task of classifying the soul's qualitative apprehensions in a way that will order and systematise the findings of empirical and mathematical science. There is nothing wrong with this aspiration in itself, except that in Digby's hands (as Coleridge complains) it becomes merely a pedantic system, a set of formal terms juxtaposed to the mathematico-corpuscular hypothesis, consistent with it in the end simply because not touching it. There is no way to reconcile body and spirit in Digby's terms. Instead of ordering from above, Digby's metaphysics is cut off from below, and falls prey to the tyranny of an atomic determinism.

Despite his lack of mathematical rigour and technical exper-tise, Browne, by contrast, retains for metaphysics a creative vision. The correspondences, likeness principles, hierarchies, analogies, middle entities (spirits of the universe, of plants, lodestones and angels), are, in his view, full participants in our everyday world, which is fraught with myriad interpenetrations of occult forms and energies, such as the eye of imagination can grasp. But Browne's writing – divorced, as we can see, from the objective discipline of 'scientific' metaphysics – threatens to become a farrago of random associations. His saving recourse is therefore to a judicious scepticism[31] by which he denies to metaphysics the clear certainties of pedantic logic or unexamined faith. His literature – genial, dreaming, unanxious and reassuring – stands between, a 'middle and participating nature' like man himself, and yet strangely disenfranchised, content to wonder at the strangeness of the predicament, preserving a balance, ventur-ing with no exorbitant certainty, either above or below. As his treatment of the cross in *Religio Medici* especially shows, Browne therefore appropriates metaphysics to the act of literature itself, as a means of enabling him to express most fully and imagina-tively his vision of man's middle state, which literature best describes. At a time when the discovery of method had, as it were, attacked metaphysics by disenchanting it, Browne's deployment of a symbol such as the metaphysical cross has the effect of something like a self-conscious re-enchantment. Browne's interest in scientific matters, we may surmise, helped to engender the wide-ranging empirical curiosity and scepticism which curtailed a thoroughgoing metaphysical inquiry. We are not, however, asked to relinquish that inquiry altogether: rather, to suspend disbelief in order to appreciate the insight which metaphysics can provide for the poet's account of the human reality which is his subject.

CHAPTER SIX

William Law's *Spirit of Love*: Rationalist Argument and Behemist Myth

I RIGOUR AND IMAGINATION IN *A SERIOUS CALL*

For William Law (1686–1761) the world without God is tragic and absurd. This is the main point of his best-known book, *A Serious Call to a Devout and Holy Life* (1729), in which he describes true devotion – the disposition, that is, of one 'who lives no longer to his own *will* . . . but to the sole will of God'.[1] Law does not cut corners: 'The short of the matter is this, either Reason and Religion prescribe *rules* and *ends* to all the ordinary actions of our life, or they do not: If they do, then it is as necessary to govern all our actions by those rules, as it is necessary to worship God' (p. 10). Among Law's 'rules' are directives for regular prayer, recommendations on the charitable use of money and time, injunctions to universal love, and, especially, an insistence on the inner nature of true religion (in a notorious phrase he points out there is 'not one command in all the Gospel for *Public Worship*' – ibid.). Religion, in brief, supplies '*strict rules* of using everything' (p. 100), and will therefore 'relieve our ignorance' by saving us 'from tormenting ourselves' (p. 99). Although Law agrees that the strict piety he advises might at first seem oppressive and anxiety-producing (p. 93), it is, he concludes, really the opposite, as the test of common experience will prove.

There is nothing exceptional about Law's general advice, which most likely draws on established spiritual authorities such as Tauler and *Theologia Germanica*, as well as contemporary French treatises by Fénelon, Antoinette Bourignan and Mme

Guyon.² And, yet, the *Serious Call* achieves genuine literary distinction. Not only was it an immediate success, but it drew acknowledgements from famous contemporaries predisposed to dislike it. Dr Johnson, for instance, picked it up 'expecting to find it a dull book (as such books generally are), and perhaps to laugh at it', but soon found Law 'quite an overmatch for me'. Gibbon, more grudgingly, praised Law 'as a wit and a scholar' who might rank among the 'most agreeable and ingenious writers of the times' were it not for his 'enthusiasm'.³

Law's book, indeed, answers readily enough to both these judgements, for (as Johnson saw) it treats the perennial themes of devotional literature in a striking and topical manner, while also achieving a distinctive style or 'wit'. Characteristically, Law conveys a vigorous and challenging sense of a man who knows where he stands, but he is not a boring dogmatist, for he wants to act, as he says with a kind of elegant bluntness, 'with regard to the use of the world, because that is what everybody can see' (p. 13). He appeals repeatedly to 'common life', acknowledging that not everyone lives 'unto God' in the same way, but according to 'their several callings' (p. 31), and he energetically proclaims the plain reasonableness of such teaching. The book begins by announcing 'our strict duty to live by *reason*' (p. 8), and ends by reassuring us that our actions have no worth 'but so far as they are instances of our obedience to reason' (p. 272).

Given such forthrightness, Law not surprisingly is quick to affirm the 'absurdity' (p. 8) of departures from his principles.⁴ He has a merciless eye for the *'mixture* of Ridicule in the lives of many People' (p. 8) for whom religion is a matter of occasional or half-hearted observance, and a good deal that is interesting in *A Serious Call* derives from his satiric portraits of the less than strictly pious: 'About prides, superiorities and affronts,' says C. S. Lewis, 'there's no book better than Law's *Serious Call to a Devout and Holy Life* where you'll find all of us pinned like butterflies on cards.'⁵ How to make such 'pinning' at the same time an act of charity of course presents difficulties, but Law partly meets these by directing his satire at types rather than individuals. Flavia, for instance, the bourgeois lady of moderate means and orthodox opinions, 'will sometimes read a *book* of *Piety*, if it is a short one, if it is much commended for *style* and *language*, and she can tell where to *borrow* it' (p. 58). Law's vigorous diction counterpoints the lady's nerveless vacillation, and the effect is of a strong mind quickly despatching a trivial one. Flavia, however, remains sufficiently generalised for there to be little sense of personal malice: Law, we feel, appreciates her psychology in so far as it discloses the kind of folly which he can condemn on principle. And, yet, the satiric portraits make clear that he well knew religion is a matter not just of principles but also of personalities. He is therefore content to allow imagination its uses to 'correct our minds' by permitting us to look at 'that which is contrary' (p. 109) to rational behaviour. In this, he is plainly enough of the age of Pope,[6] except that Pope retains an affection for the glittering society which he at once mocks and affirms, while Law deliberately sets his face against the *beau monde* altogether. He did not write to entertain the fashionable, and he did not (even grudgingly) like the world he satirised. Flatus, for instance, is a well-off gentleman in pursuit of happiness which he never finds. His 'wandering imagination' (p. 107) is taken up by an interminable series of projects, during each of which he tells his friends he 'never was so delighted in anything in his life' (p. 108). For sheer inconsistency, arrogance, gentlemanly petulance and incorrigible folly ('he is always cheated, and is satisfied with nothing' – p. 107) there is nobody in literature so much like Flatus as Kenneth Grahame's Mr Toad. But, whereas Mr Toad is lovable, Flatus (by Law's express directive) is not: 'I hope, that every particular folly that you here see, will naturally turn itself into an argument, for the wisdom and happiness of a religious life' (p. 109).

As exemplified by the treatment of Flatus, however, Law's principles clearly put a strain on his writerly practice, for Law's strenuous judgement stands at odds with the sense that Flatus's behaviour is incorrigible, given his circumstances and a lifetime of bad habits. Acute as Law's psychological portraiture is, it must remain sufficiently general to admit reproach in the name of reason. Despite his gifts of imagination, therefore, Law remains a rigorist, and one result is that, although we might often admire *A Serious Call*, we might just as often find it as difficult to love as it was difficult for Law to love his incorrigible, foolish gentleman.

Law's strictness, we may surmise, was first of all temperamental, and in his early career he re-enforced a natural ascetic inclination by appeal to certain ideas which he discovered in the French Oratorian Nicolas Malebranche. Not until he read Jacob Boehme at about the age of fifty did Law discover for himself a commonplace of the spiritual life which St Teresa,[7] among others, describes as of deep importance to the education of discernment: we should seek direction from those who are like-minded in belief, but whose temperaments are *not* like our own, otherwise we shall find our prejudices merely confirmed. The young Law, however, was content to confirm his prejudices, and his leanings towards rigorism are first evident in an early list of rules written at about the age of eighteen, in which, already, the basic teachings of *A Serious Call* are before us.[8] 'To fix it deep in my Mind', the first rule tells us, 'that I have one business upon my hands – to seek for eternal happiness, by doing the Will of God.' Law then warns himself not to waste time and not to eat or drink too much, and assures himself 'that no condition of this Life is for enjoyment, but for trial'. He is to pray regularly, forbear from evil speaking, and be humble. Rule 9 is an avowal 'To spend as little time as I possibly can, among such persons as can receive no benefit from me, nor I from them.'

Although it is frequently claimed that Law mellowed as he got older, the disposition expressed by these rules, as by the general rigorism of *A Serious Call*, remains characteristic. The routine, for instance, at King's Cliffe (the country house to which Law retired in 1740), was an attempt to live strictly according to principle.[9] There, among other things, Law ran a charity school in which a child who told a lie or was undutiful to its parents stood chained to the wall for a morning, before asking forgiveness on its knees.[10] Mellowness, we conclude, is relative; Law's charity-school library would no doubt have excluded *Wind in the Willows*.

And yet there are clear differences between Law's writings of the late and early periods. As C. S. Lewis says of the *Appeal to All that Doubt*, 'the *prose* of the *Serious Call* has here been all melted away and the book is saturated with delight and the sense of wonder'.[11] This opinion is frequently echoed by commentators, and there is general agreement that Law's assimilation of Jacob Boehme largely accounts for this new 'delight'. It seems, in short, that Boehme came to replace Malebranche as the main formative influence on Law's thought.[12] But what did Law find in Malebranche to begin with? Temperament, I have suggested, had something to do with the initial attraction, for Law must have recognised an affinity with the French Oratorian, similarly ascetic, concerned to put the case for reason, and disposed to see all things 'in God'. However, he also found in Malebranche a sufficiently modern way of thinking to enable him to deal with the prevailing empirical climate represented principally by Locke and Newton, and reflected in a widespread, enlightened approval of new scientific methodology and its latitudinarian corollaries among liberal theologians and Deists.[13] Certainly, the Cambridge of Law's undergraduate years, though conservative, was taken up with such concerns: 'nature rather than God, reason rather than tradition, Deism rather than Christianity, equality rather than hierarchy'.[14] Issues such as these must have put Law's rules to the test, and initially he found help among the mystics – notably John Tauler – whom he read in the Cambridge Library. Yet Law did not use mysticism to avoid hard questions raised by Deism and scientific method, but rather to answer them head on. Law's respect for Newton was high, and remained so throughout his life, so that the pressing issue was basically straightforward, having to do with the reconciliation of mystical spirituality with Newtonian science, and, in this connection, Law quickly recognised Malebranche's relevance.[15]

II MALEBRANCHISTE THEORY AND *THE CASE OF REASON*

Nicolas Malebranche (1638–1715)[16] was a French Oratorian priest of mystical sensibility and some scientific genius. On the one hand, he lived according to the precepts of the French Oratory founded by Pierre de Bérulle, based on a Teresan spirituality interpreted in a strongly theocentric fashion. Bérulle's *culte du non-moi* insisted on the exercise of severe self-abnegation in an attempt to effect what he describes as a 'Copernican revolution'[17] in the life of prayer, whereby the will is to adhere in all things to God. On the other hand, Malebranche was a disciple of Descartes, and a distinguished physicist and geometrician.[18] His attempt to reconcile a theocentric mysticism in the Bérullian–Teresan tradition with Cartesian methodology gives to his complex and rich philosophy a distinctive caste.

Malebranche accepts Descartes's separation of spiritual and extended substances, but goes further than Descartes in stressing that they cannot act on one another in any circumstance. God, rather, makes our encounter with the physical world the *occasion* for our sensitive reaction to it. Bodies do not cause sensations any more than they cause ideas. Sensations, rather, are arranged by God to correspond to our encounter with and reflection upon things, and this, briefly, is the basis of Malebranche's famous doctrine of Occasionalism. That it is fraught with problems John Locke, for one, was quick to point out in the name of common sense.[19] And yet Malebranche is not without his own relevance and depth. For instance, he saw clearly the danger to faith of the new Cartesian method having relegated God to a celestial realm effectively divorced from a world which men would increasingly come to see as a vast array of interacting masses deployed to no discernible final purpose in the infinite emptiness of space.[20] At the same time, he knew he could not turn his back on science; the future lay with it, and what the mystics taught must find expression, accordingly, in terms of its precepts and methods.

For this reason, Malebranche chose to be firmer than Descartes on the question of the soul's interaction with body, and weaker on the question of our autonomy as thinking beings. In the first case, Descartes, by means of the pineal-gland theory, had posited a mechanism for linking the world of extension to the world of thought.[21] Malebranche refused to follow suit, on the strictly rationalist grounds that, by definition, thinking and extended substances excluded each other. Malebranche gained by so doing the right to refuse a 'horizontal' solution to epistemology based on our direct experience of bodies. God, rather (instead of being relegated to the ultra-transcendence of *causa sui*), was intimately present in our every act of perception and cognition. We sense and perceive and think, in short, all things *in God*.

In the second case, Malebranche weakened Descartes's 'methodical' argument that we have a clear, intuitive idea of ourselves just as we have a clear idea of extension. Malebranche instead insisted that, because all things are from God, we are in ourselves nothing, and consequently have no idea of ourselves at all, but only a confused sensation of our continuing identity. This lack of self-knowledge is a direct consequence of our depths being hidden in Christ, and Malebranche goes on to single out the illusions of self-sufficiency to which scientists in particular fall prey by following alternative solutions:

I could, by considering my own modifications attentively,

become acquainted with physics and several sciences which consist only in the knowledge of the relations of extension, as you know quite well. In a word, I should be a light unto myself, and I cannot think of that without a kind of horror.

Malebranche's two major modifications of Descartes thus serve the same end, for both insist that man in nature is not self-sufficient. 'Of ourselves we can do nothing, hence of ourselves we ought to will nothing.'[22] Our depths being hidden with Christ in God, only through adherence to God's will in all things can we be truly ourselves.

Malebranche, however, is more interesting for the witness he bears to the value both of science and of mystical spirituality than for his success in formulating a theory to synthesise them. On the one hand his thought runs counter to the progress of method towards a mechanistic and anthropocentric view of the universe; on the other, he is an enthusiastic proponent of empirical and rationalist procedures, being quite prepared to follow Bacon's experimental practice, and having a high regard for Newton, whose *Opticks*, for instance, enabled him to rewrite his own treatise on light in a more satisfying and coherent manner.[23] But it is one among many such curiosities in the thought of the period that Malebranche's theory of 'all things in God' should have enabled him to feel comfortable with a scientific method destined, effectively, to banish God from the fabric of creation. All things in God, as Hume was later to appreciate with fine irony, is not so very far from nothing at all in God. Rationalism, it seems, no less than empiricism, provides no theological guarantees one way or the other.

When Law embraced Malebranche's theories at Cambridge, he was not as astute as Hume, though he did, eventually, come to appreciate the consequences for his own position of something like a Humean critique. Clearly, however, he was captivated by Malebranche's insight that mysticism needed to be interpreted in the language of science and reason for a scientific and rational age. Law thus looked to Malebranche for instruction on how to think about Newton and Tauler together, in a manner appropriate to his own personal 'Rules'. Consequently, in 1729, Law told his friend John Byrom that through Malebranche he was able to keep his 'act' at Cambridge on 'Omnia videmus in Deo.'[24] Malebranche the rationalist, the elegant prose-stylist, the ascetic who preached the way of self-abnegation and who taught that we are to see even our sensations and perceptions 'in God' therefore becomes part of the intellectual substance itself of the *Serious Call*, Law's rigorous masterpiece of Englightenment spirituality. But the Malebranchiste premises soon gave rise to certain specific problems having to do with the place of reason in the spiritual life.

A critic has counted more than 340 uses of the word 'reason' in *A Serious Call*,[25] and, as have seen, Law felt that, if piety were not reasonable, it was nothing: 'All men therefore, as men, have one and the same *important* business, to act up to the excellency of their rational nature, and to make *reason* and *order* the law of all their designs and actions' (p. 88). An essential part of this 'important business', we have also seen, lies in humbly conforming our wills to God and denying all pretensions to self-sufficiency. Thus, says Law, 'it is as great an offence against truth, and the reason of things, for a man . . . to lay claim to any degrees of glory, as to pretend to the honour of creating himself' (p. 166).

If this line of enquiry is pressed, however, reason soon finds itself embarrassed, for its seems (in so far as it is *our own* reason) to be effective only in proving its own impotency and lack of self-sufficiency, which is to say, its unreliability in proving anything. The Deist Tindal warned against just such a predicament in reverse: 'The very attempt to destroy reason is a demonstration that men have nothing but reason to turn to.'[26] Not surprisingly, therefore, the status of reason became the main subject in Law's controversial attack on Tindal's *Christianity as Old as the Creation* (1730). Nothing if not honest about facing matters directly, Law called his work simply *The Case of Reason, or, Natural Religion Fairly and Fully Stated* (1731), and it is a clearly argued (ironically 'reasonable') attack on the effectiveness of reason in religion.

Tindal's position is mainly that the best religion is founded on nature, and that the Bible helps us to see the natural fitness of things. Law begins by setting out a series of propositions to make clear how he is offended by such trust 'upon the *sufficiency* . . . of Reason'.[27] Reliance on the 'authority of his own Reason', Law thinks, is man's 'greatest vanity' (p. 59), and leads to atheism:

This argument, if it were allowed, leads directly to *atheism*. For if a revelation cannot be divine, if it contains anything mysterious, whose fitness and necessity cannot be explained by human reason, then neither *creation* nor *providence* can be proved to be divine, for they are both of them more mysterious than the Christian revelation. And revelation itself is *therefore* mysterious because creation and providence cannot be delivered from mystery.   (p. 103)

Law never tires of calling our attention to mystery in this trenchantly reasonable style, and of castigating the monstrous vanity of reason's arrogation to itself of the task of '*infallibly* discovering everything' (p. 61). 'These relations are both very plain and very mysterious,' he writes, 'they are very plain and certain, as to the *reality* of their existence; and highly mysterious and inconceivable, as to the *manner* of their existence' (p. 71). This is clearly true. It does not, however, imply that reason itself is otiose (Tindal would be quick to point out that only reason could put such a clear case against reason); rather, that we are unfit, as Law says, to judge God's 'methods' (p. 67) by reason's method, and that '*clear ideas*' (p. 71) do not unravel divine mystery, for God is beyond mathematical demonstration and cannot be understood by the interrogation of natural causes.

Already, despite Law's concern to see all things 'in God', the Cartesian deity (piously affirmed as beyond thought and then, conveniently, relegated to the unthinkable) begins to loom larger than Malebranche's amazing Occasionalist magician, present to us in every thought and sensation. The burden of the mystery alone, Law says, is sufficient proof of divinity against reason, and, among the many mysteries which throw us upon God's mercy and inscrutable providence, the problem of suffering and evil is paramount. Reason cannot explain sin (p. 73), misery, weakness and suffering (p. 61), nor the '*diseases* and mortality of human bodies' (p. 64). Answers come only from 'some *incomprehensible depth* of divine goodness' (p. 61), without which, Law concludes, man is inconsolable.

III   HUME'S *DIALOGUES* AND LAW'S PREDICAMENT

It is instructive at this point to consider how close *The Case of Reason* (in which the intellectual premises of Law's early career are exposed, thus, to fresh, self-critical scrutiny), comes in certain respects to Hume.[28] The allegiance would of course have surprised Law, but the author of *Dialogues on Natural Religion* would have appreciated the ironic affinity. Indeed, Demea, the spokesman for orthodoxy in Hume's *Dialogues*, could well be modelled on the confident indignation and lucid energy of Law in *The Case of Reason*. Demea, like Law, insists on mystery and on the limits of reason against Cleanthes, Hume's spokesman for natural religion: 'the question is not concerning the *being* but the *nature* of God. This, I affirm, from the infirmities of human understanding, to be altogether incomprehensible and unknown to us.'[29] The words could very well be Law's own, and Demea even goes on to quote Malebranche in support of his position (p. 141). Law's other favourite assertions follow, predictably: 'pride and self-sufficiency' (p. 131) are results of a religion based on nature and reason, which leads only to atheism; God, rather, 'exceeds all analogy, and even comprehension' (p. 168), and, although Demea does not relish the label 'mystic' which Cleanthes applies to him, he accedes, 'None but we mystics, as you were pleased to call us, can account for this strange mixture of phenomena, by deriving it from attributes, infinitely perfect, but incomprehensible' (p. 199).

The crucial fact, however, is that Hume treats Demea ironically. The sceptical Philo (who is closest to Hume's opinion[30]) is coyly aware that Demea's agreement with his own position is really a measure of their radical differences. Demea is just slow on the uptake. The reader, by contrast, detects Philo's attitude through a certain refinement of tone: 'Let Demea's principles be improved and cultivated: Let us become thoroughly sensible of the weakness, blindness, and narrow limits of human reason' (p. 131), says Philo, with the kind of sinister generosity of a man prepared to encourage the full display of his opponent's folly before turning the tables on him. The tone, here, is sufficient indication for an alert reader, but Hume underscores the intent by having the student narrator soon after record Cleanthes' bemused reaction, 'as if he perceived some raillery or artificial malice in the reasonings of Philo' (p. 132). Demea, indeed, is the butt of manifold ironies. Philo mocks his enthusiasm while encouraging his scepticism; Cleanthes, who enjoys Philo's joke, taunts Demea further by asking how his brand of mysticism, maintaining the 'absolute incomprehensibility of the Deity'

(p. 158), differs from scepticism or atheism. Finally, Hume has Demea himself pronounce that 'atheist and sceptic' (p. 139) are almost synonymous, not seeing that his own arguments against reason in the name of transcendent mystery themselves amount to such scepticism.

There is both amusement and mild suspense in the way Demea's case against reason is made to accompany Philo's agnosticism until, at last, Philo points out that reason is too weak to mount any reliable hypotheses at all about God, and total suspension of judgement is therefore the most reasonable conclusion (p. 186). The final confrontation, however (which prefaces Demea's departure from the company), is moral rather than epistemological, and focuses on the questions of suffering and evil, on which Hume allows Philo a vehement and anguished statement. Philo talks of hospitals and diseases, malefactors and debtors, of wars, tyrannies, famines and pestilence (p. 196), and asks how, then, can the old questions of Epicurus be answered: 'Is he [God] willing to prevent evil, but not able? then he is impotent. Is he able, but not willing? then he is malevolent. Is he both able and willing? whence then is evil?' (p. 198). In the face of 'perpetual war' between creatures, and 'Oppression, injustice, contempt, contumely, violence, sedition, war, calumny, treachery, fraud' (p. 195) among humans, how can we conclude anything certain about God's benevolence, and 'to what purpose establish the natural attributes of the Deity, while the moral are still doubtful and uncertain' (p. 199)? Arguing on such grounds, Philo is even permitted a moment of elation: 'Here I triumph' (p. 201).

This (as in Law's *Case of Reason*) is again the decisive issue. Law had thought (with trepidation) that man would be driven by suffering to God, because, if left to his own devices and without consolation, his naked egotism and self-sufficient reason would make an intolerable place of the world. Hume feared naked egotism no less, but thought that the self-righteousness of the world's Demeas had already caused inordinate suffering through hypocrisy and superstition (the repeated fact of religious history is that 'The sacredness of the cause sanctifies every measure which can be made use of to promote it' – p. 222). And yet Law, in turn, is as exercised as Philo about the evils perpetrated by institutionalised religion,[31] just as Philo is (in the end) prepared to admit the value of 'true religion' – the sort, that is, which regulates the heart, and works silently within men to 'humanize their conduct' (p. 220). It seems that the closer we look the more we see how, despite their differences, Law and Hume are of one spirit at least in their apprehension of dangers built into the human desire for excessive certainty.

I am aware, however, that so far I have equated Hume and Philo in an uncritical manner: to insist on their identity is risky, even though it seems plain that Philo does express his creator's most characteristic, wry turn of mind. But for that very reason it is appropriate now to call attention to the fact that Hume does not in the end claim victory for himself through Philo, for that would, in turn, court an overhasty and insufficiently judicious certainty. Thus, in the famous conclusion to the *Dialogues*, Hume has the student narrator say that 'Philo's principles are more probable than Demea's; but that those of Cleanthes approach still nearer to the truth' (p. 228). The narrator's reliability (his student opinions are necessarily half-baked) itself requires cautious assessment, but Cleanthes, the reasonable man who maintains a sense of wonder at the beauty and order of creation together with a willingness to argue for his beliefs in an intelligent creator, and who puts an optimistic face on things, is not dismissed. It is as if Hume here acknowledges the potentially debilitating effects of systematic scepticism. 'My sentiments', says Philo at one point, 'are not worth being made a mystery of' (p. 203). In certain circumstances such a statement could be reassuring, but it is a cold and banal rationalism that is no more responsive to the wonder of human intelligence than that. The same trustworthy but lacklustre reassurance recurs soon after when Philo warns against hypotheses: 'All that belongs to human understanding, in this deep ignorance and obscurity, is to be sceptical, or at least cautious; and not to admit of any hypothesis, whatever' (p. 205). This is especially the case, says Philo, with regard to the causes of evil: 'None of them appear to human reason, in the last degree, necessary or unavoidable; nor can we suppose them such, without the utmost licence of imagination' (ibid.). Hume, we conclude, is more complex than Philo, if only because the *Dialogues* are imaginative.[32] To have no imagination and no hypotheses would be, in the end, diminishing. Also, as we see, total scepticism and total belief in an incomprehensible deity can be surprisingly similar (and potentially debilitating) positions, dependent on very similar arguments. It therefore seems that

Law, no less than Hume, in order to avoid the claim for total certainty from rebounding and striking out his own teeth, must admit to his own case against reason the leavening, humanising activity of imagination. For Law, this involved in part a relinquishment of Malebranchiste method – already under duress, as we see, in Law's arguments with the Deists – and advocacy of the strange, compelling visionary metaphysics of Jacob Boehme.

Initially, I was uncritical about equating Hume and Philo, and now, before turning to Boehme, I must acknowledge having done the same thing by suggesting a direct equivalence between Law and Demea. Admittedly, Demea is very like Law, and both seem unaware of the ironic reversals which they court by arguing for God with the weapons of clear reason, rigorously applied. But Law in *The Case of Reason* is (like Hume in the *Dialogues*) haunted by the deficiencies of such an approach, and is repeatedly worried by the question of imagination. He seems, indeed, to realise that imagination has a part to play in bringing men to God, and yet he cannot quite admit it to his critique of natural religion because the jargon of 'analogy' and 'metaphor' smacks too much of easy relativism and worldliness. Malebranche's thought, besides, held imagination in low regard, and, although Law was not a doctrinaire Malebranchiste, the theory of 'All things in God' discouraged undue reliance on imagination, the function of which is to mediate *between* things and God.

Law is clearly perturbed. On the one hand, he repeatedly declares the deficiencies of imagination: God, after all, 'governs the world, not according to our weak imaginations, but according to his own infinite perfections' (p. 99). On the other, he admits that the 'ineffable, and incomprehensible' (p. 78) truths need to be mediated to us in a manner befitting our capacities – that is, 'imperfectly, yet *truly* and usefully' (p. 79). Elsewhere he writes, one feels with inadvertent rather than calculated ambivalence,

> All these enquiries are, by the nature of things, made impossible to us, so long as we have no light but from our own natural capacities, and we cannot take upon us to be *knowing*, and *philosophers*, in these matters, but by deserting our Reason, and giving ourselves up to *vision* and *imagination*.   (p. 74)

On first reading, this seems to recommend imagination: really to be 'knowing' involves the relinquishment of reason's arid processes for a higher inspiration, in a fashion which Blake might approve. But actually Law intends the opposite, as the next paragraph makes clear: imagination and vision in their turn are delusory, and tell us as little as reason about '*how* our souls shall live in the beatific presence of God' (ibid.). Giving ourselves up turns out to be not abandonment to a higher form of knowledge, but another form of escape.

I should hesitate to proclaim an Empsonian ambiguity for Law here, were it not for the fact that the passage in the sense in which I first read it is so exactly prophetic of Law's own progress towards the 'Blakean', through Boehme. The inadvertent suggestion of imagination's value thus stands in ambivalent relationship to the assertion of imagination's deficiency. Throughout *The Case of Reason* one feels Law being carried by the clarity and vigour of his own reasoning as on a wave, despite himself, towards a conclusion rather like Demea's, the naïveté of which he at the same time suspects. His hesitation, which we detect in his uncertainty about imagination, is confirmed by the one sure thing Law learned from his debate with the Deists: that wrangling arguments on such subjects are endless, and fruitless. For, as John Hoyles points out, Law came to see Deism as a paper tiger which was soon reduced to the *papier maché* orthodoxy from which it briefly emerged.[33] In *The Way to Divine Knowledge* (1752), Law confides of his controversies on such subjects:

> For I had frequently a Consciousness rising up within me, that the Debate was equally vain on both Sides, doing no more real Good to the one than to the other, not being able to imagine, that a Set of scholastic, logical Opinions about History, Facts, Doctrines, and Institutions of the Church, or a Set of logical Objections against them, were of any Significancy towards making the Soul of Man either an eternal Angel of Heaven, or an eternal Devil of Hell. (*Works*, VII, 153)

In his *Address to the Clergy*, Law repeats that mere '*Scholastic*' (*Works*, IX, 19) argument of this sort gives rise to phariseeism, and, so, to the '*Religion of Self*' which is, he assures us once more, 'the Fullness of Atheism' (p. 20). The real debate, after all, was not between the Deists' natural religion and Malebranche's 'All things in God', but between 'All things in God' and atheism, which is to say, nothing in God.[34]

That Law should have arrived at such a position is not surprising when we consider the shift that occurred between the relative optimism about reason in the *Serious Call*, and the relative denigration of it in *The Case of Reason*. He knew, however (and maintained to the end of his days), that he could not just give up on reason, even though he came to see he could not rely on it either. Reason, in short, is double-edged, and in *The Case of Reason* there is some indication that Law appreciated this fact. He is fond, for instance, of reducing Tindal's positions to comic tautology (p. 66), of showing how Tindal actually proves the reverse of what was intended (p. 62), of how reason, on certain issues, is *'equally perplexed'* when faced with deciding which of two ways is better (p. 65). Underlying Law's argument for reason's inadequacy to explain mystery, then, is a further sense of reason's even more disturbing ambivalence.

IV   BOEHME'S METAPHYSICS AND *THE SPIRIT OF LOVE*

As is well known, Law's discovery of Jacob Boehme was a revelation of such import as to enable us to distinguish clearly between Law's pre-Boehme satirical and controversial works, and the post-Boehme writings in which imagination and reason are reconciled in a mature spirituality.[35] But, although Law explicitly acknowledges Boehme's influence, he never defends it on rational grounds.[36] Boehme's writing is, rather, a solution to reason's perplexities, not a series of propositions for reason to debate. Law finds in Boehme, that is, a truth compelling to imagination, and, just as Hume refuses total victory to Philo but engages us imaginatively in reason's ironically fragmented hall of reflecting mirrors, so Law avoids the strict certainties of Demea by way of Boehme's metaphysical myth of man's cosmic fall and redemption. For Law, Boehme's metaphysics pre-eminently represent the mystery before which reason balks, but which affects the heart, so that the understanding can gradually open.[37] Just as (in the *Answer to Dr Trapp*) Law says Adam fell because 'his Imagination wandered after the Secrets of this outward World' (*Works*, vi, 18), so, conversely, the work of redirecting imagination to truth is fundamental to repairing the consequences of Adam's departure from it.

There are several useful summaries of Boehme's visionary metaphysics, and it will suffice here to epitomise the main features.[38] Behind all manifestation, Boehme tells us, is the Abyss of Godhead, the *Ungrund*. The unknowable will of this Abyss is God the Father, a fiery principle made manifest and softened by the Son's light, mediated by Spirit. This threefold divine energy gives birth to eternal nature, and, thence, by emanation involving seven properties, the creatures are made manifest, each recapitulating, according to its capacity, the triune Godhead. Three of the seven properties are dark (equivalent to nature without God), and three are light (God manifest in the creatures): the mediating fourth, the 'lightning flash', turns the dark ternary towards light. The fall of angels and men is to be understood in context of these seven properties. Lucifer's jealousy of the Son and desire to know the source of God's will caused the fire principle in himself to burn up as wrath, precipitating a catastrophic chain reaction through the creation under Lucifer's control, as the dark principle was expressed in isolation from the light. We learn then of a second creation, and of Adam's fall from the androgynous state of his paradisal body into the divisions and separations to which flesh is heir, and how the material world was subsequently crystallised out by God into its present form to impose a limit to the fall. Christ, the cosmic redeemer whose seed is in each of us, was afterwards born as a man to conquer the fiery self-will, and passed through the states of fallen human nature – at last reassuming, after death, the paradisal body, an act which all men should strive to imitate.

Boehme insists that desire and imagination directed towards Christ are the foundation of true religion, and distinguishes between *Verstand* and *Vernunft*, a higher (intuitive) and lower (discursive) reason. Boehme realises, however, that manifestation in every form involves contrariety: desire itself is in a state of dynamic tension, potentially agonising and self-divisive, potentially the delightful harmony between part and whole. Just so, reason stands in relation to wisdom. Law does not, therefore, champion Boehme at the expense of a cogent use of reason, as we see, for instance, in *The Way to Divine Knowledge*, the work which most clearly outlines Law's Behemenism. Academicus (the scholarly antagonist) protests that, if Boehme's teaching is true, it cannot be contrary to reason, to which Theophilus (Law's spokesman) replies that 'natural Reason' has 'no higher a Nature or Birth than *natural Doubting*' (*Works*, VII, 201). We are not to renounce reason (p. 189); rather, to appreciate its inevitably antinomous structure and to know that spiritual life is its own vindication, which reason itself cannot affect.

The key question now is, what kind of epistemological status does Law accord to Boehme? The great appeal of Malebranche had lain in the fact that he seemed to marry a genuinely rationalist, modern method to a true spirituality. But, especially when faced with the incomprehensibility of evil and suffering, Law's Malebranchiste rationalism became over-rigorous and self-righteous, or sceptically aware of its own weakness. Yet, in turning to Boehme, Law did not relinquish his desire to discover a way to deal with spiritual truths in an age of science. He insists, therefore, that Boehme's thought accounts for natural phenomena, claiming, even, that Newton had borrowed from Boehme in formulating the laws of attraction, repulsion and movement of natural bodies. In explaining the 'Laws of *Matter* and *Motion*', Law confides, 'the illustrious Sir *Isaac* ploughed with *Behmen's* Heifer'.[39] The diagnosis is of course fanciful, but indicates all the more strongly for that Law's desire to reconcile scientific discovery with spiritual truth. Boehme is thus introduced as a kind of hypothesis in a Cartesian sense: an explanation, that is, which renders the phenomena intelligible, and is justified by its own inner clarity and consistency.

Law's own pronouncements on Boehme are, in this respect, interesting. In *Some Animadversions on Dr Trapp's Late Reply*, he makes clear that Boehme was 'no Messenger from God of any Thing *new* in Religion'; his theories are not '*necessary* to be received, or as a Rule of Faith and Manners' (*Works*, VI, 205–6). At the same time, Boehme experienced genuine insight into 'the grounds and Reasons' of Religion and Nature, and, as we learn emphatically in *The Way to Divine Knowledge*, his intuitions are not just '*notional*', but constitute truth that can be seen only when 'you stand where he stood' (VII, 188). Boehme is true, that is, because of his power to move the heart (spiritually) and save the appearances (scientifically). Law thus boldly complements Malebranche's methodical spirituality by introducing a metaphysical vision of the cosmic origins of sin, suffering, and redemption. He offers this vision as an achievement of imagination, neither 'notional' nor 'necessary', but none the less compelling. To his enduring credit, he saw that no other solution would do: in a world filled with suffering, the method of natural science must seek to improve the human lot by gaining control of nature and by understanding nature's laws. But, so long as method cannot explain the fact of suffering itself, the gap between reason and mystery needs to be bridged by imagination, from which the heart finds direction, and which must, with increasingly self-conscious explicitness, be deployed to protect method from its own potentially anti-human excesses.

It is difficult, in brief compass, to give a just sense of the literary impact of Law's late writings as they attempt such a synthesis. But one first notices their grandeur and tolerance, their scope and moving sense of the frailty and nobility of human nature. The *Spirit of Love (Works*, VIII), in this respect, is Law's masterpiece. In it, the old themes remain evident: we are to see all things in God, 'For *every Creature that lives, must have its Life* in and from *God, and therefore God must be in every Creature*' (p. 56); the way to God is by conforming our will to his in the 'Spirit of Love, which is God himself living and working in you' (p. 31); to make progress in things spiritual we must acknowledge the 'absolute Necessity of the Gospel-Doctrine of the Cross', which is the '*one Morality* that does Man any Good' (p. 30); such teaching is severe, but did not the compassionate Jesus tell us to pluck out the eye and cut off the hand that offends us, and if Jesus 'had been wanting in this Severity, He had been wanting in true Love towards Man' (p. 80). The fact of evil and the sense of sin and suffering remain present throughout, and Law sees the 'Spirit of wrath' through the 'whole Universe of Things', from the sore of an animal body to 'a *Tempest* of the Elements' (p. 42). Such evil cannot be explained or resolved 'in the Way of Reasoning' (p. 22), for a 'clear Idea' does not put us in living possession of a thing, but rather allows us more readily to be side-tracked by the deceptive imagination (p. 23). Man's greatest enemy, Law repeats, is the lure of self-sufficiency, for 'the natural Man must of all Necessity be for ever and ever in the Hell of his own Hunger, Anguish, Contrariety and Self-Torment' (pp. 30–1).

These are, by now, familiar matters, but in the *Spirit of Love* they are qualified and expanded in the light of Boehme's metaphysics, in a way which relieves the struggling *ratio* of its burden of anxiety and strain. Men are moved, Law has come to see, not just by the force of argument, but by the beauty and coherency which the texture of thought itself can express. Thus, although Law initially criticises the Deists for erecting a '*wooden God*', he quickly withdraws from contention on that kind of point: 'I say not this (as is too commonly done) in the Spirit of Accusation, or to raise an Odium. No, by no Means. I have the utmost Aversion to such a Procedure' (p. 93). Elsewhere, he disavows the 'Wrangle of a rational Debate' and the 'contentions' it breeds (p. 3), preferring to stir up the spirit of love, the one thing needful.

The particular qualities which emerge from Law's deliberate stirring of love are, as I have said, grandeur and tolerance, and these depend especially on his descriptions of the cosmic context of redemption. Material nature, torn apart by tempests and ravenous beasts, is a concrete manifestation of the primordial, selfish turning towards the dark principle:

> I said the *Serpents* of Covetousness, Envy, Pride, and Wrath, because they are alone the *real, dreadful, original* Serpents; and all earthly Serpents are but transitory, partial, and weak Out-Births of them. All evil earthly Beasts, are but short-lived Images, or creaturely Eruptions of that hellish Disorder, that is broken out from the fallen spiritual World; and by their manifold Variety, they show us that *Multiplicity* of Evil, that lies in the Womb of that Abyss of dark Rage, which (N. B.) has *no Maker*, but the three first Properties of Nature, fallen from God, and working in their own Darkness.
>
> So that all evil, mischievous, ravenous, venomous Beasts, though they have no Life, but what begins in and from this material World, and totally ends at the Death of their Bodies, yet have they no Malignity in their earthly temporary Nature, but from those *same wrathful* Properties of fallen Nature, which *live* and *work* in our eternal fallen Souls. And therefore, though they are as different from us, as Time from Eternity, yet wherever we see them, we see so many infallible Proofs of the *Fall* of Nature, and the *Reality* of Hell. For was there no Hell broken out in spiritual Nature, not only no evil Beast, but no bestial Life, could ever have come into Existence.

(pp. 120–1)

Law does not withdraw our attention here from nature's

manifest terrors, and the sheer scope of the catastrophe in which man is involved and by which he is surrounded is rendered physically immediate. Redemption, indeed, must correct the physical disorders of nature itself: 'for there is nothing that is *supernatural*, however mysterious', Law says, but 'Nature set right, or made to be that which it ought to be' (p. 83). In this sense, redemption is the 'most demonstrable Thing in all Nature' (p. 29), the aim, that is, of all true apprehension of nature's laws, and from this point of view Law sees no contention between the discoveries of Newton and those of the metaphysicians.

The 'wrath' so evident throughout fallen nature, Law now goes on to suggest, does not exist in God, who can will only good (p. 36). Theophilus insists on this point, and here Law notably departs from Boehme, whose theory did allow a wrathful deity. You must 'stick close to the absolute Impossibility of Wrath having any Existence in God' (p. 37), says Theophilus, and on this ground Law constructs his doctrine of atonement, which 'declares a God, that is all Love' (p. 83) while radically criticising traditional attempts to interpret the atonement as a ransom or bargain whereby the Son pays a debt to purchase mankind's redemption:

Again, This Account which the *Schools* give of the Sacrifice of Christ, made to atone a Wrath in the Deity by the infinite Value of Christ's Death, is that alone which helps *Socinians, Deists* and Infidels of all Kinds, to such Cavils and Objections to the Mystery of our Redemption, as neither have, nor can be silenced by the most able Defenders of that scholastic Fiction. The Learning of a *Grotius* or *Stillingfleet*, when defending such an Account of the Atonement and Satisfaction, rather increases than lessens the Objections to this Mystery: But if you take this Matter as it truly is in itself, *viz.*, That God is in Himself all Love and Goodness, therefore can be nothing else but all Love and Goodness towards fallen Man, and that fallen Man is subject to no Pain or Misery, either present or to come, but what is the natural, unavoidable, essential Effect of his own evil and disordered Nature, impossible to be altered by himself, and that the infinite, never-ceasing Love of God, has given Jesus Christ in *all his Process*, as the highest, and only possible Means, that Heaven and Earth can afford, to save Man from himself, from his own Evil, Misery, and Death, and restore to him his original Divine Life; when you look at this Matter in this true Light, then a God, all Love, and an Atonement for Sin by Christ, not made to pacify a Wrath in God, but to bring forth, fulfil, and restore Righteousness in the Creature that had lost it, have every Thing in them that can make the Providence of God adorable, and the State of Man comfortable. (pp. 82–3)

Law insists that Christ is the seed of God in man, and that redemption began when God assured Adam that the serpent's head would be crushed. Jesus was thus a unique historical realisation of Christ, 'the highest, most natural, and efficacious Means, through all the Possibility of Things, that the infinite Love and Wisdom of God could use, to put an End to Sin, and Death, and Hell, and restore to Man his first Divine State or Life' (p. 83). By enduring the worst that the fiery wrath of fallen nature could do to him, Jesus preserved Adam's original spirit beyond physical death. Thus 'his Sufferings, his Death, and Cross, were the *Fullness* of his Victory over all the Works of the Devil' (p. 90). Law does not underestimate the reality of Christ's suffering, but insists that it was on our *account*, and not *in our place*, the culmination of God's supernatural direction to man on how nature should be brought back to its original state 'in God'. Humanity thus continues to stand, with Jesus, in the midst of nature's contraries, 'in the midst of Heaven and Hell' (p. 119), and there is no release from the struggles of the human heart (pp. 99, 112), whose every inclination is either to love or to wrath, to God or fallen Lucifer.

It is possible sometimes to detect a certain forced optimism in all this. 'Had I an hundred Lives,' says the persuaded Theognes, 'I could with more Ease part with them all, by suffering an hundred Deaths, than give up this lovely Idea of God' (p. 38). 'You have struck a most amazing Light into my Mind' (p. 63), he later avers, by putting the matter 'now in open Daylight' in a way which, says Eusebius, 'has entirely prevented my ever having one more anxious Thought' (p. 104). Theognes and Eusebius admittedly do not speak for Law, but there is no hint here (as there is with Hume) that Law is exploiting their naïveté for rhetorical purposes. The sense is that they have been brought to see the light, even though the full force of the cosmic drama which Theophilus puts before them (and us) has the effect of refusing to man in his middle state that freedom from 'anxious Thought' which Eusebius, in his moment of enthusiasm, claims as his own.

Boehme therefore provides Law with a metaphysical myth, which is a hypothesis. It is the result of intuition, and is to be tested empirically; it is freely chosen and accorded the status of truth, though not of 'necessary' truth. Law's appreciation both of Malebranche and of Newton – of the problem of method, that is, in its rationalist and empiricist forms – bore in upon him the fact of modern man's spiritual isolation in a material world viewed increasingly as an inanimate conjunction of atomic mass and naked force within an empty and infinite space, under the aegis of an incomprehensible deity. By reaction, Law came to see the importance of a vision such as Boehme's for satisfying the perennial desire for imaginative coherence and depth in a post-Enlightenment world.

Law, then, found in Boehme a way to enrich his vision charitably and with tolerance, while suggesting a means of reconciling the achievements of Newton with the spiritual traditions of the Christian past. Hume's challenge to Demea, we recall, had centred on the incomprehensibility of suffering and natural evil, before which Philo could best recommend suspension of judgement. This position remains central to the *Dialogues*, which permit, none the less, a certain free play to imagination as a means of avoiding the illusory comfort of total scepticism. We are right to feel wonder and awe before questions of such magnitude. Law's response to the same predicament likewise acknowledges the imperfection of human solutions to the terrible phenomena of nature's wrath, while pointing also to the grandeur of the mystery. We are free to disbelieve in Boehme, but through him an alternative to scepticism is presented. The very solution itself, however, calls attention to the difficulty of the problem, and then asks for our assent to a metaphysical myth, both systematic and imaginative, to awaken in us a renewed sense of man's middle state, both in the world, and yet not altogether of it.

CHAPTER SEVEN
Conclusion

In the foregoing pages I have attempted first to say something about literature, and then about some literary responses to certain intellectual and cultural challenges posed by the rise of science in England during the Renaissance. My central claim can be put simply. It is that literature gives us the most complex verbal expression of human experience and, in so far as it is concerned with matters of belief, reaffirms our paradoxical 'middle state'. It discourages us, that is, from relinquishing an essential human tension either by putting all the responsibility for determining human worth in God's hands and none in man's, or by putting it all in man's ability to describe the physical determinants of his existence.

There is, of course, some genuine intellectual satisfaction in being able to conclude that the most important human problems *are* worked out in advance because subject to unalterable law, either through the decrees of a divine will (in which case human reality is mainly spiritual) or through the inevitable workings of mechanical nature (in which case it is mainly material). Calvin's *Institutes* are redolent of this kind of satisfaction, as we find for instance in the cool certainty of his unperturbed logic assuring us that we deserve only God's hatred and the flames of eternal torment. But there is a kindred effect in numerous passages of 'the atheist' Hobbes, describing with trenchant eagerness how human beings exist basically in a turmoil of brutish appetites in contention for sheer material power. In both cases the lesson is disturbingly incongruous with the unflinching intellectual clarity of the language expressing it, so that one effect of reading these authors is to feel that, despite their evident distinction, they are somehow similarly dangerous, though for opposite reasons.

Literature, I want to say, resists the two kinds of total

determinism which these opinions represent, by showing us how, in the true complexity of human experience, we in fact always do treat our spiritual and psychological lives as to some degree our own responsibility and as part of what the world means. Our theoretical attempts to reduce psychological and spiritual reality to mechanical operations are continually outstripped by our infinitely more surprising conscious human selves. And yet the thoroughgoing predestinationist, like his cousin, the thoroughgoing materialist, is impossible to refute directly because his logic is circular and his case complete. The main point against him is, simply, that his view is insufficiently large and he distorts the truth he would command by having to lacerate and confine it so that it can be commanded. By contrast, all that is whole and unconfined in human experience, in so far as language can grasp it, is the province of literature to make real.

So far I have claimed nothing more than that literature is broadening and imaginative. But even such a modest assertion will bear repetition if only because we so repeatedly encounter temptations to relinquish the kind of reality it describes in favour of some particular ideological simplification. People need to pursue ideals, though not too vigorously: there is truth in Artaud's maxim that cruelty is an idea in action. From such a point of view, the literary achievement of the five authors discussed in this book I believe is salutary because broadening, and broadening because an imaginatively persuasive re-creation of human experience, especially in so far as such experience deals with the certainties and beliefs upon which men act and judge.

Thus Thomas More's *Richard III* provides a moral and religious denunciation of tyranny, though More also gives us a view of a tyrant's progress which resists any clear or satisfying application of the religious lesson the narrator would bring to it. We do not deny that Richard is godless, but we must acknowledge that in daily experience the ways of God are far from plain. Ordinary people are all too often in tacit complicity with misdeeds they would abhor when seen in the light of moral or religious absolutes. Such abhorrence implies that we are morally responsible, but the half lights of language which More so brilliantly explores through his use of dramatic irony, multiple points of view, litotes, metaphors of colouring and framing and so on, also show how we are often compelled by meanings that unfold beyond our knowledge. And, yet, such tyrannies of language make no stronger a final claim on us in *Richard III* than does the anti-hagiographical exemplum, and it is a mark of More's literary skill that we acknowledge the fascinating and fully rendered interplay of both principles simultaneously.

In a similar manner, Ben Jonson, who confesses in *Discoveries* that a good life is a main argument, creates in *Bartholomew Fair* a moral argument which has the texture of real life. Jonson is fascinated by the human comedy attendant upon an unavoidable warfare between the body's physical urgencies and the mind's ideal prescriptions. Consequently, we see among the fairdwellers a spectacle of an incorrigible, outlandish and bewildering physical energy which constitutes part of the human enormity with which judgement must perpetually strive to deal. And yet the Fair has its own reprobate kind of appeal, just as the monomaniac attempts – for instance, by Overdo – to legislate and judge every human action have their own kind of repugnant ferocity, redeemed only to the degree that they spill over into farce. Jonson's appreciation of the body's irreducible irrationality, however, is no mere recommendation of anarchy, for the play values judgement and order, as is indicated by the constant concern about licences, and by the invitation to the King to judge favourably (and so to licence) the performance itself. Jonson's subject is therefore in a special sense the comic dehumanisation of judgement under the influence either of the body's mindless agitation or over-rigorous conformity. These alternatives are represented by the vapours and puppets: extremes, that is, of senseless foolery and of insensible rigidity which partly prevent judgement and to which, partly, bad judgement drives us. Nevertheless, as the series of masque-like revelations at the conclusion demonstrates, good judgement is a possible human achievement. Jonson's art therefore calls attention alike to the necessity of our acknowledging the limitations of over-regulation from above, and of wholesale deregulation from below. Humanity discovers itself most truly, not by ignoring the compelling claims these opposites make on us, but by finding a balance between them.

Donne's preoccupation with the motif of the heart leads him to the same kinds of problems as Jonson, though Donne faces them in a more explicitly theological manner. The soaring and anguished poetry of the *Anniversaries* is to some extent self-consciously a victim of its own witty extravagance, and I have taken Donne's treatment of the heart as a key to his interpretation of man's incarnate condition, unable to attain sufficient spiritual solace or to embrace wholesale materialism. A complex veering of tone, which combines overreaching hyperbole and dramatic scepticism, implied protest and energetic faith, creates in these poems the impress of a restlessly dual allegiance of body and soul, spirit and matter, resistant alike to temptations of spiritual pride and sensualist despair.

Sir Thomas Browne's *Religio Medici* resembles the *Anniversaries* in that Browne also is concerned with man's 'amphibious' nature, poised between 'a corporall and spirituall essence', somehow reconciling the extremes in itself. With Browne, however, Donne's type of anxiety and protest yields to tolerant reassurance and acceptance. For Browne, contraries graciously become the life of one another, fused in his 'easie' metaphysical definitions in a manner expressing the unresolved and perplexing nature of the human quest, as well as accepting it with a tender whimsy. Browne's fascination with the reconciliation of dualities finds expression especially in the metaphysical symbol of the cross, the controlling figure in *Religio Medici*, whereby the paradoxes of experience, the antinomies and antitheses among which we must labour, are as 'right lines' and 'decussations' which require for completion the circle which the cross bears within its arms. In *Religio Medici*, Browne's style itself is at once an elaborately expansive entanglement in paradox and a leisurely, circular structure. Browne thus yields neither to inert literalism nor to aerobic abstraction, and the *Religio Medici* confirms the creatively tentative status of human knowledge, neither reducible to scepticism's 'extream of despair' nor to false dogmatism's excessive certainties.

For William Law, imagination constitutes a special problem because he explicitly distrusted it. None the less, in his early and immensely popular devotional classic, *A Serious Call*, he allows imagination to 'correct our minds' by showing us the self-condemning follies of human behaviour which transgresses the plain and reasonable dictates of true piety. There is, however, a degree of strain in *A Serious Call*, between Law's rationally argued rigorism and his satirical, imaginative practice, and we detect here the basic terms of a lifelong enquiry wherein he investigates the possibility of expressing a mystical spirituality for a rationalist and scientific age. As Law came to see how unreliable was reason for making his mystical case, and as the problem of natural and moral evil pressed upon him, he increasingly sought a means to engage more fully the humanising activity of imagination, and this he accomplished especially by adapting to his purposes the writings of Jacob Boehme. One result is a distinctive grandeur and tolerance in Law's late writings, combined with a sense of the nobility and frailty of human nature. This combination at once relieves reason of anxiety and strain, while helping to interpret the human position, poised uncertainly and poignantly between an incomprehensible deity and an increasingly mechanised, Newtonian universe.

These five authors have in common, then, at least their consistent insight into human imagination as an index of our incarnate condition, dissatisfied with raw materialism, though incapable of an assured and continuing transcendence of the material state. But I have also claimed, throughout this study, that the literature under discussion is, in a particular way, a response to certain intellectual and cultural challenges posed by the rise of science and the 'discovery of method'.

First, the 'discovery of method' in Renaissance England I have taken to mean a certain efficient organisation of knowledge based on an assumption of responsibility for a mathematical and empirical investigation of nature, and espousing a corpuscular theory of matter. Despite historical complexities, the discovery of method was revolutionary, and its progress depended on a distinctive anti-metaphysical bias. This bias is especially evident in the widespread attack on scholastic terminology: on the kind of language, that is, which offered abstract reasons why we find the world intelligible, instead of how we are to describe, quantitatively, the movement of mass in space. One result is that the scientific revolution polarised God and nature in a novel and distinct manner. For, in so far as the world picture is mechanised, our knowledge of nature is determined from below by the laws of impact and motion; correspondingly, our saving knowledge of God is determined from above by divine fiat upon which our understanding of physical nature has no direct bearing.

Although men of letters did not respond equally to the challenges of this new intellectual climate, literature in seventeenth-century England is, in general, marked by a novel intensity of self-reflexiveness often explicitly suggestive of a response to such issues. Literature, as it were, comes to know itself in a special sense dedicated to expressing the human condition, resistant alike to the twin determinisms of mere grace and mere materialism. Certainly, the self-reflexive ingenuity, anxiety and exuberant energy with which our five authors in particular express the 'middle and participating nature' of human knowledge seem to me stimulated by their contact, as I have described in each case, with issues raised by the scientific revolution. And this contention brings me finally to the relationship between literature and metaphysics, for the discovery of method, as we see, did not prevent literature from seeking metaphysical satisfaction. Poetry, especially when concerned with religious faith, naturally seeks to express the mystery of created being, of God's ordering the world towards the higher perfections. Otherwise, poets can express only their powerlessness to deal with the world in religious terms, a wholly transcendent God being inaccessible to them as to anyone else. But in effectively destroying the cultural pertinacity of such a corporately assured metaphysical attitude to the world as had characterised medieval intellectual discourse, the discovery of method made poets free in a new way to question the relationship of poetry to metaphysics, and of fictive images to logical truth.

We can see the beginning of such a development in Thomas More. Like many Humanists, More is attracted to a theory (which Erasmus refers to as 'method') based on openness and co-operation, ordinary speech and common meaning, developed by scientific study of philology and explicitly anti-scholastic. However, More is also convinced that plainness and clarity are never enough, because abuses can be defended against only by those who know the unreliability of language, and its multiple ironies. He consequently promotes a critical attitude to language, is suspicious of intellectual elitism, desires knowledge based on common sense and plain speech, co-operatively developed and with a strong secular orientation. Clearly, this programme is not much concerned with experiment or mathematics, but More none the less helped to develop in England a version of continental Humanism by which the discovery of method was nurtured. In this context *Richard III*, as a work of literature, provides striking expression of problems involved in reconciling secular behaviour with religious instruction. As More felt a chasm increasingly opening between these realms, he sought a vocabulary for reconciliation in traditional metaphysics, a fact which his polemical works – especially on the Eucharist – demonstrate. He thus returned to a corporate metaphysical language which he held to be self-evidently true. But it is clear that in having to return to it he also stood apart from it. Traditional metaphysics is thus not so much self-evident as it is a body of knowledge which we need to be persuaded to accept if we are to maintain an ordered sense of God's presence in and through the world, as well as beyond and outside it.

Ben Jonson shared something of More's Humanist idealism, and the court masques offer an explicit depiction – allegorical, metaphysical and Platonist – of virtues to which we are asked to conform. But Jonson's masques are less complex than his comedies, which take such pleasure in revealing how human beings are victimised by the mechanical operations of their bodies so that their attempts to conform to ideals only make their behaviour ridiculous. As we see, however, *Bartholomew Fair* suggests that free human judgement is possible, and Jonson presents us with a series of masque-like unfoldings coming to rest in the King, in the course of which sound judgement is increasingly evident. And, yet, Jonson self-consciously deploys this masque-like, metaphysical effect especially to make clear how difficult is the problem of free will and determinism, a problem to which new anti-Galenist attitudes to human physiology had drawn his attention, and which *Bartholomew Fair* presents so provocatively. For, in so far as the discovery of method extends its influence to physiology, it invites us to interpret the body's actions as mechanical, and thus stands opposed to traditional humoral theory with its metaphysically based language of 'qualities'. As we have seen, medical handbooks of Jonson's time richly express the quandary of a traditional Galenism fundamentally disturbed by developments in anatomy growing directly from the discovery of method. Such a climate of opinion is reflected everywhere in Jonson's comedies and, partly, enables him to depict with such vigour and completeness the duress under which a humanist meliorism is placed by a mechanical, reductionist view of the human passions.

Similarly, in Donne's writing the human heart is a key motif for representing the human predicament, for the heart is disenfranchised by science on the one hand and by a Calvinist doctrine of grace on the other. Donne consequently attempts, in his treatment of Elizabeth Drury, to *make* of the dead girl a metaphysical symbol sufficient to bear the weight of such experience. But his deliberate symbolic fabrication succeeds less in assuaging the fears and uncertainties of the human condition by mediating confidently between heaven and earth than in drawing our attention to (and its energy from) those very fears and uncertainties.

Although Sir Thomas Browne regards the new science more favourably than Donne, he is none the less reactionary because he remains such a fond, old-fashioned metaphysician. Browne's mixed attitudes to science and metaphysics become especially clear by comparison with Sir Kenelm Digby's *Two Treatises*. As a philosopher, Digby insists on a rigorous approach to metaphysics which he tries (unsuccessfully) to reconcile with the theories of Descartes and Hobbes. Digby's thought, moreover, is pedestrian and inert; Browne, by contrast, is a poet, and retains for metaphysics a creative vision. But, in making of metaphysics something more imaginative than systematic, he also stresses its subjectivity – its freedom from scientific truth – in a typically modern way, thereby thematising the problem itself of the truth value of metaphysical language.

Finally, William Law in *A Serious Call* attempts to combine the certainty of reasoned discourse and scientific method with traditional mystical spirituality through Nicolas Malebranche. Law's synthesis, however, is flawed, as he comes to realise in controversy with Tindal. In arguing, subsequently, that Newton had used Boehme to formulate the laws of attraction and repulsion of bodies, Law attempts to reconcile sanctity with science through a metaphysical myth deliberately chosen from the visionary 'Teutonic philospher' and presented as a hypothesis to enable his literature to describe the heavenly purposes of created nature. *The Spirit of Love* makes clear both the ennobling function of Law's metaphysical myth for his literary practice, and the clarity of his understanding that we, as readers, must also face the problems of belief entailed by the arbitrariness of his choice of such a myth to serve his ends.

My aims in this study have, therefore, been threefold. First, to discover something of the value of the literature under discussion as a broadening and humane experience affirming the creative imagination. Second, to suggest that this literature offers a commentary on the discovery of method by helping to express the subjective life of ideas, and in being freshly aware of itself as preventing the absolute ideologies of spirit and matter as I have described them in relation to some basic tenets of the new science. Finally, I have suggested a developing self-consciousness among my five authors with respect to the relationship of metaphysics to poetry, a development which I maintain is closely linked to the discovery of method, and which intimates also, I believe, some of the most challenging issues faced by the subsequent course of modern literary history.

Notes

CHAPTER ONE: INTRODUCTION

1. See C. S. Lewis, 'Bluspels and Flalansferes: A Semantic Nightmare', *Selected Literary Essays*, ed. Walter Hooper (Cambridge: Cambridge University Press, 1969) pp. 251–65.
2. See, further, Keith Thomas, *Religion and the Decline of Magic. Studies in Popular Beliefs in Sixteenth and Seventeenth Century England* (London: Weidenfeld and Nicolson, 1971) pp. 177ff.
3. Ibid., p. 182.
4. Harvey did not see the heart simply as a pump, and neither did Descartes; the development of such an idea was gradual. See Hugh Kearney, *Science and Change 1500–1700* (London: Weidenfeld and Nicolson, 1971) pp. 80–8, 158–60; Herbert Butterfield, *The Origins of Modern Science, 1300–1800*, new edn (London: G. Bell, 1957; first published 1949) ch. 3, 'The Study of the Heart down to William Harvey', pp. 37ff.
5. See Owen Barfield, *Saving the Appearances* (New York: Harcourt, Brace and World, 1965) pp. 15ff., 71–92, *et passim*; Butterfield, *The Origins of Modern Science*, p. 5; Thomas S. Kuhn, *The Structure of Scientific Revolutions*, 2nd, enlarged edn (Chicago: University of Chicago Press, 1970) pp. 111ff.; Alexandre Koyré, *From the Closed World to the Infinite Universe* (Baltimore: Johns Hopkins Press, 1957) esp. pp. 28ff., and *Metaphysics and Measurement. Essays in Scientific Revolution* (Cambridge, Mass.: Harvard University Press, 1968) p. 3.
6. See Frank E. Manuel, *A Portrait of Isaac Newton* (Cambridge, Mass.: Harvard University Press, 1968) pp. 264ff., on the secularisation of science under Newton's influence, and esp. p. 290; J. E. McGuire and P. M. Rattansi, 'Newton and the Pipes of Pan', *Notes and Records of the Royal Society*, 21 (1966) 108–43; B. J. T. Dobbs, *The Foundations of Newton's Alchemy, or 'The Hunting of the Greene Lyon'* (Cambridge: Cambridge University Press, 1975).
7. For the function of the textbook tradition in reducing and clarifying scientific knowledge, see Kuhn, *The Structure of Scientific Revolutions*, pp. 136ff., and Walter J. Ong, SJ, *Ramus, Method and the Decay of Dialogue* (Cambridge, Mass.: Harvard University Press, 1958) p. 164.
8. See Andrea Dworkin, *Pornography. Men Possessing Women* (New York: G. Putnam's Sons, 1979) p. 143, on pornography and witch-hunting; Susan Griffin, *Pornography and Silence. Culture's Revenge Against Nature* (New York: Harper and Row, 1981) pp. 78–80. Also Brian Easlea, in *Witch*

Hunting, Magic and the New Philosophy: An Introduction to Debates of the Scientific Revolution 1470–1750 (Hassocks, Sussex: Harvester Press; and Atlantic Highlands, NJ: Humanities Press, 1980), describes the sexist side of the scientific revolution, showing how the existence of an increasingly transcendent God was confirmed on earth by the presence of witches, Satan's agents, and how new philosophers contrived to gain power over nature by reducing it to barren matter whose secrets they sought to possess. See also Easlea's *Science and Sexual Oppression. Patriarchy's Confrontation with Woman and Nature* (London: Weidenfeld and Nicolson, 1981) esp. ch. 3, 'Male Sexism and the Seventeenth-Century Scientific Revolution', pp. 65–89.

9. I draw here on Kuhn, *The Structure of Scientific Revolutions*, p. 99, which summarises the issue.
10. Ibid., p. 149.
11. Karl R. Popper, *Objective Knowledge. An Evolutionary Approach* (Oxford: Clarendon Press, 1972) pp. 16, 25. See also pp. 53, 155, 210.
12. See Popper, *Objective Knowledge*, pp. 77–81; Michael Polanyi, *Personal Knowledge. Towards a Post-Critical Philosophy* (New York: Harper Torchbooks, 1964; first published 1958), on the open-endedness of scientific enquiry. For a discussion of Polanyi, see Patrick Grant, *Six Modern Authors and Problems of Belief* (London: Macmillan, 1979) pp. 132ff. I am aware also of objections that can be raised against Popper. Anthony O'Hear, *Karl Popper* (London: Routledge and Kegan Paul, 1980), argues that Popper gets into difficulty by rejecting the justification of theories while claiming also that science progresses towards objective truth. Popper insists that all knowledge is theory-impregnated, and thereby overlooks the role of everyday observation statements in connecting language to the common world which we all share. Paul Feyerabend, *Against Method* (London: New Left Books, 1975), attacks Popper and the 'critical rationalists' (p. 172) for running the risk of turning man 'into a miserable, unfriendly, self-righteous mechanism without charm and humour' (p. 175). Also, Feyerabend points out that scientific discovery often starts not with a problem but with some irrelevant, even playful, activity, and that Popper's falsification theory, strictly applied, would prevent science even from beginning (see chs 8–12). Science, in short, is 'more "sloppy" and "irrational" than its methodological image' (p. 179), and Feyerabend calls for a kind of pluralistic anarchism. My argument is in sympathy with Feyerabend's desire to avoid seeing scientific method as a kind of dogmatism, by suggesting that literature shows us the threatening aspects of method so raised to an absolute. At the same time, it is necessary to acknowledge the remarkable successes of science in order to appreciate how easily enthusiasm could harden into prejudice. Something of this hardening is already evident in the scientific revolution itself. Popper's remarks, for the purposes of this chapter, serve therefore to draw attention to a transformational model of scientific development which, as I now proceed to point out, is itself subject to interpretation.
13. See Bruno Snell, *The Discovery of the Mind. The Greek Origins of European Thought*, trs. T. G. Rosenmeyer (Oxford: Basil Blackwell, 1953). Also Hans-Georg Gadamer, *Dialogue and Dialectic: Eight Hermeneutical Studies on*

Plato, trs. P. Christopher Smith (New Haven, Conn.: Yale University Press, 1980) esp. chs 1 and 2, suggests that Plato's Dialogues must be understood with respect to *logos*, the full play of language in bringing the subject matter to light, a process which includes the provocation of debate by illogical statements and dramatic interchange of a sort which is opposed to methodological deduction. Gadamer holds that Plato requires us to submit to the multivalency of language and to the primacy of *logos* in this wide and undifferentiated sense.

14. Neal W. Gilbert, *Renaissance Concepts of Method* (New York: Columbia University Press, 1960). Page numbers are cited in the text. See also Angelo Crescini, *Il Problema Metodologico alle Origini della Scienza Moderna* (Rome: Edizioni dell'Ateneo, 1972).

15. Butterfield, *The Origins of Modern Science*, pp. vii–viii.

16. See Alexandre Koyré, *Études Galiléennes* (Paris: Hermann, 1966; first published 1939) pp. 47ff., and *Metaphysics and Measurement*, pp. 31ff., *et passim*; Anneliese Maier, *On the Threshold of Exact Science*, ed. and trs. Steven D. Sargent (Philadelphia: University of Pennsylvania Press, 1982) esp. ch. 5, 'Galileo and the Scholastic Theory of Impetus', pp. 103ff.

17. For Bacon's originality, see Thomas S. Kuhn, *The Essential Tension. Selected Studies in Scientific Tradition and Change* (Chicago: University of Chicago Press, 1977), Part I, ch. 3, 'Mathematical versus Experimental Traditions in the Development of Physical Science', pp. 31ff., and esp. p. 41. For Kepler, see E. A. Burtt, *The Metaphysical Foundations of Modern Physical Science* (New York: Doubleday, 1954) p. 58; Max Caspar, *Kepler*, ed. and trs. C. Doris Hellman (London: Abelard-Schuman, 1950) pp. 129ff., 387ff.

18. Stephen Toulmin and June Goodfield, in *The Architecture of Matter* (New York: Harper and Row, 1962) p. 165, point this out, and cite the conclusion to the *Principia*: 'At the same time, remembering my own insignificance, I make no positive affirmations, but submit all my own opinions to the authority of the Catholic church and the judgement of wiser men.' For Descartes, see L. J. Beck, *The Method of Descartes. A Study of the 'Regulae'* (Oxford: Clarendon Press, 1952) p. 29; Kuno Fischer, *History of Modern Philosophy. Descartes and his School*, trs. J. P. Gordy, ed. Noah Porter (London: T. Fisher Unwin, 1887) pp. 382, 397. The reduction of seventeenth-century mathematical physics to mediaeval antecedents is a highly technical business. Pierre Duhem, *Le Système du Monde*, 10 vols (Paris: Hermann, 1913–59), discovered so many anticipations of Galileo in Buriden and Oresme and the fourteenth-century philosophers of Paris and Oxford that he virtually declared that the seventeenth-century revolution took place in the fourteenth century. Galileo's originality was defended with subtlety and sophisticated scholarship by Koyré in *Études Galiléennes*, and the intensive, precise researches of Maier in, for example, *On the Threshold of Exact Science*. Maier argues for the originality of the seventeenth-century revolution in exact science, but holds that a fourteenth-century revolution of a philosophical sort anticipated the major methodological positions of the later movement. She insists on avoiding anachronistic interpretations of late mediaeval thought, and sees it as retaining certain metaphysical presuppositions which had the effect of rendering the fourteenth-century revolution speculative rather than practi-

cal; on the threshold, that is, of exact science. Maier thus sees a twofold emancipation from Aristotelian metaphysics: the first, in the fourteenth century, rejected certain specific Aristotelian positions; the second, in the seventeenth century, rejected the basic principles of Aristotelian natural philosophy in a manner which was not possible for the scholastics. See also A. C. Crombie, *Robert Grosseteste and the Origins of Experimental Science 1100–1700* (Oxford: Clarendon Press, 1953); Stephen Toulmin and Jane Goodfield, *The Fabric of the Heavens. The Development of Astronomy and Dynamics* (New York: Harper and Row, 1961) esp. pp. 210ff., on 'continuous progress' through the Middle Ages.

19. Ong, *Ramus, Method and the Decay of Dialogue*, p. 275.
20. Giorgio de Santillana, 'The Role of Art in the Scientific Renaissance', in *Critical Problems in the History of Science*, ed. Marshall Clagett (Madison: University of Wisconsin Press, 1959) pp. 33–65. Page numbers are cited in the text.
21. See *The Assayer*, trs. Stillman Drake, in *Discoveries and Opinions of Galileo* (New York: Doubleday, 1957) pp. 237–8.
22. We should recall here that Copernicus, although revolutionary, did not know about elliptical orbits, necessary to 'save the appearances'. According to Arthur Koestler's fascinating account in *The Sleepwalkers. A History of Man's Changing Vision of the Universe* (Harmondsworth: Penguin, 1975; first published 1959) p. 318, Kepler's laws are the landmark:

> They divorced astronomy from theology, and married astronomy to physics. Lastly, they put an end to the nightmare that had haunted cosmology for the last two millennia: the obsession with spheres turning on spheres, and substituted a vision of material bodies not unlike the earth, freely floating in space, moved by physical forces acting on them.

23. The mechanist content of Bacon's thought is, however, minimal. See Kearney, *Science and Change*, p. 90.
24. For specific treatment of this general development, see Marie Boas, *The Scientific Renaissance 1450–1630* (London: Collins, 1962); Burtt, *The Metaphysical Foundations of Modern Physical Science*; E. J. Dijksterhuis, *The Mechanization of the World Picture*, trs. C. Dikshoorn (Oxford: Clarendon Press, 1961); A. Rupert Hall, *From Galileo to Newton, 1630–1720* (London: Collins, 1963). For the drift to corpuscular theory see Kuhn, *The Essential Tension*, pp. 43–4. For the philosophical aspect of seventeenth-century mechanics, see René Dugas, *Mechanics in the Seventeenth Century*, trs. Freda Jacquot (Neuchâtel: Editions du Griffon; and New York: Central Book Company, 1958); and Marie Boas, 'The Establishment of the Mechanical Philosophy', *Osiris*, x (1952) 412–54.
25. A. R. Hall, *The Scientific Revolution 1500–1700. The Formation of the Modern Scientific Attitude* (London: Longmans, Green, 1954) p. xvii.
26. See Richard S. Westfall, *Science and Religion in Seventeenth-Century England* (Ann Arbor: University of Michigan Press, 1973; first published 1958), which shows how the leading English scientists were at first confident about maintaining the Christian belief which their science in fact eventually undermined.

27. I include here the development of nominalism and of Terminist logic. For an account of the effects of late mediaeval logic on the rise of science, see Rita Guerlac, *Juan Luis Vives against the Pseudodialecticians. A Humanist Attack on Mediaeval Logic* (Dordrecht, London and Boston, Mass.: D. Reidel, 1979).

28. Thomas Hobbes, *Leviathan*, ed. C. B. Macpherson (Harmondsworth: Pelican, 1968) i.2 (p. 88).

29. Galileo's distinction is made in *The Assayer*. See S. Drake, *Discoveries and Opinions*, p. 274. For Locke, see *An Essay Concerning Human Understanding*, ed. Alexander Campbell Fraser, 2 vols (New York: Dover, 1959) ii.8.23. See also Dijksterhuis, *Mechanization of the World Picture*, pp. 431ff., on 'The Mechanisation of Qualities'.

30. See Richard A. Watson, *The Downfall of Cartesianism 1683–1712: A Study of Epistemological Issues in Late 17th Century Cartesianism* (The Hague: Martinus Nijhoff, 1966) p. 2, *et passim*.

31. I draw on Jacques Maritain, *The Degrees of Knowledge*, trs. Bernard Wall and Margot R. Adamson (London: Geoffrey Bles, 1937) p. 60.

32. René Descartes, *Meditations*, trs. Arthur Wollaston (Harmondsworth: Penguin, 1960) 4 (pp. 136–7).

33. Francis Bacon: *Advancement of Learning*, i ('To the King'), in *The Works of Francis Bacon*, 14 vols, ed. James Spedding, Robert Leslie Ellis and Douglas Denton Heath (London: Longman, 1858) iii, 267; and *The New Organon*, 'Aphorisms Concerning the Interpretation of Nature and the Kingdom of Man', xlviii, in *Works*, iv, 57. The methodological division of final causes from secondary causes was, however, a late mediaeval development, as Maier points out in *On the Threshold of Exact Science*, p. 166.

34. Burtt, *The Metaphysical Foundations of Modern Physical Science*, p. 306.

35. See Dijksterhuis, *Mechanization of the World Picture*, p. 497: 'whenever it [classical science] . . . formulated principles of a teleological character, it was always this teleological interpretation of the observed regularity that remained the weak point'. On the *cogito*, see A. J. Ayer, 'Cogito, Ergo Sum', *Analysis*, 14 (1953) 27–31; Bertrand Russell, *History of Western Philosophy and its Connection with Political and Social Circumstances from the Earliest Times to the Present Day*, 2nd edn (London: George Allen and Unwin, 1961; first published 1946) p. 550. For Locke, see Douglas Greenlee, 'Locke's Idea of "Idea" ', in *Locke on Human Understanding. Selected Essays*, ed. J. C. Tipton (Oxford: Oxford University Press, 1977) pp. 41ff. For Henry More, see Flora Isabel Mackinnon, *The Philosophical Writings of Henry More* (New York: Oxford University Press, 1925), and *Philosophical Poems of Henry More, Comprising 'Psychozoia' and Minor Poems*, ed. G. Bullough, Publications of the University of Manchester, English Series, no. 20 (Manchester, 1931).

36. A. D. Nuttall, *Overheard by God. Fiction and Prayer in Herbert, Milton, Dante and St John* (London and New York: Methuen, 1980) p. 23.

37. See Rudolf Otto, *The Idea of the Holy*, trs. J. W. Harvey (Aberdeen: H. W. Turner, 1974), for this famous phrase. See also R. C. Zaehner, *Our Savage God* (London: Collins, 1974), for a disturbing statement of the struggle between traditional theology and the omnipotent God whose ways confound us.

38. R. K. Merton, *Science, Technology, and Society in Seventeenth-Century England* (New York: Howard Fertig, 1970). The 1970 edn has a bibliography dealing with the controversy which has continued since the book's first appearance in 1938. See also Douglas S. Kemsley, 'Religious Influences in the Rise of Modern Science: A Review and Criticism, Particularly of the "Protestant–Puritan Ethic" Theory', *Annals of Science*, 24 (1968) 199–226.
39. The conclusion becomes explicit in Julien Offray De la Mettrie, *L'Homme Machine* (Leyden, 1748). See also Dijksterhuis, *Mechanization of the World Picture, passim*; and Toulmin and Goodfield, *The Architecture of Matter*, p. 169: 'the problem of life and the mind–body problem took central places in philosophical biology and psychology in a way they had never done before.'
40. See Nuttall, *Overheard by God*, esp. pp. 62ff. I am also indebted to A. D. Nuttall for a note making the above point on poetry and secondary qualities.

CHAPTER TWO: THOMAS MORE'S 'RICHARD III'

1. Nicholas Harpsfield, *The Life and Death of Sir Thomas Moore, Knight, Sometimes Lord High Chancellor of England*, ed. Elsie Vaughan Hitchcock, intro. by R. W. Chambers, *Early English Text Society*, old ser., no. 186 (London, New York and Toronto: Oxford University Press, 1932) p. 204.
2. See Louis L. Martz, 'Thomas More: The Tower Works', in *St Thomas More: Action and Contemplation*, ed. Richard S. Sylvester (New Haven, Conn., and London: Yale University Press for St John's University, 1972) p. 61, describing More's letters from the Tower as 'some of his finest works of art', partly because 'they show the most artful regard for the presence of two or three or more different audiences', including his jailers and Cromwell himself. Besides the letters to Margaret, see the letter to Dr Nicholas Wilson in *The Correspondence of Sir Thomas More*, ed. Elizabeth Frances Rogers (Princeton, NJ: Princeton University Press, 1947) no. 208, pp. 533ff. More was not unafraid of physical pain: see *Correspondence*, no. 210, p. 543; no. 206, p. 530; no. 211, p. 546. And see *De Tristitia Christi*, ed. and trs. Clarence H. Miller, in *The Complete Works of St Thomas More*, xiv.1 (New Haven, Conn., and London: Yale University Press, 1976) 57–9; *A Dialogue of Comfort*, ed. Louis Martz and Frank Manley, *Complete Works*, xii (1976) 244ff. Walter M. Gordon, 'Tragic Perspective in Thomas More's Dialogue with Margaret in the Tower', *Cithara*, 17.2 (1978) 3–12, deals with the tension and complexity of More's attempt to reconcile his earthly and heavenly loves in the context of his fears and anxieties.
3. Harpsfield, *Life*, p. 203.
4. *The Life of John Picus Erle of Myrandula*, in *The Workes of Sir Thomas More Knyght, Sometyme Lorde Chancellour of England, Wrytten by him in the Englysh Tonge* (London, 1557) pp. 5, 8, 22.
5. More, *Correspondence*, no. 208, p. 537.
6. More, *A Dialogue of Comfort*, i.17, in *Complete Works*, xii, 57.
7. The *Epigrammata* of 1518 show considerable concern with tyranny. See *The Latin Epigrams of Thomas More*, ed. Leicester Bradner and Charles Arthur

Lynch (Chicago: University of Chicago Press, 1953) nos 62, 91, 92, 96, 97, 102, 103, 124, 144, 182, 211, 222, 227, cited also in *The History of King Richard III*, ed. Richard S. Sylvester, in *Complete Works*, II (1963) xcix. See also Judith P. Jones, *Thomas More* (Boston, Mass.: Twayne, 1979) p. 34. Erasmus tells us that More always loathed tyranny: see *Erasmi Epistolae*, 12 vols, ed. P. S. and H. M. Allen *et al.* (Oxford: Clarendon Press, 1906–58) IV, 15. See also Stephen Gresham, 'The Dramaturgy of Tyranny: More's *Richard III* and Sackville's Complaint of Buckingham', in *Quincentennial Essays on St Thomas More*, ed. Michael J. Moore (Boone, NC: Albion, 1978) esp. pp. 40–2.

8. See W. Roper, *The Life of Sir Thomas More, Knight*, in *Lives of St Thomas More*, ed. E. E. Reynolds (London: Dent, 1963) pp. 4–5; R. W. Chambers, *Thomas More* (London: Jonathan Cape, 1935) pp. 87, 151–2. For the view that More's political advancement depended on his success at such advocacy, see William Nelson, 'Thomas More, Grammarian and Orator', in *Essential Articles for the Study of Thomas More*, ed. R. S. Sylvester and G. P. Marc'hadour (Hamden, Conn.: Archon, 1977) pp. 150–60.

9. See, for instance, *A Dialogue Concerning Heresies*, in *Workes of Sir Thomas More Knyght*, p. 284; *Responsio ad Lutherum*, ed. John M. Headley, trs. Sister Scholastica Mandeville, I.18, in *Complete Works*, v.1 (1969) 271. And see Stephen Greenblatt, *Renaissance Self-Fashioning* (Chicago: University of Chicago Press, 1980) pp. 63–4.

10. More, *Correspondence*, no. 199, p. 499. For More's tendencies towards conciliarism, see *Sir Thomas More: Action and Contemplation*, p. 7. John M. Headley, in *Complete Works*, v.2 (1969) 760ff., suggests that More's idea of the Church developed and required revisions.

11. See Richard J. Schoeck, 'Thomas More's *Dialogue of Comfort* and the Problem of the Real Grand Turk', *English Miscellany*, 1969, pp. 23–37; and Alistair Fox, *Thomas More: History and Providence* (Oxford: Basil Blackwell, 1982) pp. 233ff., suggesting that the Turk comes to stand for tribulation in general.

12. More, *Treatise on the Passion*, ed. Garry E. Haupt, in *Complete Works*, XIII (1976) 13, 140, 150. See *St Thomas More: Selected Letters*, ed. Elizabeth Frances Rogers (New Haven, Conn., and London: Yale University Press, 1961) no. 46, p. 180, where More tells Erasmus how determined he is to be hateful to heretics; G. R. Elton, 'Thomas More, Councillor', in *Sir Thomas More: Action and Contemplation*, p. 111: 'Heresy, as it were, came to the rescue, and from late 1528 onwards More presented himself to the world as England's leading controversialist.' See also, Chambers, *Thomas More*, pp. 186ff., 254.

13. For More's hopes under Henry VIII, and his support of the invasion, see Chambers, *Thomas More*, p. 203; and Robert P. Adams, *The Better Part of Valor* (Seattle: University of Washington Press, 1962) pp. 38–42, 211–13.

14. See Willis J. Egan, SJ, 'Thomas More: Other Worldling and Prophet of Secularity', *Moreana*, XIII (1976) 102–7.

15. See, for instance, Walter J. Ong, *Ramus, Method, and the Decay of Dialogue* (Cambridge, Mass.: Harvard University Press, 1958) pp. 167 (the Humanists themselves 'seldom realised the full implication of their position') and 225ff. Neal W. Gilbert, *Renaissance Concepts of Method* (New York:

Columbia University Press, 1960) p. 67, discusses the influence of Humanism on the concept of method. See esp. pp. 83ff., for the impact of Humanist teaching on mathematics and the theory of scientific demonstration. See also E. J. Dijksterhuis, *The Mechanization of the World Picture*, trs. C. Dikshoorn (Oxford: Clarendon Press, 1961) pp. 223–5. A good account of the intellectual ferment caused by Humanism, and its complex effects on the new science, is provided by Antonia McLean, *Humanism and the Rise of Science in Tudor England* (London: Heinemann, 1972).

16. For the *de casibus* tradition, see L. Dean, 'Literary Problems in More's *Richard III*', *Publications of the Modern Language Association*, LIII (1943) 22–41, repr. in *Essential Articles for the Study of Thomas More*, pp. 315ff.; A. R. Myers, 'The Character of Richard III', *History Today*, 4 (1954) 509–21; Gresham, in *Quincentennial Essays on St Thomas More*, pp. 35–42. Paul Murray Kendall, *Richard III* (London: George Allen and Unwin, 1955) p. 423, points to the 'stunning vitality of More's literary talent' in inverting the advice-to-princes genre. Robert Reiter, 'On the Genre of Thomas More's *Richard III*', *Moreana*, xxv (1970) 15–16, sees the work as an inversion of the conventional mediaeval saint's life. For Humanist history, see C. S. Lewis, *English Literature in the Sixteenth Century, Excluding Drama* (Oxford: Clarendon Press, 1954) p. 167; Richard S. Sylvester, in his edn of More's *The History of King Richard III*, in *Complete Works*, II, lxv–civ; Damian Grace, 'On Interpreting St Thomas More's *History of King Richard the Third*', in *European History and its Historians*, ed. Frank McGregor and Nicholas Wright (Adelaide: Adelaide University Union Press, 1977) pp. 11–22, and 'Is *Richard III* a "Satirical Drama"?' *Moreana*, xv (1978) 31–7. Elizabeth Story Donno, 'Thomas More and *Richard III*', *Renaissance Quarterly*, 35 (1982) 401–7, argues that More writes history not in a mediaeval or Tudor manner, but on the model of a sixteenth-century declamation, in an epideictic vein, as a *vituperatio*, and on the model of a paradoxical encomium.

17. A. W. Chambers, 'The Continuity of English Prose from Alfred to More and his School', in Harpsfield, *Life*, p. liii.

18. Ibid., pp. cxxii and cliii.

19. For discussion of the two versions, see Sylvester, in his edn of *Richard III*, pp. 1ff., suggesting that both versions were written together; Alison Hanham, *Richard III and his Early Historians, 1483–1535* (Oxford: Clarendon Press, 1975) pp. 198ff., suggesting (against Sylvester) that More wrote an English draft first. Michael A. Anderegg reviews Hanham's argument in *Moreana*, xv (1978) 39–46. Fox, in *Thomas More: History and Providence*, pp. 104ff., argues that the Latin Arundel is first, or concurrent with the English, and that More then developed the Latin Louvain. Questioning the historicity of More's account are Myers, in *History Today*, 4, 509–21; Murray, in *Richard III*; and Jeremy Potter, in *Good King Richard* (London: Constable, 1983). But compare A. L. Rowse, *Bosworth Field and the Wars of the Roses* (London: Macmillan, 1966) pp. 152–3, 257–9, which accepts the general account as reliable. For specific historical inaccuracies, see A. F. Pollard, 'The Making of Sir Thomas More's *Richard III*', in *Historical Essays in Honour of James Tait*, ed. J. G. Edwards, V. H. Galbraith and E. F. Jacob

(Manchester, for subscribers, 1933) pp. 223–38, repr. in *Essential Articles for the Study of Thomas More*, pp. 421–31.

20. There is a tradition of commentary interpreting *Richard III* as drama. See Chambers, *Thomas More*, p. 117; Walter M. Gordon, 'Exemplum Narrative and Thomas More's *History of King Richard III*', *Clio*, 9 (1979) 75–88; Hanham, *Richard III and his Early Historians*, 174ff.; Arthur Noel Kincaid, 'The Dramatic Structure of Sir Thomas More's *History of King Richard III*', *Studies in English Literature*, 12 (1972) 223–42; Myers, in *History Today*, 4, 509–21; Pollard, in *Essential Articles for the Study of Thomas More*, pp. 426ff.; M. M. Reese, *The Cease of Majesty* (New York: St Martin's Press, 1961) p. 46; W. G. Zeeveld, review of Sylvester's edn of *Richard III*, in *Moreana*, I (1963) 64–9.

21. All quotations are from Sylvester's edn, and page numbers are indicated in the text.

22. See Sylvester, in his edn of *Richard III*, pp. lxix; xcix–civ.

23. On this general point, see Donald A. Stauffer, *English Biography before 1700* (Cambridge: Mass.: Harvard University Press, 1930), on More's 'delicacy of presentation' (p. 39) and 'dramatic and psychological skill' (p. 40); Gordon, in *Clio*, 9, 75–88; James L. Harner, 'The Place of "Shore's Wife" in More's *The History of King Richard III*', *Moreana*, XIX (1982) 69–76.

24. Fox, *Thomas More: History and Providence*, pp. 75ff., argues that any engagement with politics forces us to compromise with evil, and in *Richard III* a 'massive failure of free will' in the body politic enables Richard to succeed. This point anticipates mine, though I read Fox's study after first writing this chapter. Our arguments differ in that Fox analyses More's concern with history and providence, while I deal with a linguistic problem, but I defer to Fox where we overlap.

25. Ibid. Fox mentions the imprudent marriage, and an anti-heroic portrait of Edward.

26. I summarise here the interesting article by Kincaid, 'The Dramatic Structure of Sir Thomas More's *History of King Richard III*', in *Studies in English Literature*, 12, 223–42. See also Hanham, *Richard III and his Early Historians*, esp. pp. 174ff., treating the work as a satirical drama in five acts.

27. More often presents his opponents as bad actors. See Richard S. Sylvester, 'A Part of his Own: Thomas More's Literary Personality in his Early Works', *Moreana*, IV (1967) 29–42.

28. See Greenblatt, *Renaissance Self-Fashioning*, pp. 17ff., treating More in context of Holbein's *The Ambassadors*; and Ernest B. Gilman, *The Curious Perspective, Literary and Pictorial Art in the Seventeenth Century* (New Haven, Conn.: Yale University Press, 1978) *passim*.

29. Elizabeth McCutcheon, 'Denying the Contrary: More's Use of Litotes in *Utopia*', *Moreana*, XXXI–II (1971) 107–21. See also John Carey, 'Sixteenth and Seventeenth Century Prose', in *English Poetry and Prose*, ed. Christopher Ricks (London: Barrie and Jenkins, 1970) pp. 341ff., on the use of double negatives to create an 'atmosphere of whispered rumour'.

30. See Sylvester, in his edn of *Richard III*, pp. lxvff. Donno, in *Renaissance Quarterly*, 35, 423, argues that More's appeal to such phrases as 'men say', 'some say' is designed to produce uncertainty.

31. See Fox, *Thomas More: History and Providence*, pp. 101ff., for a fascinating account of More's awareness that the judicial murder of the third Duke of Buckingham echoes the career of the second Duke as *Richard III* records it. Fox argues that More came to see how Morton's interference in events was morally compromising (p. 104), and that More's own duties connected with the execution of the third Duke caused him to become disillusioned with the hope of maintaining moral integrity in a political forum.

32. See Richard J. Schoeck, *The Achievement of Thomas More: Aspects of his Life and Works*, English Literary Studies, no. 7 (British Columbia: University of Victoria, 1976) p. 53, on More and Erasmus restoring 'the full play and reach of irony to Western letters'. See also Adams, *The Better Part of Valor*, pp. 34–5, on More and Erasmus bringing 'irony into literature'. Both Schoeck and Adams here allude to, and reaffirm, the opinion of J. A. K. Thompson, *Irony: An Historical Introduction* (London: George Allen and Unwin, 1926) p. 66.

33. See *Compendium Vitae* in Desiderius Erasmus, *Christian Humanism and the Reformation*, ed. John C. Olin (Gloucester, Mass.: Peter Smith, 1973) pp. 22–30. Page numbers are cited in the text. See also Johan Huizinga, *Erasmus and the Age of Reformation* (New York: Harper and Row, 1957) pp. 4ff., *et passim*.

34. See *Antibarbarorum Liber*, trs. Margaret Mann Phillips as *The Antibarbarians*, in *Collected Works of Erasmus*, xxiii (Toronto: University of Toronto Press, 1978) 28ff., 42ff. Erasmus suggests that violence and negligence in education produce violence and sedition in the state.

35. *The Paraclesis*, in Erasmus, *Christian Humanism*. Page numbers are cited in the text.

36. See Marjorie O'Rourke Boyle, *Erasmus on Language and Method in Theology* (Toronto: University of Toronto Press, 1977), for a discussion of Erasmus's 'bold transformation of the new philology into theological method' (p. 8). Boyle argues that 'the historical impact of waning scholasticism and emerging humanism was methodological, and only subsequently involved in doctrinal dispute' (p. 15).

37. See *Erasmus against War*, ed. J. W. Mackail (Boston, Mass.: Merrymount Press, 1907) pp. 38–9. Erasmus says the mischief of war has come about 'little and little' (p. 38). First, 'learning and cunning crept in', supposedly to refute heretics, developing then to 'an ambitious pleasure of brawling disputations', until at last 'Aristotle was altogether received into the middle of divinity, and so received, that his authority is almost reputed holier than the authority of Christ' (p. 39).

38. Erasmus, *The Lives of Vitrier . . . and John Colet*, trs. J. H. Lupton (London: G. Bell, 1883) pp. 21–2, for Colet's study of the scholastics, and pp. 32–3 for his attack on them. For an account of his preaching, see p. 25.

39. Erasmus, *The Praise of Folly*, trs. Betty Radice, intro. A. H. T. Levi (Harmondsworth: Penguin, 1971) p. 152. Page numbers are henceforth cited in the text.

40. *Erasmi Epistolae*, i, 431–2, no. 200; *The Complaint of Peace*, trs. Thomas Paynell (London, 1559) sig. Di ff.; *The 'Julius Exclusus' of Erasmus*, trs. Paul Pascal, intro. J. Kelley Sowards (Bloomington: Indiana University Press, 1968) pp. 72ff., 81–2, 88, *et passim*.

41. Letter to Jodocus on Luther, in Erasmus, *Christian Humanism*, p. 263.
42. Richard J. Schoeck, 'The Place of Erasmus Today', in *Erasmus of Rotterdam*, ed. Richard L. De Molen (New York: Twayne, 1971) p. 80, cites Julian Benda, *La Trahison des Clercs*, trs. R. Aldington (New York: William Morrow, 1928) p. 80, on Erasmus being 'a great patrician of the mind'. See also James D. Tracy, 'Erasmus the Humanist', in the same collection, p. 38, on Erasmus's theory of education being aristocratic. H. A. Mason, *Humanism and Poetry in the Early Tudor Period* (London: Routledge and Kegan Paul, 1959), maintains that Humanism at large was a learned and elitist game.
43. *Letter to Paul Volz*, in Erasmus, *Christian Humanism*, pp. 123, 127, 123.
44. See, further, Sister Geraldine Thompson, *Under Pretext of Praise* (Toronto: University of Toronto Press, 1973), for an account of Erasmus's ironic practice, and his cautious attitude to traditional truths and symbols, which he respects, even though treating them ironically. Also, Jean-Claude Margolin, 'The Method of "Words and Things" in Erasmus's *De Pueris Instituendis* (1529) and Comenius's *Orbis Sensualium Pictus* (1658)', in *Essays on the Works of Erasmus*, ed. Richard L. De Molen (New Haven, Conn., and London: Yale University Press, 1978) pp. 221–38, for Erasmus's empirical treatment of language, and the links (extending through Francis Bacon) between his pedagogical methodology and that of Comenius.
45. See *St Thomas More: Selected Letters*, pp. 8–64. Page numbers are henceforth cited in the text.
46. *Juan Luis Vives against the Pseudodialecticians. A Humanist Attack on Mediaeval Logic*, ed. and trs. Rita Guerlac (Dordrecht, London and Boston, Mass.: D. Reidel, 1979). This edn contains translations of *Against the Pseudodialecticians* and *On Dialectic*, III.v, vi, vii, from *The Causes and Corruption of the Arts*. I draw on both treatises, and page numbers are cited in the text.
47. Ibid., pp. 34–5, 42.
48. Gordon, in *Clio*, 9, 77, notices that the exemplum theory runs aground when one realises 'the history would serve just as well for the Machiavel'. E. Harris Harbison, 'The Intellectual as Social Reformer: Machiavelli and Thomas More', *Revue Internationale de Philosophie*, 44 (1957) 1–46, sees the two men as inaugurating modern political thinking, but contrasts More's morality with Machiavelli's realism. Recall that Shakespeare's Richard says he will 'set the murderous Machiavel to school' (*Henry VI Part Three*, III.ii.193).
49. *Correspondence*, no. 190. Page numbers are cited in the text.
50. More, *Treatise on the Passion*, ed. Garry E. Haupt, in *Complete Works*, XIII. Page numbers are cited in the text.
51. More, however, was not simply an old-fashioned metaphysician: see Walter M. Gordon, 'A Scholastic Problem in Thomas More's Controversy with John Frith', *Harvard Theological Review*, 69 (1976) 131–49. Gordon points out that 'Underlying this stout corpus of materials lay a variety of metaphysical presuppositions used in support of the differing [scholastic] schools' (p. 135), but More's job was to offer a popular defence of tradition, and so it would be wrong to 'assign More a place in any of the scholastic traditions' (p. 143). None the less, as Gordon also points out, George Joye, who entered the debate on Frith's side, 'scoffs at the "Thomistical papists"'

and their "Thomistical mystery" and the "strange Thomistical sense" which More makes of Christ's words' (p. 145). This sense of More's implicit affirmation of general scholastic principles within a non-technical discussion is exactly my point.

52. Louis L. Martz, 'Thomas More: The Sacramental Life', *Thought*, 52 (1977) 302.

53. Edward Halle, *The Union of the Two Noble and Illustrate Famelies etc.* (London, 1548) sig. ppp4v., cited by Sylvester in *Moreana*, IV, 30.

54. See, however, Robert P. Adams, 'The Social Responsibilities of Science in *Utopia, New Atlantis*, and After', *Journal of the History of Ideas* x (1949) 374–98, for similarities (and differences) between More's and Bacon's interest in empirical science. Also, Mario Praz, *The Flaming Heart* (New York: Doubleday Anchor, 1958) p. 97, calls attention briefly to More's scientific point of view. And see Paul Lawrence Rose, 'Erasmians and Mathematicians at Cambridge in the Early Sixteenth Century', *Sixteenth Century Journal*, VIII, Supplement (1977) 47–59, on the Humanist contribution to the development of maths at Cambridge. Rose points out that More was a noted patron of mathematics (p. 59). The first 'arithmetical book' (p. 51) printed in English, *De Arte Supputandi* (London, 1522), was dedicated to More; the mathematician Nicholas Kratzer 'was a member of More's family circle', and More 'often discussed mathematics with Henry VIII' (ibid.). See also Ong, *Ramus, Method, and the Decay of Dialogue, passim*; Gilbert, *Renaissance Concepts of Method*, pp. 83ff.

55. See Schoeck, in *Erasmus of Rotterdam*, pp. 77ff., on Erasmus's maintaining a sense of living tradition; this is not present in More's polemical writings, where tradition 'is now a repository which must be safeguarded' (p. 87).

CHAPTER THREE: BEN JONSON'S 'BARTHOLOMEW FAIR'

1. W. David Kay, 'Jonson's Urbane Gallants: Humanistic Contexts for *Epicoene*', *Huntingdon Library Quarterly*, 39 (1976) 251–66, places Jonson's practice in the context of Humanist ideals, which were under pressure when Jonson wrote. A later article by the same author, 'Jonson, Erasmus, and Religious Controversy: *Discoveries*, Lines 1046–1062', *English Language Notes*, 17 (1979–80) 108–12, demonstrates Jonson's interest in Humanist debate, and cites a remark of Thomas More's as possibly echoed by Jonson. See also Alan C. Dessen, *Jonson's Moral Comedy* (Evanston, Ill.: Northwestern University Press, 1971), which broadly emphasises Jonson's concern with morality.

2. *Timber: or Discoveries*, title page, ed. C. H. Herford and Percy and Evelyn Simpson, *Ben Jonson*, 11 vols (Oxford: Clarendon Press, 1925–52) VIII, 561. All quotations from Jonson's work are from this edition, and references are henceforth indicated in the text.

3. See J. B. Bamborough, *Ben Jonson* (London: Hutchinson, 1970) p. 174: 'Jonson has good claims to be called the first English "Man of Letters", the first professional writer, that is, wholly dedicated to his craft and relying on his exercise of it to establish his place in society.'

4. Jonson, *Epigrammes*, i, iii, xvii, xviii.

5. *Epigrammes*, ci, xiv, lxxvi; *The Forest*, ii; *Epigrammes*, cxxx, iv and li.
6. Stephen Orgel, *The Illusion of Power. Political Theatre in the English Renaissance* (Berkeley, Calif.: University of California Press, 1975), and *The Jonsonian Masque* (Cambridge, Mass.: Harvard University Press, 1965).
7. See also Enid Welsford, *The Court Masque* (New York: Russell and Russell, 1962); John C. Meagher, *Method and Meaning in Jonson's Masques* (Notre Dame, Indiana: University of Notre Dame Press, 1966).
8. This point is argued for instance by Edward B. Partridge, *The Broken Compass* (London: Chatto and Windus, 1958) p. 235: 'His major comedies seem now like antimasques to the Renaissance masque of the Golden Age – grotesque violations of the exalted vision.'
9. T. S. Eliot, 'Ben Jonson', in *Selected Essays*, 3rd edn (London: Faber and Faber, 1951) p. 153.
10. Jonson, 'On Gut', *Epigrammes*, cxviii.
11. For an extreme but influential description of this side of Jonson, see Edmund Wilson, 'Morose Ben Jonson', in *The Triple Thinkers. Twelve Essays on Literary Subjects* (New York: Oxford University Press, 1948) pp. 213–32.
12. Not only is Bacon cited with approval in *Discoveries*, but Jonson's style, full of gnomic pithiness, of *sententiae* extended to small essays giving the impression of an individual mind freely in pursuit of learning, soaked in experience, publicly responsible and ready for action, is recognisably Baconian.
13. See Owsei Temkin, *Galenism: Rise and Decline of a Medical Philosophy* (Ithaca, NY, and London: Cornell University Press, 1973) pp. 134ff., *et passim*. Temkin points out, for instance, that Copernicus's heliocentric system replaced the Ptolemaic, but that Vesalius's theories, though highly innovative, developed from Galenism.
14. Jonson, *The Magnetic Lady*, Induction, l. 99. The Boy says, 'The *Author*, beginning his studies of this kind, with *every man in his Humour*; and after, *every man out of his Humour*.'
15. See Peggy Knapp, 'Ben Jonson and the Publicke Riot', *Journal of English Literary History*, 46 (1979) 578: 'Yet it is not easy to discover from the plays what Jonson would have regarded as an ideal, or even an acceptable, mode of life.' See also C. G. Thayer, *Ben Jonson: Studies in the Plays* (Norman: University of Oklahoma Press, 1963) p. 19, on the implied moral norm which exists outside the action of *Every Man in his Humour*.
16. For Renaissance theories of the gentleman, see Ruth Kelso, *The Doctrine of the English Gentleman in the Sixteenth Century* (Gloucester, Mass.: Peter Smith, 1964; first published 1929); Fritz Caspari, *Humanism and the Social Order in Tudor England* (Chicago: University of Chicago Press, 1954); Lewis Einstein, *Tudor Ideals* (New York: Russell and Russell, 1962).
17. See Roger Ascham, *The Scholemaster*, ed. Rev. Dr Giles, in *The Whole Works of Roger Ascham*, 3 vols (London: John Russell Smith, 1865) III, 123–4.
18. *Ben Jonson*, ed. Herford and Simpson, IX, Appendix 391ff. J. B. Bamborough, *The Little World of Man* (London: Longmans, Green, 1952), provides a useful account of humoral theory.
19. See especially Temkin, *Galenism*, ch. 3 and 4, pp. 95ff. The following account draws on Temkin's study.

20. Ibid., p. 139.
21. Bernardinus Telesius, *De Rerum Natura*, ed. Vincenzo Spampanato (Modena: A. F. Formiggini, 1910–23) 5.1–3; Thomas Campanella, *De Sensu Rerum et Magia, Libri Quatuor*, ed. Tobias Adami (Frankfurt, 1620) 9.70. Cited in Temkin, *Galenism*, pp. 145–6.
22. For a general account, see Anthony Levi, SJ, *French Moralists: The Theory of the Passions, 1585–1649* (Oxford: Clarendon Press, 1964).
23. Lily B. Campbell, *Shakespeare's Tragic Heroes: Slaves of Passion* (1952; Gloucester, Mass.: Peter Smith, 1973, repr.).
24. See Paul H. Kocher, *Science and Religion in Elizabethan England* (San Marino, Calif.: Huntington Library, 1953) pp. 239–57.
25. *Advancement of Learning*, ed. James Spedding, Robert Leslie Ellis and Douglas Denton Heath, IV.2, in *The Works of Francis Bacon*, 14 vols (London: Longman, 1858) IV, 388.
26. Keith Thomas, *Religion and the Decline of Magic. Studies in Popular Beliefs in Sixteenth and Seventeenth Century England* (London: Weidenfeld and Nicolson, 1971) p. 210.
27. For Elizabeth Jackson, see Thomas, *Religion and the Decline of Magic*, p. 537; for Marthe Brossier, see Patrick Grant, *Images and Ideas in Literature of the English Renaissance* (Amherst: University of Massachusetts Press; and London: Macmillan, 1979) pp. 107ff.
28. Contemporary treatises on phlebotomy show a marked preoccupation with the relationship between astrology and free will. Physicians should have knowledge of how the stars and planets affect temperament, but must not conclude that the patient's will is thereby determined. This problem is of course perennial, but the degree to which phlebotomists of the sixteenth and seventeenth centuries insist on it deserves further attention. See, for instance, Martinus Hellingus, *De Phlebotomia* (Marburg, 1594) ch. 3, pp. liii–liv; Horatius Argenius, *De Ratione Curandi per Sanguinis Missionem* (Frankfurt, 1598) pp. 90, 16ff.; Simon Harward, *Phlebotomy: or, A Treatise on Letting of Bloud* (London, 1601) pp. 94ff.; David de Planis Campi, *Discours de la Phlebotomie* (Paris, 1621) pp. 41ff.
29. Bacon, *Advancement of Learning*, IV.2, in *Works*, IV, 382–3, 385.
30. Ibid., p. 385.
31. *The Masculine Birth of Time*, trs. Benjamin Farrington, 2, in *The Philosophy of Francis Bacon* (Chicago: University of Chicago Press, 1964) p. 64. For the original, see *Temporis Partis Masculus*, 2, in *Works*, III, 531.
32. Ibid., p. 532.
33. Bacon, *Advancement of Learning*, IV.2, in *Works*, IV, 383.
34. John Purcell, *A Treatise on Vapours or, Hysterick Fits* (London: H. Newman and N. Cox, 1702) Preface.
35. See, further, John D. Redwine Jr, 'Beyond Psychology: the Moral Basis of Jonson's Theory of Humour Characterisation', *Journal of English Literary History*, 28 (1961) 316–34; Robert Shenk, 'The Habits and Ben Jonson's Humours', *Journal of Mediaeval and Renaissance Studies*, 8 (1978) 115–36.
36. See John J. Enck, *Jonson and the Comic Truth* (Madison: University of Wisconsin Press, 1957) p. 189; Jonas Barish, *Ben Jonson and the Language of Prose Comedy* (Cambridge, Mass.: Harvard University Press, 1960) pp. 188, 230; Thayer, *Jonson: Studies in the Plays*, pp. 128–56; Brian Gibbon,

Jacobean City Comedy: A Study of Satiric Plays by Jonson, Marston, and Middleton (Cambridge, Mass.: Harvard University Press, 1968) pp. 179–91. Other interpretations, however, stress morality before mellowness. See, for instance, Robert E. Knoll, *Ben Jonson's Plays: An Introduction* (Lincoln, Nebr.: University of Nebraska Press, 1964) p. 147; Jackson I. Cope, 'Bartholomew Fair as Blasphemy', *Renaissance Drama*, 8 (1965) 127–52; Dessen, *Jonson's Moral Comedy*, pp. 128ff.; Knapp, in *Journal of English Literary History*, 46, 589ff. W. David Kay, 'Bartholomew Fair: Ben Jonson in Praise of Folly', *English Literary Renaissance*, 1976, pp. 299–316, argues for a complex Erasmian atmosphere which lacks Erasmus's transcendent dimension.

37. There is a good deal of commentary on the play's structure. See, for instance, Knoll, *Ben Jonson's Plays*, p. 151, on Jonson's handling of multiple intrigues, which increasingly crowd the stage. Richard Levin, 'The Structure of Bartholomew Fair', *Publication of the Modern Language Association*, LXXX (1965) 172–9, points out how groups of people break up, with individual members then joining their duplicates from another group. Ian Donaldson, *The World Upside Down* (Oxford: Clarendon Press, 1970) p. 58, argues that excitement arises from our not knowing who is in charge, and that Jonson contrives a hall-of-mirrors effect. Joel H. Kaplan, 'Dramatic and Moral Energy in Ben Jonson's *Bartholomew Fair*', *Renaissance Drama*, new ser., 3 (1970) 141–3, examines Jonson's handling of tempo; R. B. Parker, 'The Themes and Staging of Bartholomew Fair', *University of Toronto Quarterly*, 39 (1970) 293–309, discusses the staging. Guy Hamel, 'Order and Judgement in *Bartholomew Fair*', *University of Toronto Quarterly*, 43 (1973–4) 48–67, discusses the 'fine balance of delicately opposed obligations' (p. 48) and Jonson's use of the vacant and crowded stage. G. W. Hibbard, in his edn of *Bartholomew Fair* (London: Ernest Benn, 1977) pp. xviii ff., sees the characters as either fair-dwellers or visitors, and distinguishes three locales and three groups of visitors.

38. See William Blissett, 'Your Majesty is Welcome to a Fair', *The Elizabethan Theatre*, IV, ed. G. R. Hibbard (Toronto: Macmillan, 1974) esp. pp. 98ff., on the quality of merriment depending on the quality of the audience's adjudication. See also Donaldson, *The World Upside Down*, pp. 46ff., on the play's two distinct audiences: those who see only the noisy farce, and those who grasp the play's own reflections on the kind of entertainment it provides.

39. See Thayer, *Ben Jonson*, p. 132. For Ursula's booth in relation to bourgeois repression, see Judith K. Gardiner, 'Infantile Sexuality, Adult Critics, and *Bartholomew Fair*', *Literature and Psychology*, 4 (1974) 24–31.

40. See W. J. Passingham, *London's Markets. Their Origin and History* (London: Sampson, Low, Marston, 1935) p. 6.

41. William Austen, 'The Origin of Markets and Fairs, and the Early History of those at Luton', *Home Counties Magazine*, XIV (1912) 41. R. W. Muncey, *Our Old English Fairs* (London: Sheldon Press, 1936) pp. 7–19, offers an interesting collection of acts and proclamations dealing with the legislation of fairs.

42. Henry Morley, *Memoirs of Bartholomew Fair* (London: Chapman and Hall, 1859) p. 118.

43. See ibid., p. 136; and Cornelius Walford, *Fairs Past and Present. A Chapter in the History of Commerce* (New York: Burt Franklin, 1967; first published 1883) pp. 184ff. See also pp. 190ff., where Walford cites the City of London Proclamation of 1604, which is full of Jonsonian detail about measurement, bordering on the absurd. *The Lawes of the Market* (London, 1595), in *The English Experience*, no. 676 (Amsterdam: Theatrum Orbis Terrarum, 1974), is likewise instructive and amusing.

44. See Walford, *Fairs Past and Present*, p. 190; Morley, *Memoirs*, p. 139.

45. Austen, in *Home Counties Magazine*, xiv, 106.

46. See George Speaight, *The History of the English Puppet Theatre* (London: George G. Harrap, 1955) pp. 15, 21, 40–1. I draw here on Speaight's account, which, in turn, draws a good deal on Jonson (pp. 52ff.).

47. Preface to the translation of Hero's *Automata* (1589). Cited in Speaight, *English Puppet Theatre*, p. 39.

48. John Evelyn, *The Diary of John Evelyn*, ed. E. S. De Beer, 6 vols (Oxford: Clarendon Press, 1955) ii, 99. See also ii, 112–13; iii, 30.

49. Characters of the actors, ll. 80–1.

50. Speaight, *English Puppet Theatre*, p. 65.

51. The effects puppets have on us are interestingly described on a general, structural model by Roger-Daniel Bensky in *Recherches sur les Structures et la Symbolisme de la Marionette* (Paris: A.-G. Nizet, 1971). Bensky points to George Sand's reaction to marionettes (she described them as 'une chose triste et même effrayante') and goes on to analyse the 'sentiment vertigineux' which arises from 'un trop grand rapprochement de l'homme et de l'objet' (p. 120). Puppets, Bensky wants to say, cause us to be aware of ourselves paradoxically as objects who are also subjects, and to be aware of a certain 'déhumanisation toujours menaçante' (p. 121). Jonson develops just such a disturbing response in a variety of ways in *Bartholomew Fair* by confronting us not only with a puppet show, but with a play in which the puppets are more human than some of the characters, who are, in turn, more puppet-like than the puppets.

52. See Blissett, in *The Elizabethan Theatre*, iv, 96ff., for a discussion of vapours in relation to meteorology, and especially evaporation. Blissett cites S. K. Heninger, *A Handbook of Renaissance Meteorology* (Durham, NC: Duke University Press, 1960). See James E. Robinson, '*Bartholomew Fair*: Comedy of Vapours', *Studies in English Literature* 1 (1961) 65–80, for the connection between vapours and humours, and also Shenk, in *Journal of Mediaeval and Renaissance Studies*, 8, 115–36. Barish, *Ben Jonson and the Language of Prose Comedy*, comments on the 'disorderly gregariousness' (p. 231) which helps to reduce us to automata, like the puppets.

53. Carroll Storrs Alden, in her edn of *Bartholomew Fair* (New Haven, Conn.: Yale University Press, 1904) p. 172.

54. Blissett, in *The Elizabethan Theatre*, iv, 105. Donaldson, in *The World Upside Down*, p. 71, also sees the play as anti-masque.

55. Sir John Harington gives a wonderful (though doubtless touched-up) account in a letter to 'Mr Secretary Barlow, 1606', *Nugae Antiquae*, ed. Henry Harington, 3 vols (Hildesheim: Georg Olms, 1968; first published 1779) ii, 127–9:

One day, a great feast was held, and after dinner the representation of Solomon his Temple and the coming of the Queen of Sheba was made, or, as I may better say, was meant to have been made, before their Majesties, by device of the Earl of Salisbury and others. But alass! as all earthly thinges do fail to poor mortals in enjoyment, so did prove our presentment hereof. The Lady who did play the Queens part did carry most precious gifts to both their Majesties; but, forgetting the steppes arising to the canopy, overset her caskets into his Danish Majestyies lap, and fell at his feet, tho I rather think it was in his face. Much was the hurry and confusion; cloths and napkins were at hand to make all clean. His Majesty then got up and woud dance with the Queen of Sheba, but he fell down and humbled himself before her, and was carried to an inner chamber and laid on a bed of state; which was not a little defiled with the presents of the Queen which had been bestowed on his garments; such as wine, cream, jelly, beverage, cakes, spices, and other good matters. The entertainment and show went forward, and most of the presenters went backward, or fell down, wine did so occupy their upper chambers. Now did appear, in rich dress, Hope, Faith, and Charity: Hope did assay to speak, but wine rendered her endeavours so feeble that she withdrew and hoped the King would excuse her brevity. Faith was then all alone, for I am certain she was not joyned with good works; and left the Court in a staggering condition. Charity came to the Kings feet, and seemed to cover the multitude of sins her sisters had committed: In some sorte she made obeysance and brought giftes, but said she would return home again, as there was no gift which heaven had not already given his Majesty; she then returned to Hope and Faith, who were both sick and spewing in the lower hall.

56. The combined self-indulgence and self-consciousness with which monarchs sought this kind of re-enforcement perhaps indicates a diminishing confidence in the validity of the metaphysical foundations upon which their absolute claims rested. In the history of that diminishment at large, we may conjecture, the discovery of method had a part to play.

CHAPTER FOUR: JOHN DONNE'S 'ANNIVERSARIES'

1. Ben Jonson, *Conversations with William Drummond of Hawthornden*, 45, in *Ben Jonson*, ed. C. H. Herford and Percy and Evelyn Simpson, 11 vols (Oxford: Clarendon Press, 1925–52) I, 133.

2. Edmund Gosse, *The Life and Letters of John Donne*, 2 vols (London: William Heinemann, 1899) I, 305–6.

3. There is a minor critical tradition of attempts to make symbolic sense of Elizabeth Drury. Louis L. Martz, *The Poetry of Meditation* (New Haven, Conn., Yale University Press, 1954) pp. 211–48, presented the crucial argument that the poems are meditative exercises, but that *The First Anniversarie* fails to make an appropriate symbol of the girl. In 'Donne's *Anniversaries* Revisited', in *That Subtile Wreath. Lectures Presented at the Quatercentenary Celebration of the Birth of John Donne*, ed. Margaret W.

Pepperdene (Decatur, Ga.: Agnes Scott College, 1972) pp. 29–55, Martz reviews discussion of the *Anniversaries* subsequent to his original interpretation, and concludes that Donne deliberately enacts a failure of the meditative process to teach us contempt of the world. Charles M. Coffin, *John Donne and the New Philosophy* (New York: Humanities Press, 1958; first published 1937), pp. 258, 276, suggests that the girl figures forth Christ. William Empson, *Some Versions of Pastoral* (London: Chatto and Windus, 1950) p. 84, argues that she is the *Logos*. D. W. Harding, 'Coherence of Theme in Donne's Poetry', *Kenyon Review*, 13 (1951) 427–44, argues that she is the idea of motherhood. Marius Bewley, 'Religious Cynicism in Donne's Poetry', *Kenyon Review*, 14 (1952) 619–46, suggests that she covertly represents the Catholic Church, and also identifies her with Queen Elizabeth. Marjorie Hope Nicolson, *The Breaking of the Circle*, rev. edn (New York: Columbia University Press, 1960) pp. 81–122, deals with the impact of the new science on the poem, and suggests that the dead girl symbolises Queen Elizabeth, and is associated with Astraea. Frank Manley, *John Donne: The Anniversaries* (Baltimore: Johns Hopkins Press, 1963), esp. pp. 20ff., suggests she is Wisdom. Richard E. Hughes, *The Progress of the Soul. The Interior Career of John Donne* (New York: William Morrow, 1968) pp. 208ff., suggests St Lucy. Barbara Kiefer Lewalski, *Donne's 'Anniversaries' and the Poetry of Praise. The Creation of a Symbolic Mode* (Princeton, NJ: Princeton University Press, 1973), maintains she is the Image of God restored in the regenerate soul. John Carey, *John Donne. Life, Mind and Art* (London: Faber and Faber, 1981) pp. 102–4, suggests that the poems are venal exercises in extravagant hyperbole, and that symbol-hunting makes nonsense of them.

4. *Conversations*, 47, in *Ben Jonson*, ed. Herford and Simpson, I, 133.

5. Manley, *Donne: The Anniversaries*, p. 7.

6. Lewalski, *Donne's 'Anniversaries'*.

7. P. G. Stanwood, ' "Essential Joye" in Donne's *Anniversaries*', *Texas Studies in Literature and Language*, 13 (1971) 227–38, also suggests that the poems are centrally concerned with grace.

8. Lewalski, *Donne's 'Anniversaries'*, p. 161. Patrick Cruttwell, *The Shakespearean Moment and its Place in the Poetry of the 17th Century* (London: Chatto and Windus, 1954) pp. 73–106, compares the *Anniversaries* with Shakespeare's last plays, and notices, with respect to Platonic symbolism, that the *Anniversaries* show 'Donne's own personal version, modernised, intellectualised, infused with tinctures of bitterness and irony, of the old Spenserian Platonism from which he had revolted at the start of his career' (p. 75).

9. A. D. Nuttall, *Overheard by God. Fiction and Prayer in Herbert, Milton, Dante and St John* (London: Methuen, 1980), esp. ch. 1, 'The Temple', pp. 1–82. For the idea that the poems are about poetry itself, see Ruth A. Fox, 'Donne's *Anniversaries* and the Art of Living', *Journal of English Literary History*, 3 (1971) esp. p. 531; and Antony F. Bellette, 'Art and Imitation in Donne's *Anniversaries*', *Studies in English Literature* 15 (1975) 84–5.

10. All references to the *Elegies* and *Songs and Sonnets* are to Helen Gardner's edn, *John Donne. The Elegies and the Songs and Sonnets* (Oxford: Clarendon Press, 1965). Line numbers are cited in the text.

11. All references to the *Epithalamions* and *Anniversaries* are to *John Donne. The Epithalamions, Anniversaries and Epicides*, ed. W. Milgate (Oxford: Clarendon Press, 1978). Line numbers are indicated in the text. *FA = The First Anniversarie; SA = The Second Anniversarie*.

12. On 'The Exstasie' and its tradition, see Merritt Y. Hughes, 'The Lineage of "The Extasie" ', *Modern Language Review*, xvii (1932) 1–5; A. J. Smith, 'The Metaphysic of Love', *Review of English Studies*, new ser., ix (1958) 362–75; Helen Gardner, 'The Argument about "The Ecstasy" ', in *Elizabethan and Jacobean Studies Presented to F. P. Wilson*, ed. Herbert Davis and Helen Gardner (Oxford: Clarendon Press, 1959) pp. 279–306; George Williamson, 'The Convention of "The Ecstasie" ', in *Seventeenth Century Contexts*, rev. edn (Chicago: University of Chicago Press, 1969) pp. 63–77.

13. See Gardner, in her edn of *Songs and Sonnets*, Appendix D, 'The Ecstasy', p. 264.

14. For a summary of opinions on the seductive intent, see Gardner, in her edn of *Songs and Sonnets*, pp. 259–65. She concludes that there is a suggestion of seduction, but that the poem's main point is 'to explore imaginatively the notion of ecstasy as he had met it in his Neoplatonic reading' (p. 261).

15. For a full account of Galen's theory of blood flow, see Rudolph E. Siegel, MD, *Galen's System of Medicine and Physiology, an Analysis of his Doctrines on Blood Flow, Respiration, Humours, and Internal Diseases* (Basel: Karger, 1968), and *Galen on Psychology, Psychopathology, and Function and Diseases of the Nervous System* (Basel: Karger, 1973) pp. 35ff. For the function of the spirit in linking soul and body, see J. B. Bamborough, *The Little World of Man* (London: Longmans, Green, 1952) pp. 54–7.

16. Carey, *John Donne*, pp. 138, 164, argues for the deliberate oddness of the imagery, and connects 'The Exstasie' and the *Anniversaries* by comparing the ecstatic lovers' cemented hands with Elizabeth Drury's thinking flesh. It is perhaps worth noting that Helkiah Crooke, in *Microcosmographia. A Description of the Body of Man* (London, 1615) p. 367, describes the heart as a 'fountaine of . . . Spirit', positioned in the middle of the body, 'in a Noble place as it were a Prince' (p. 368). Perhaps Donne's famous, cryptic line 'Else a great Prince in prison lies' refers to the heart seated thus in the centre of the body, where it was conventionally considered to be a ruler.

17. The *Divine Poems* are cited from Helen Gardner's edn, *John Donne. The Divine Poems* (Oxford: Clarendon Press, 1952).

18. Quotations from the *Sermons* are cited from *The Sermons of John Donne*, ed. George R. Potter and Evelyn M. Simpson, 10 vols (Berkeley, Calif., and Los Angeles: University of California Press, 1953–62). Volume and page numbers are cited in the text.

19. Karl Rahner, *Theological Investigations*, iii: *The Theology of the Spiritual Life*, trs. Karl H. and Boniface Kruger (London: Darton, Longman and Todd, 1967) p. 323.

20. See *Dictionnaire de Spiritualité et Mystique, Doctrine et Histoire* (Paris: G. Beauchesne, 1932–) col. 2289: 'tel saint Augustin, demeurés très fidèles à la langue de la philosophie grecque, *cor* sera en concurrence constante, et cela durant tout le moyen âge, avec les termes *anima, animus, mens, intellectus* et *ratio*, au point d'en devenir pratiquement synonyme'. See also A. Guillaumont, 'Les Sens des Noms du Coeur dans l'Antiquité', in *Le Coeur*,

Études Carmélitaines (1950) pp. 67ff. The following account draws on these two sources.

21. Gregory, *Moralia*, xxv.8.20 (*Patrologia Latina*, 76, 332cd; 28, 19, 474b); Cassiodorus, *In Psalmos*, LXXII.26 (*Patrologia Latina*, 70, 523cd); Peter Lombard, *Summa Sententiarum*, III, 27.5; Isidore of Seville, *Etymologiae*, XI.i.118 (*Patrologia Latina*, 82, 411c).

22. See E. Gilson, *La Théologie Mystique de Saint Bernard* (Paris: J. Vrin, 1934) pp. 124–5.

23. Hugh of St Victor, *De Modo Orandi*, 1 (*PL*, 176, 977b).

24. Richard of St Victor, *De Statu Interioris Hominis*, 1, 2.

25. For St Bonaventure, see *In Epiphaniam Sermo 3*; *Vitis Mystica*, chs 3, 24; *Collationes in Hexaemeron*, II.32.

26. Thomas Aquinas, *Summa Theologica*, 2ᵃ, 2ᵃᵉ, 9.44a, 5: 'Actus voluntatis, quae hic significatur per *cor.*' See further, M.-D. Chenu, 'Les Catégories Affectives dans la Langue de l'École', in *Le Coeur*, pp. 123–8, for a discussion of the complexities of Aquinas's teaching, and especially the distinction between *voluntas ut natura* and *voluntas ut ratio*.

27. See Dante, *Vita Nuova*, 4 (1st sonnet), 20 (10th sonnet) and 33 (17th sonnet). For Petrarch, see Donald L. Guss, *John Donne, Petrarchist. Italianate Conceits and Love Theory in 'The Songs and Sonnets'* (Detroit: Wayne State University Press, 1966) pp. 103ff.

28. Barbara Kiefer Lewalski, *Protestant Poetics and the Seventeenth-Century Lyric* (Princeton, NJ: Princeton University Press, 1979) p. 197. Further references are cited in the text.

29. For Donne's Franciscan readings, see Patrick Grant, *The Transformation of Sin. Studies in Donne, Herbert, Vaughan and Traherne* (Amherst: University of Massachusetts Press; Montreal: McGill–Queen's University Press, 1974) pp. 40ff. For Donne's heavy reliance on St Bernard, see p. 56.

30. Following Aquinas, the Jesuits stressed the importance of educating the heart. For the impact of the Jesuits on Donne, see esp. Carey, *John Donne*, who makes a strong case for the lifelong effects on Donne of his 'apostasie' from the religion of his childhood. See pp. 15ff., *et passim*.

31. Georgette de Montenay, *Emblemes ou Devises Chrestiennes*, ed. John Harden, intro. by C. N. Smith, Continental Emblem Books no. 15 (Menston, Yorks: Scolar Press, 1973; first published (1571). Page numbers are cited in the text.

32. For the following examples from Montenay, see ibid., pp. 5, 29, 78, 44.

33. Empson, *Some Versions of Pastoral*, p. 84. See also Empson's article 'Donne the Spaceman', *Kenyon Review*, 19 (1957) 337–99, for a provocative interpretation of Donne's tacitly unorthodox sentiments. The anguish and disturbance felt by Donne's contemporaries on such issues is suggested by Don Cameron Allen, 'The Degeneration of Man and Renaissance Pessimism', *Studies in Philology*, XXXV (1938) 202–22; Victor Harris, *All Coherence Gone* (Chicago: University of Chicago Press, 1949); Robert Ornstein, 'Donne, Montaigne and Natural Law', *Journal of English and Germanic Philology*, LV (1956) 213–29.

34. Donne, *Biathanatos* (New York: Facsimile Text Society, 1930). Page numbers are cited in the text. For further reflections on *Biathanatos* and Donne's unorthodox tendencies, see George Williamson, 'The Libertine

Donne: Comments on *Biathanatos'*, *Philological Quarterly*, XIII (1934) 276–91; Ernest W. Sullivan, 'The Genesis and Transmission of Donne's *Biathanatos'*, *Library*, 31 (1976) 52–72.

35. Janel M. Mueller, 'Death and the Maiden: The Metaphysics of Christian Symbolism in Donne's *Anniversaries'*, *Modern Philology* 72 (1974–5) 280–6, a review article dealing with Lewalski, *Donne's 'Anniversaries'*, suggests that the *Anniversarie* poems remain flawed precisely by Donne's failure to 'focus the metaphysical problem of evil as a genuinely human problem in Elizabeth Drury' (p. 285). See also Patrick Mahoney, 'The *Anniversaries*: Donne's Rhetorical Approach to Evil', *Journal of English and Germanic Philology*, 68 (1969) 407–13, repr. in *Essential Articles for the Study of John Donne's Poetry*, ed. John R. Roberts (Hamden, Conn.: Archon, 1975) pp. 363–7, which suggests that the main evil addressed by the poems is the decay of our mental faculties, and that the poems attempt to address readers who share this condition. Kitty Datta, 'Love and Asceticism in Donne's Poetry: The Divine Analogy', *Critical Quarterly*, 19 (1977) 5–25, suggests that the tensions in the poems partly relate to Donne's ambivalent attitude to women (p. 14), and sees the language as 'the reverse of the sacred parody described by Martz, in which language of secular love poetry is applied to the divine Beloved. Instead, divine language is being applied to human life' (p. 17), and the result is an ambivalent parody of religious praise.

36. For further suggestions on the self-reflexiveness of the *Anniversaries*, see Carol M. Sickerman, 'Donne's Timeless Anniversaries', *University of Toronto Quarterly*, 39 (1970) 127–43, repr. in *Essential Articles for the Study of John Donne's Poetry*, pp. 374–86, which conceives of the poems as 'searching', and as expressing the anguished discovery of failure; Rosalie L. Colie, 'The Rhetoric of Transcendence', *Philological Quarterly*, XLIII (1964) 145–70, repr. in *Essential Articles for the Study of John Donne's Poetry*, pp. 199–219, deals with the poems in context of the self-referential epistemology of the period. See also Ruth A. Fox, 'Donne's *Anniversaries* and the Art of Living', *Journal of English Literary History*, 38 (1971) 528–41, on the poems becoming verse 'by negating themselves' (p. 530), and on Elizabeth Drury giving 'her soul to verse' (p. 531).

37. Manley brings this up, in *Donne: The Anniversaries*, p. 11, and so does Harold Love, in 'The Argument of Donne's *First Anniversary'*, *Modern Philology*, 64 (1966) 125–31, repr. in *Essential Articles for the Study of John Donne's Poetry* p. 357.

38. Ibid. The idea of the heart is touched upon by other critics – for instance, by Martz, in *That Subtile Wreath*, p. 38 (with a reference to Harold Love); and by Lewalski, in *Donne's 'Anniversaries'*, pp. 248ff., 262.

39. Lewalski (ibid., p. 158) calls attention to Donne's 'retreat from the Spenserian allegorical mode in poetry with its multiple levels or juxtaposed planes of meaning'.

40. Coffin, *John Donne and the New Philosophy*, pp. 88ff.

41. *John Donne. Ignatius his Conclave*, ed. T. S. Healy, SJ (Oxford: Clarendon Press, 1969) pp. 7, 81.

42. Ibid., p. 15.

43. *John Donne. Paradoxes and Problems*, ed. Helen Peters (Oxford: Clarendon Press, 1980) p. 33; *Ignatius his Conclave* p. 7.

44. See Milgate, in his edn of *Epithalamions, Anniversaries and Epicides*, p. 143, note to *FA*, ll.259–60.
45. Ibid., p. 141, note to *FA*, l. 221. Gilbert is also alluded to in *Essays in Divinity*, ed. Evelyn M. Simpson (Oxford: Clarendon Press, 1952) p. 34.
46. See Coffin, *John Donne and the New Philosophy*, p. 185; and Empson, in *Kenyon Review*, 19, 337–99.
47. Gardner, in her edn of the *Divine Poems*, p. 13.
48. For Paracelsus, see D. C. Allen, 'John Donne's Knowledge of Renaissance Medicine', *Journal of English and Germanic Philology*, 42 (1943) 322–42, repr. in *Essential Articles for the Study of John Donne's Poetry*, pp. 93ff.; W. A. Murray, 'Donne and Paracelsus, An Essay in Interpretation', *Review of English Studies*, 25 (1949) 185ff.
49. Donne, *Letters to Severall Persons of Honour* (London, 1651) pp. 13–15.
50. Donne: *Biathanatos*, p. 172; *Ignatius his Conclave*, p. 19.
51. See Coffin, *John Donne and the New Philosophy*, pp. 180ff., Cruttwell, *The Shakespearean Moment*, p. 89; Carey, *John Donne*, pp. 231ff.
52. See Simon Harward, *Phlebotomy: or, A Treatise of Letting of Bloud* (London, 1601), p. 93: 'as in *Aries* the head, *Taurus* the neck, *Gemini* the shoulders and armes, *Cancer* the breast, stomach and ribs, *Leo* the heart . . .'; David de Planis Campi, *Discours de la Phlebotomie* (Paris, 1621), trs. E. W. (London, 1658) pp. 42, 85: 'As the sun is in the middle of the Planets; so is the heart (which is subject to it) placed in the middle of man', '*Sol*, hot and dry, governs the Heart'.
53. *Batman uppon Bartholome, his Booke De Proprietatibus Rerum* (London, 1582) p. 126.
54. Henricus Cornelius Agrippa, *De Occulta Philosophia Libri Tres* (Strasbourg, 1531) p. clxxiiii.
55. See John Russell Brown's edn of *Henry V*, v.ii. 164–7, in Signet *Classic Shakespeare* (New York: Harcourt Brace Jovanovich, 1972) p. 799.
56. Robert Burton, *The Anatomy of Melancholy*, ed. Floyd Dell and Paul Jordan-Smith, i.i.2.4 (New York: Tudor, 1955) p. 133.
57. Samuel Purchas, *Microcosmos or the Historie of Man* (London, 1619) p. 50.
58. W. S. C. Copeman, *Doctors and Disease in Tudor Times* (London: Dawson, 1960) p. 89.
59. John Davies of Hereford, *Microcosmos*, in *The Complete Works of John Davies of Hereford*, ed. Alexander B. Grosart, 2 vols (Edinburgh: Chertsey Worthies' Library, 1878) i, 28.
60. See, for instance, Montenay, *Emblemes*, p. 8; Herman Hugo, *Pia Desideria*, ed. John Harder, intro. by Hester M. Black, Continental Emblem Books no. 11 (Menston, Yorks: Scolar Press, 1971; first published 1624) Preface.
61. *Paracelsus, Selected Writings*, ed. Jolande Jacobi, trans. Norbert Guterman, Bollingen Series xxviii 2nd edn (New York: Pantheon Books, 1958) pp. 124, 122.

CHAPTER FIVE: THOMAS BROWNE'S 'RELIGIO MEDICI'

1. Sir Kenelm Digby, *Observations upon Religio Medici* (London, 1644). Page numbers are cited in the text. For a full account of Digby, see R. T.

Petersson, *Sir Kenelm Digby. The Ornament of England 1603–1665* (London: Jonathan Cape, 1956).

2. *Aubrey's Brief Lives*, ed. Oliver Lawson Dick (Harmondsworth: Penguin, 1962) p. 187.

3. See Frank Livingstone Huntley, *Sir Thomas Browne. A Biographical and Critical Study* (Ann Arbor: University of Michigan Press, 1962) p. 146: 'Thanks to the Latin translation of Religio in 1644 by John Merryweather, and to the inevitable linking of the names of Dorset, Digby, and Howell to his own, Dr Thomas Browne gained a European reputation.'

4. *Coleridge on the Seventeenth Century*, ed. Roberta Florence Brinkley, intro. by Louis I. Bredvold (Durham, NC: Duke University Press, 1955) p. 438. Page numbers are henceforth cited in the text.

5. Herbert Butterfield, *The Origins of Modern Science, 1300–1800*, new edn (London: G. Bell, 1957; first published 1949) p. 118.

6. Browne, *Religio Medici*, I.33. All quotations from Browne are from Geoffrey Keynes's rev. edn, *The Works of Sir Thomas Browne*, 4 vols (London: Faber and Faber, 1964), referred to as *Works* and cited by volume and page, except in the case of *Religio Medici*, which is cited by part and section number.

7. See Leonard Nathanson, *The Strategy of Truth. A Study of Sir Thomas Browne* (Chicago and London: University of Chicago Press, 1967) p. 6: 'And the issue is further complicated by Browne's explicit distrust of imaginative literature and his continual inveighing in *Vulgar Errors* against metaphorical language as one of the deadly enemies of truth.' For the same suspicion of rhetoric in *Religio Medici*, see John R. Mulder, *The Temple of the Mind. Education and Literary Taste in Seventeenth-Century England* (New York: Pegasus, 1969) pp. 54ff.

8. Browne might not have approved of the title, which appears in the 1642 edns, but is dropped in 1643. But after 1643 the book was republished or reissued numerous times, and the title stayed with it. See *Sir Thomas Browne. Religio Medici and Other Works*, ed. L. C. Martin (Oxford: Clarendon Press, 1964) p. xv.

9. Browne warns against atheism, which he sees as a consequence of too much concern for secondary causes (*Religio Medici*, I.19). On the physician as atheist, see Paul H. Kocher, *Science and Religion in Elizabethan England* (San Marino, Calif.: Huntington Library, 1953) pp. 239–57.

10. For a further development of this position, see Stanley E. Fish, *Self-Consuming Artifacts. The Experience of Seventeenth-Century Literature* (Berkeley, Calif.: University of California Press, 1972) pp. 353ff. Leonard Nathanson, 'Sir Thomas Browne and the Ethics of Knowledge', in *Approaches to Sir Thomas Browne. The Ann Arbor Tercentenary Lectures and Essays*, ed. C. A. Patrides (Columbia, Miss.: University of Missouri Press, 1982) pp. 12ff., argues that Browne's paradoxical balance is a way of validating intellectual activity itself. John R. Knott, Jr, 'Sir Thomas Browne and the Labyrinth of Truth', ibid., pp. 19–30, suggests that the truth lies in the labyrinthine search.

11. There is some debate about how modern and Baconian Browne was. Almonte C. Howell, 'Sir Thomas Browne and Seventeenth-Century Scientific Thought', *Studies in Philology*, 20 (1925) 61–80, along with Alwin

Thaler, 'Sir Thomas Browne and the Elizabethans', *Studies in Philology*, 28 (1931) 87–117, and Egon Stephen Merton, *Science and Imagination in Sir Thomas Browne* (New York: King's Crown Press, 1949), argues for a strong Baconian and modern cast to Browne's thinking. William P. Dunn, *Sir Thomas Browne* (Minneapolis: University of Minnesota Press, 1950; first published 1926) pp. 7ff., holds that Browne inherited the weaknesses of the mediaeval scholastic method which Bacon analyses so well, and this view is maintained by Basil Willey, *The Seventeenth Century Background* (Harmondsworth: Penguin, 1964; first published 1934) p. 47. More recent studies tend to confirm this opinion, seeing Browne as caught up, willy-nilly, with new scientific trends but maintaining assumptions out of character with them. See Joan Bennett, *Sir Thomas Browne* (Cambridge: Cambridge University Press, 1962) pp. 127–38; Frank L. Huntley, *Sir Thomas Browne*, esp. pp. 86ff.; Nathanson, *The Strategy of Truth*, p. 156; Achsah Guibbory, 'Sir Thomas Browne's *Pseudodoxia Epidemica* and the Circle of Knowledge', *Texas Studies in Literature and Language*, 18 (1976) 486–99, shows that, although *Pseudodoxia Epidemica* seems at first to be Baconian, it is based on certain epistemological assumptions which undermine Bacon's ideal advancement of learning. Marie Boas Hall, 'Thomas Browne Naturalist', in *Approaches to Sir Thomas Browne*, pp. 178–87, claims that Browne is a collector of facts, and that he had no interest in Baconian progress or in current methodological debate.

12. As Mulder points out in detail in *The Temple of the Mind*, pp. 54ff.
13. Merton, *Science and Imagination in Browne*, p. 21.
14. There are thus good reasons for placing Browne among the Baconians. Browne's early critic Alexander Ross, in *Arcana Microcosmi – with a Refutation of Doctor Browne's Vulgar Errors, the Lord Bacon's Natural History, and Doctor Harvey's Book de Generatione* (London, 1652), places him in such company. Browne's home laboratory was visited and described by John Evelyn on 17 October 1671: *The Diary of John Evelyn*, ed. E. S. De Beer, 6 vols (Oxford: Clarendon Press, 1955) III, 594. The *Pseudodoxia Epidemica* joins with those 'who endeavour the advancement of Learning' by means of 'experimentall and judicious knowledge' ('To the Reader', *Works*, II, 6), and is evidently touched by Baconianism. In a letter, Browne praises Harvey's discovery of the circulation of the blood (*Works*, IV, 255), and F. Huntley, 'Sir Thomas Browne's Early Reputation as a Scientist', *Seventeenth Century News*, Spring 1978, pp. 22–3, indicates that by 1652 Browne was known outside England for scientific enquiry.
15. Anne Drury Hall, 'Epistle, Meditation, and Sir Thomas Browne's *Religio Medici*', *Publications of the Modern Language Association*, XCIV (1979) 234–46.
16. Laurence A. Breiner, 'The Generation of Metaphor in Thomas Browne', *Modern Language Quarterly*, 38 (1977) 261–75, argues, I believe correctly, that Browne's tropes share 'a covert "master figure" '. C. A. Patrides, ' "The Best Part of Nothing": Sir Thomas Browne and the Strategy of Indirection', in *Approaches to Sir Thomas Browne*, pp. 43–4, argues that order is a 'major preoccupation' in *Religio Medici*, and that Browne already anticipates the *Garden of Cyrus*.
17. Deborah Joanne Griebel's unpublished MA thesis, 'Contrary Devotion: An Analysis of Binary Structure in the Works of Sir Thomas Browne' (British

Columbia: University of Victoria, 1979), ch. 2, 'Religio Medici: The Paradox of Faith and Works', pp. 26ff., discusses the *Religio Medici* in terms of Browne's paradoxical oppositions becoming elaborate circular arguments, so that the tension between opposites is resolved. The circle, which suggests this resolution, can, however, threaten constriction. The chapter does not deal with the cross, but the reading of Browne's relation of faith to works in terms of doctrinal paradox resolved by circular figures is, I believe, correct. See also N. J. Endicott, 'Some Aspects of Self-Revelation and Self-Portraiture in *Religio Medici*', in *Essays in English Literature from the Renaissance to the Victorian Age. Presented to A. S. P. Woodhouse*, ed. Millar MacLure and F. W. Watt (Toronto: University of Toronto Press, 1964) p. 93: 'It is only from the whole effect of the circling movement of his mind, as we follow and participate in the exact phrasing, that we find (or think we find) the author.'

18. Fish, *Self-Consuming Artifacts*, p. 371.
19. Austin Warren, 'The Styles of Sir Thomas Browne', in *Seventeenth-Century Prose. Modern Essays in Criticism*, ed. Stanley E. Fish (New York: Oxford University Press, 1971) pp. 413–23, argues that Browne cultivates high, middle and low styles. J. R. Mulryne, 'The Play of Mind: Self and Audience in *Religio Medici*', in *Approaches to Sir Thomas Browne*, pp. 60ff., discusses Browne's literary persona.
20. Guibbory, in *Texas Studies in Literature and Language*, 18, 486–99.
21. *Coleridge on the Seventeenth Century*, p. 448.
22. See Petersson, *Sir Kenelm Digby*, p. 120.
23. Ibid., p. 122. See Marjorie Nicolson, 'The Early Stage of Cartesianism in England', *Studies in Philology*, 26 (1929) 357.
24. Sir Kenelm Digby, *Two Treatises, in the One of Which, the Nature of Bodies; In the Other, The Nature of Mans Soule; is looked into: in Way of Discovery, of the Immortality of Reasonable Soules* (Paris, 1644). All quotations from the *Two Treatises* are from this edn, and are cited in the text.
25. Sir Kenelm Digby, *Of the Sympathetic Powder* (London, 1669). See Lester S. King, *The Road to Medical Enlightenment 1650–1695* (London: Macdonald, 1970) pp. 140–5.
26. Digby, *Of the Sympathetic Powder*, p. 191.
27. See Petersson, *Sir Kenelm Digby*, p. 184. Digby does not mention Bacon, but Petersson claims he was Baconian (p. 182).
28. Ibid., p. 124. For Descartes's remark, see *Oeuvres de Descartes*, ed. C. Adam and P. Tannery, 11 vols (Paris: J. Vrin, 1969; first published 1897–1909) ii, 398.
29. See Digby, *Observations upon Religio Medici*, p. 24. Digby was writing the *Two Treatises* at the time when he composed the *Observations*. See Huntley, *Sir Thomas Browne*, p. 138.
30. In *Two Treatises*, pp. 116–17, Digby remarks, 'we have always one foote upon the ground; so as the other may be sure of firme footing before it settle. Whereas, they that for more hast will leape over rugged passages and broken ground; when both their feete are in the ayre, can not helpe themselves, but must light as chance throweth them'. The remark is not directed at Browne, but it nicely indicates Digby's attitude to Browne's metaphysics.

31. See Dominick Grundy, 'Scepticism in Two Essays by Montaigne and Sir Thomas Browne', *Journal of the History of Ideas*, 34 (1973) 529–42; Bennett, *Sir Thomas Browne*, pp. 66, 129, 184; Endicott, in *Essays in English Literature from the Renaissance to the Victorian Age*, p. 89.

CHAPTER SIX: WILLIAM LAW'S 'SPIRIT OF LOVE'

1. *A Serious Call to a Devout and Holy Life*, in *The Works of William Law*, 9 vols (Setley, Hants: G. Moreton, 1892–3; first published 1762) IV, 7. Page numbers are cited in the text.
2. A. Keith Walker, *William Law: His Life and Thought* (London: SPCK, 1973) p. 67. Law is careful, however, to avoid Quietism. See *A Serious Call*, p. 153: 'you ought not to say, that I encourage that *quietism* by placing religion in the heart'. Desirée Hirst, *Hidden Riches. Traditional Symbolism from the Renaissance to Blake* (London: Eyre and Spottiswoode, 1964) pp. 196ff., maintains that Law's work represents an attempt to keep in touch with the mainstream of Christian spirituality. See also Arthur W. Hopkinson, *About William Law* (London: SPCK, 1948) p. 75, on Law's mystical readings.
3. James Boswell, *Life of Johnson*, ed. R. W. Chapman, corrected by J. D. Fleeman (London: Oxford University Press, 1970) pp. 50–1; Edward Gibbon, *Memoirs of my Life*, ed. George Bonnard (London: Thomas Nelson, 1966) p. 22. See also Katherine C. Balderston, 'Dr Johnson and William Law', *Publications of the Modern Language Association*, LXXV (1960) 302–94. For a brief summary of the indebtedness of Wesley, Whitefield, Pope, Johnson, Blake and Coleridge to Law, see John Sitter, *Literary Loneliness in Mid-Eighteenth-Century England* (Ithaca, NY, and London: Cornell University Press, 1982) pp. 50ff.
4. See Colin Wilson, *Religion and the Rebel* (Westport, Conn.: Greenwood Press, 1957) p. 212: 'This is a clean, hard-hitting prose. In its clarity, it has something in common with Shaw.' See also Gerald Bullett, *The English Mystics* (London: Michael Joseph, 1950) p. 138.
5. C. S. Lewis, *Letters to an American Lady*, ed. Clyde S. Kilby (Grand Rapids, Mich.: William B. Eerdmans, 1967) p. 43.
6. For the influence of Law on Pope, see Benjamin Boyce, *The Character Sketches in Pope's Poems* (Durham, NC: Duke University Press, 1962) pp. 49ff.
7. St Teresa of Avila, *Interior Castle*, trs. E. Allison Peers (New York: Image, 1961) p. 68.
8. These 'Rules for my Future Conduct' are printed in the 'Prefatory Memoir', *Works*, I, v.
9. See Walker, *William Law*, p. 169: 'The dominant purpose of Law's move was to set up a holy household and to live according to the principles of the *Serious Call*, with devotion and charity as the twin pillars of existence.'
10. See C. Walton, *Notes and Materials for an Adequate Biography of William Law* (London: privately printed, 1854) pp. 429–41.
11. *The Letters of C. S. Lewis*, ed. W. H. Lewis (London: Geoffrey Bles, 1966) p. 143. See also Charles Williams, *Descent of the Dove* (Grand Rapids, Mich.:

William B. Eerdmans, 1939) p. 195, who claims that a few books from Law's later phase 'form perhaps one of the best statements of the pure Christian religion that have ever been issued'.

12. This does not mean, however, that Malebranche was rejected. Law held throughout his life, for instance, to the Malebranchiste 'Omnia videmus in Deo.'

13. For this background to Law, see Henri Talon, *William Law. A Study in Literary Craftsmanship* (New York: Rockliff, 1948), ch. 2, 'The Background', pp. 7ff.; N. Sykes, *Church and State in England in the Eighteenth Century* (Cambridge: Cambridge University Press, 1934); Walker, *William Law*, 'Early Years and Cultural Background', pp. 1ff.

14. Ibid., p. 6.

15. John Byrom, *Private Journal and Literary Remains*, ed. Richard Parkinson, 2 vols (Manchester: Chetham Society, 1854–7) I, 23, which deals with Law's early acquaintance with Malebranche. John Hoyles, *The Edges of Augustanism. The Aesthetics of Spirituality in Thomas Ken, John Byrom and William Law* (The Hague: Martinus Nijhoff, 1972) p. 104, deals with the fact that 'A cult of Malebranche appears to have developed among the second generation of non-jurors who organised themselves as such after the 1715 Hanoverian settlement.'

16. For a summary of Malebranche, see Patrick Grant, *Images and Ideas in Literature of the English Renaissance* (Amherst: University of Massachusetts Press; and London: Macmillan, 1979) pp. 175ff. Useful accounts of Malebranche's thought can be found in R. W. Church, *A Study in the Philosophy of Malebranche* (New York and London: Kennikat Press, 1970; first published 1931); and Frederick Copleston, *A History of Philosophy*, IV: *Descartes to Leibniz* (London: Burns and Oates, 1960) ch. 9, 'Malebranche', pp. 180–204. For Malebranche's spirituality, see Pierre Blanchard, *L'Attention à Dieu selon Malebranche* (Paris: Desclée de Brouwer, 1956); and Maurice Blondel, 'L'Anti-Cartésianisme de Malebranche', *Revue de Métaphysique et de Morale*, 1916, pp. 1–26. For the relationship between science and religion in Malebranche, see Beatrice K. Rome, *The Philosophy of Malebranche. A Study of his Integration of Faith, Reason and Experimental Observation* (Chicago: Henry Regnery, 1963); Michael E. Hobart, *Science and Religion in the Thought of Nicolas Malebranche* (Chapel Hill: University of North Carolina Press, 1982).

17. *Oeuvres Complètes de Bérulle*, ed. J. P. Migne (Paris, 1886) col. 161.

18. See especially André Robinet, *Malebranche de l'Académie des Sciences* (Paris: J. Vrin, 1970).

19. See *Remarks upon Some of Mr Norris's Books, Wherein he Asserts P. Malebranche's Opinion of our Seeing All Things in God*, in *The Works of John Locke. A New Edition*, 10 vols (London: Thomas Tegg, 1823) X, 247–59; and *An Examination of P. Malebranche's Opinion of Seeing All Things in God*, ibid., IX, 211ff. Thomas Reid, *Essays on the Intellectual Powers of Man*, 2 vols (Dublin, 1786) I, 142, says of Locke's *Examination*, 'whether it was written in haste, or after the vigour of his understanding was impaired by age, there is less of strength and solidity in it, than in most of his writings'. Yet Locke is shrewd in arguing that the curious structure of the eye and ear remains unexplained if, as Malebranche holds, God operates in the most direct and

simplest ways, and that the doctrine of knowing all things in God refutes common experience by implying that we know what God's ideas are, but not the ideas in our own understanding. See also, Joseph Moreau, 'Le Réalisme de Malebranche et la Fonction de l'Idée', *Revue de Metaphysique et de Morale*, 1946, pp. 97–141.

20. For Malebranche's knowledge of Bacon, Descartes and Newton, see Rome, *The Philosophy of Malebranche*, esp. ch. 1, 'Scientific Method', pp. 7ff.; Robinet, *Malebranche de l'Académie des Sciences*, pp. 212, 294ff., 318ff., *et passim*.

21. For a discussion of whether Descartes's argument 'does not undermine the very goal that he sought', see Rome, *The Philosophy of Malebranche*, pp. 48ff.

22. Malebranche, *Dialogues on Metaphysics and on Religion*, trs. Morris Ginsberg (London: George Allen and Unwin, 1923) pp. 147, 196.

23. See Robinet, *Malebranche de l'Académie des Sciences*, pp. 299ff.

24. Byrom, *Journal*, I.2, 337.

25. Walker, *William Law*, p. 66.

26. Matthew Tindal, *Christianity as Old as the Creation, or the Gospel a Republication of the Religion of Nature* (1730) p. 179.

27. Law, *The Case of Reason*, in *Works*, II, 57. Page numbers are henceforth cited in the text.

28. Sitter, *Literary Loneliness in Mid-Eighteenth-Century England*, pt I, 'Writing and Belief', pp. 19ff., points this out: I agree that Law's 'fideism balances Hume's skepticism both as counterweight and as complement' (p. 11).

29. David Hume, *Dialogues Concerning Natural Religion*, ed. Norman Kemp Smith, 2nd edn, with supplement (New York: Social Sciences Publishers, 1948) p. 141. Page numbers are henceforth cited in the text.

30. See Smith, ibid., pp. 57ff., for a summary of Philo's character in relation to his creator. Hume, however, does not identify himself with Philo: see below, and note 32.

31. See, for instance, Law's *An Humble, Earnest, and Affectionate Address to the Clergy* (1761), in *Works*, IX, 82–3.

32. For Hume's literary accomplishments, see Michael Morrisroe, Jr, 'Hume's Rhetorical Strategy: A Solution to the *Dialogues Concerning Natural Religion*', *Texas Studies in Literature and Language*, 11 (1969) 963–74, and 'Rhetorical Methods in Hume's Works on Religion', *Philosophy and Rhetoric*, 2 (1969) 121–38. See also Sitter, *Literary Loneliness in Mid-Eighteenth-Century England*, ch. 1, 'Hume's Stylistic Emergence', pp. 19ff.

33. Hoyles, *The Edges of Augustanism*, p. 90.

34. Walker, *William Law*, p. 140, notices a developing compassion on Law's part towards the Deists.

35. For accounts of Boehme's influence on Law, see J. H. Overton, *The Life and Opinions of William Law* (London: Longmans, Green, 1881) pp. 140ff.; Caroline Spurgeon, *Mysticism in English Literature* (Cambridge: Cambridge University Press, 1913) pp. 91ff; Stephen Hobhouse, 'Fides et Ratio, the Book which Introduced Jacob Boehme to William Law', *Journal of Theological Studies*, 37 (1934) 350–68, and (ed.) *Selected Mystical Writings of William Law* (London: C. W. Daniel, 1938) pp. 303ff.; J. Brazier Green, *John Wesley and William Law* (London: Epworth, 1945) pp. 93ff.; Henri Talon,

William Law: A Study in Literary Craftsmanship, pp. 58ff.; Peter Malekin, 'Jacob Boehme's Influence on William Law', *Studia Neophilologica*, 36 (1964) 245–60; Walker, *William Law*, pp. 96ff.

36. See, for instance, Law's *The Way to Divine Knowledge* (1762), in *Works*, VII, 201: Academicus says that, if Boehme's works 'contain the *Ground* and *Philosophy* of all Nature, and all Creatures; surely they must not only allow the Use of our Reason, but call for the highest and most acute Exercise of it'. To which Theophilus (Law's spokesman) replies that, 'if the *Mystery is the deep Ground of* all Things', then 'no Acuteness or Ability of Natural Reason can so much as look into it'.

37. See Walton, *Notes and Materials*, p. 26.

38. See, for instance, John Joseph Stoudt, *Sunrise to Eternity* (Philadelphia: University of Pennsylvania Press, 1957); Malekin, in *Studia Neophilologica*, 36, 249ff.; Walker, *William Law*, pp. 96ff.; Patrick Grant, *Literature of Mysticism in Western Tradition* (London: Macmillan, 1983) pp. 86ff.

39. Law, *The Spirit of Love*, in *Works*, VIII, 19. See also, *Some Animadversions upon Dr Trapp's Late Reply* (1740), ibid., VI, 201:

> The illustrious Sir *Isaac Newton*, when he wrote his *Principia*, and published to the World his great Doctrine of *Attraction*, and those *Laws of Nature* by which the *Planets* began, and continue to move in their Orbits, could have told the World, that the *true and infallible* Ground of what he there advanced, was to be found in the *Teutonic Theosopher*.

> On Newton's possible knowledge of Boehme, see Hobhouse, in his edn of *Selected Mystical Writings of Law*, pp. 397ff.; H. McLachlan, *Sir Isaac Newton, Theological Manuscripts* (Liverpool: Liverpool University Press, 1950) pp. 20–1; S. Hutin, *Les Disciples Anglais de Jacob Boehme* (Paris: Editions Denöel, 1960) pp. 142–50; Walker, *William Law*, p. 106.

Index

Agrippa, Cornelius, 98
Analytical geometry, 10
Anatomy, 51, 56, 57, 60, 61, 75, 152
Aquinas, Thomas, St, 1, 88
Aristotle, 8, 12, 37, 57, 61, 103, 106, 107, 118, 119, 121, 158 n.18, 164 n.37
Ascham, Roger, 52
Aubrey, John, 92
Augustine of Hippo, St, 15, 40, 86
Averroës, 37

Bacon, Francis, 7, 8, 10, 12, 14, 16, 37, 44, 50, 58, 60, 61, 107, 109, 115, 118, 130, 167 n.12
Baldi, Guastalla, 69
Barrough, Philip, 56
Batman, Stephen, 69, 98
Bergson, Henri, 75
Bernard of Clairvaux, St, 86, 88
Bérulle, Pierre de, 128
Blake, William, 15, 137
Bodin, Jean, 7
Boehme, Jacob, 126, 136, 137, 138ff., 153
Bonaventure, St, 86
Bourignan, Antoinette, 124
Boyle, Robert, 10
Brahe, Tycho, 10, 96
Bright, Timothy, 59, 60, 69
Brossier, Marthe, 59
Browne, Thomas, 18, 102ff., 149, 153
Bruno, Giordano, 96, 98
Burton, Robert, 98
Burtt, E, A., 14
Butterfield, Herbert, 8, 103
Byrom, John, 130

Calvin, John, 15, 16, 78, 79, 101, 146, 152

Cambridge Platonists, 2
Camden, William, 49
Campanella, Tommaso, 58
Carey, John, 91
Cassiodorus, 86
Causes, 14, 15, 44, 105, 132, 159 n.33
Chambers, R. W., 24
Chesterton, G. K., 103
Christendom, 22, 23, 37, 45, 47
Coffin, C. M., 96, 97
Coke, Edward, 67
Coleridge, Samuel Taylor, 102, 103, 104, 112, 116, 122
Colet, John, 37, 49
Constantine, 110
Copernicus, 2, 7, 9, 10, 96
Cromwell, Thomas, 21
Crooke, Helkiah, 69, 70
Cross, 109ff., 149

Davies, John, 98
Descartes, René, 2, 7, 8, 9, 12, 14, 15, 16, 102, 117, 118, 120, 128, 129, 130, 132, 140, 153
Determinism, 50, 56, 58, 61, 63, 68, 74, 75, 151, 152, 168 n.28
Digby, Kenelm, 10, 102, 103, 104, 106, 107, 108, 117ff., 153
Digges, Thomas, 96
Diogenes, 38
Donne, John, 8, 18, 77ff., 148, 149, 152, 153
Dorp, Martin, 40, 41, 42
Drury, Elizabeth, 77–9, 88ff., 153

Edward IV, 25
Einstein, Alfred, 5, 6
Eliot, T. S., 50
Elyot, Thomas, 56
Empson, William, 90, 96
Epictetus, 38

Epicurus, 134
Erasmus, 7, 35ff., 64, 65, 70, 151
Evelyn, John, 69

Falsification theory, 6, 156 n.12
Fénelon, François, 124
Ferrabosco, Alphonso, 49
Feyerabend, Paul, 156 n.12
Fish, Stanley, 112
Fox, Alistair, 30, 31, 35, 163 n.24
Freud, Sigmund, 4
Frith, John, 45

Galen, 7, 50, 51, 55–7, 60, 61, 70, 96, 152
Galileo, 8–10, 12, 13, 61, 96
Garzoni, Tommazo, 70
Gibbon, Edward, 125
Gilbert, Neal, 7
Gilbert, William, 96
Glover, Mary, 59
Grace, 15, 16, 78, 87, 95, 100, 116, 151, 152
Grahame, Kenneth, 126
Gregory, St, 86
Guibbory, A., 115
Guyon, Madame, 125

Hall, A. R., 11, 12
Harpsfield, Nicholas, 19
Harvey, Christopher, 89
Harvey, William, 2
Heart, 2, 79, 80ff., 148, 152, 155 n.3
Henry VII, 21
Henry VIII, 20, 21, 22, 25, 26, 35, 45
Herbert, George, 18, 79
Hermetic philosophy, 2
Hippocrates, 55, 56, 96
Hobbes, Thomas, 7, 10, 12, 13, 61, 102, 107, 117, 118, 146, 153
Holinshed, Raphael, 24
Homer, 3
Hooke, Robert, 10
Howard, Thomas, 25
Hoyles, John, 137
Hugh of St Victor, 86
Humanism, 22ff., 32, 35, 37, 39ff., 47ff., 57, 62, 68, 74, 151, 152, 162 n.15

Hume, David, 1, 130, 132ff., 138
Humours, 50, 51, 54–6, 58, 60, 68, 70, 75

Imagination, 2, 4, 6, 54, 104, 106, 110, 117, 120, 121, 123, 126, 135ff., 145, 147, 149, 150, 153
Isidore of Seville, 86

Jackson, Elizabeth, 59
James I, 49, 67
Jerome, St, 40
Jesuits, 7, 87
Johnson, Samuel, 125
Jones, John, 56
Jonson, Ben, 48ff., 77, 78, 91, 148, 152
Justin Martyr, 111

Kepler, Johannes, 2, 8, 10, 96, 158 n.22
King, Edward, 78
Kuhn, Thomas, 5

Law, William, 18, 124ff., 149
Lemnius, Levinus, 68, 69
Lewalski, Barbara, 78, 87, 88
Lewis, C. S., 125, 127
Locke, John, 12, 13, 15, 128
Lombard, Peter, 86
Love, Harold, 93
Lowe, Peter, 60
Loyola, Ignatius, 77
Lucy, Countess of Bedford, 49
Luther, Martin, 15, 21, 22, 43, 45, 47

McCutcheon, Elizabeth, 33
Machiavelli, Nicholas, 165 n.48
Magic, 2, 12, 58, 118
Maier, A., 157 n.18
Malebranche, Nicolas, 126, 127, 128ff., 133, 136, 137, 140, 145, 153, 181 n.19
Martz, Louis, 46
Marx, Karl, 18
Masque, 49, 50, 73, 75, 148, 152, 171 n.55
Mathematics, 9, 10, 11, 13, 14, 16, 47, 61, 105, 109, 119, 122, 123, 132, 151, 157 n.18, 166 n.54

Mechanism, 11, 12, 13, 16, 51, 57, 58, 59, 60, 61, 68, 69, 74, 109, 129, 130, 152
Meditation, 78, 109, 116
Mersenne, Marin, 102
Merton thesis, 15
Metaphysics, 2, 4, 11–15, 18, 23, 37, 44–7, 51, 57, 58, 60–2, 64, 75, 92, 95, 97, 99, 101, 103–12, 116, 117, 119–23, 138–43, 145, 149, 151–3, 158 n.18, 165 n.51, 179 n.30
Method, 1–11, 12–14, 16, 18, 35, 47, 51, 57, 61, 74, 75, 100, 105, 107, 108, 109, 119, 120–2, 129, 130, 141, 150–4, 164 n.36
Milton, John, 78
Montaigne, Michel de, 58
Montenay, Georgette de, 88, 89
More, Henry, 15
More, Thomas, 18, 19ff., 49, 75, 147, 148, 151, 152
Myth, 6, 47, 138, 145

Neo-Platonism, 2, 12, 13
Newton, Isaac, 2, 3, 5, 6, 7, 8, 10, 128, 130, 140, 143, 145, 150, 153
Nominalism, 23, 37
Nuttall, A. D., 15

Occasionalism, 132
Ockham, William of, 15, 38
Ong, Walter, 9
Orgel, Stephen, 49

Pacius, Giulio, 7
Paracelsus, 57, 60, 96, 99
Pelagius, 15
Perspective, 32, 35, 36, 40, 42, 44
Peter of Spain, 7, 41, 45
Petrarch, Francesco, 86
Plato, 1–7, 16, 49, 78, 105, 111, 112, 152, 156 n.13, 172 n.8
Pomponazzi, Pietro, 57
Pope, Alexander, 126
Popper, Karl, 5, 156 n.12
Prabury, Alice, 1
Predestination, 15, 45, 58, 61, 96, 106, 115, 132
Providence, 12, 13

Ptolemy, 7, 96
Puppets, 68ff., 148, 170 n.51
Purcell, John, 61
Purchas, Samuel, 98

Qualities, 13, 17, 51, 55, 58, 61, 119, 152

Rahner, Karl, 85
Ramus, Peter, 7, 44
Realism, 23, 37
Reformation, 8, 23, 45
Renaissance, 7, 9, 16, 18, 56, 57, 59, 61, 75, 96, 146, 150
Rhenanus, Beatus, 36
Rich, Richard, 66
Richard, III, 24ff.
Richard of St Victor, 86

Sallust, 24
Santillana, Giorgio de, 9
Science, 4, 6–18, 58, 61, 75, 78, 95, 96ff., 103, 109, 120–2, 129–30, 141, 150, 151, 153, 155 n.8, 156 n.12
Scotus, John Duns, 15, 38
Shakespeare, William, 24, 58, 98
Socrates, 2, 3, 38
Stow, John, 24
Sturm, John, 7
Suetonius, 24
Suleiman I, 21
Sylvester, Richard, 26

Tacitus, 24
Tauler, John, 124, 128, 130
Telesius, Bernardino, 58
Temkin, Owsei, 57
Teresa of Avila, St, 127, 128
Thomas, Keith, 58
Tindal, Matthew, 131, 132, 138,. 153
Tyndale, William, 45, 47
Tyranny, 21, 22ff., 31, 35–8, 43, 45, 46, 100, 147

Van Haeften, Benedict, 87
Van Helmont, Jan Baptista, 2
Van Veen, Otto, 87
Vapours, 68, 69, 70, 72ff., 148
Vesalius, Andreas, 57, 70

Index

Vives, Juan Luis, 45, 49

Wilson, Nicholas, 20

Witchcraft, 1, 4, 58, 122, 155 n.8

Wright, Thomas, 59